PINOY CAPITAL

IN THE SERIES, *Asian American History and Culture,*

EDITED BY SUCHENG CHAN, DAVID PALUMBO-LIU, MICHAEL OMI, K. SCOTT WONG, AND LINDA TRINH VŌ

~

Lisa Yun, *The Coolie Speaks: Chinese Indentured Laborers and African Slaves in Cuba*

Estella Habal, *San Francisco's International Hotel: Mobilizing the Filipino American Community in the Anti-Eviction Movement*

Thomas P. Kim, *The Racial Logic of Politics: Asian Americans and Party Competition*

Sucheng Chan, ed., *The Vietnamese American 1.5 Generation: Stories of War, Revolution, Flight, and New Beginnings*

Antonio T. Tiongson Jr., Edgardo V. Gutierrez, and Ricardo V. Gutierrez, eds., *Positively No Filipinos Allowed: Building Communities and Discourse*

Sucheng Chan, ed., *Chinese American Transnationalism: The Flow of People, Resources, and Ideas between China and America during the Exclusion Era*

Keith Lawrence and Floyd Cheung, eds., *Recovered Legacies: Authority and Identity in Early Asian American Literature*

Rajini Srikanth, *The World Next Door: South Asian American Literature and the Idea of America*

Linda Trinh Vō, *Mobilizing an Asian American Community*

Franklin S. Odo, *No Sword to Bury: Japanese Americans in Hawai'i during World War II*

Josephine Lee, Imogene L. Lim, and Yuko Matsukawa, eds., *Re/collecting Early Asian America: Essays in Cultural History*

Linda Trinh Vō and Rick Bonus, eds., *Contemporary Asian American Communities: Intersections and Divergences*

Sunaina Marr Maira, *Desis in the House: Indian American Youth Culture in New York City*

Teresa Williams-León and Cynthia Nakashima, eds., *The Sum of Our Parts: Mixed-Heritage Asian Americans*

Tung Pok Chin with Winifred C. Chin, *Paper Son: One Man's Story*

Amy Ling, ed., *Yellow Light: The Flowering of Asian American Arts*

Rick Bonus, *Locating Filipino Americans: Ethnicity and the Cultural Politics of Space*

Darrell Y. Hamamoto and Sandra Liu, eds., *Countervisions: Asian American Film Criticism*

Martin F. Manalansan, IV, ed., *Cultural Compass: Ethnographic Explorations of Asian America*

(continued on page 221)

PINOY CAPITAL

The Filipino Nation in Daly City

~

Benito M. Vergara, Jr.

TEMPLE UNIVERSITY PRESS
Philadelphia

BENITO M. VERGARA, JR. is the author of
Displaying Filipinos: Photography and Colonialism in Early 20th-Century Philippines.
He lives and works in the San Francisco Bay Area.

FOR IZZY

TEMPLE UNIVERSITY PRESS
1601 North Broad Street
Philadelphia PA 19122
www.temple.edu/tempress

⊗ The paper used in this publication meets the requirements of the American National Standard
for Information Sciences—Permanence of Paper for Printed Library Materials, ANSI Z39.48-1992

Library of Congress Cataloging-in-Publication Data

Vergara, Benito Manalo, 1970–
Pinoy capital : the Filipino nation in Daly City / Benito M. Vergara, Jr.
p. cm. — (Asian American history and culture)

Includes bibliographical references and index.
ISBN 978-1-59213-664-3 (cloth : alk. paper) — ISBN 978-1-59213-665-0 (pbk. : alk. paper)
1. Filipino Americans—California—Daly City—Social conditions.   2. Filipino
Americans—California—Daly City—Ethnic identity.   3. Immigrants—California—Daly
City—Social conditions.   4. Community life—California—Daly City.   5. Transnationalism.
6. Daly City (Calif.)—Relations—Philippines.   7. Philippines—Relations—California—Daly
City.   8. Daly City (Calif.)—Social conditions.   9. Daly City (Calif.)—Ethnic relations.   I. Title.
F869.D23V47 2009
305.89'921079469—dc22

2008014174

2 4 6 8 9 7 5 3 1

Contents

ACKNOWLEDGMENTS

Page limits force me to say "thanks" briefly. It's fitting, then, for an ethnography of place, that my more effusive acknowledgments section is elsewhere: *http:// www.thewilyfilipino.com/acknowledgments.htm* (or email me at vergara.benito@ gmail.com). After all, my gratitude exceeds the pages of this book.

And now, a list of places and names: *Ithaca*: Jojo Abinales, Jun Aguilar, Donna Amoroso, Dominique Caouette, Nick Fowler, Jeff Hadler, Jackie Hatton, Carol Hau, Lotta Hedman, Mike Montesano, Peter Vail, Erick White, Portia Wu. *The Cornell University Anthropology Department, and the Cornell Southeast Asia Program*: Benedict Anderson, Randy Barker, Ted Bestor, Jane Fajans, Viranjini Munasinghe, Beth Povinelli, Vilma Santiago-Irizarry, James Siegel, Meredith Small. Deepest thanks go to John Borneman. *Daly City*: interviewees, community leaders, city officials, activists, the staff of *Philippine News* (especially Alex and Luly Esclamado and Cherie Querol-Moreno). *San Francisco*: Darren Brown, Alice Burton, Joannie Chang, Son and Eloise Diep, Jens Hillmer, Nan Kim, Stephanie Lee, Laurel Nakamura, Jane Po, Romeo Quintana, Barb Reyes, Karen Swing, Carolyn Tran, Dorothy Wang, Mitch Wu, Luna Yasui; academic comrades Nerissa Balce, Kiko Benitez, Rick Bonus, Oca Campomanes, and Martin Manalansan. Madeline Hsu read every word in earlier drafts; I was saddened when she did not stay to read the rest. *San Francisco State University*: Lorraine Dong, Dan Gonzales, Marlon Hom, Ben Kobashigawa, Asian American Studies and Anthropology students, the League of Filipino Students SFSU chapter. *The home stretch*: Janet Francendese, Linda Vo, two Temple University Press reviewers, Lordy Rodriguez. *Home*: There are those for whom my gratitude crosses all borders, like my family in Los Baños, Laguna, and their boundless affection. The laughter of my daughter, Izzy, is where happiness can be found. Everything good in this book, and in my life, comes from her.

1

A REPEATED TURNING

~

One will hear the joke told, eventually, though it hardly ever sounds like one. It's almost always delivered casually, thrown out like an offhand rhetorical question, as a matter of incontestable fact. "You know why it's always foggy in Daly City, right? Because all the Filipinos turn on their rice cookers at the same time." This particular teller of the joke (Wally, a newspaper photographer) and I (a student of anthropology) are sitting in scuffed plastic chairs in the living room of his cramped apartment in the Pinoy capital of the United States. We are both among the 33,000 Filipino residents of Daly City, California, where one out of three people are of Filipino descent.

It is a freezing afternoon in late August, and we are looking through the damp glass of the window that faces out onto the quiet suburban street. Outside the fog swirls, tugged by the wind into gentle twists of cotton, spilling over the roofs and parallel-parked Hondas. But inside, it is warm, as it does not take much time to heat up the small room cluttered with boxes of bulk food purchased from Costco, cassette tapes, photography books, and an open *balikbayan* box addressed to Wally's parents in Quezon City. Wally, with a half-consumed bottle of beer in one hand, leans back in his chair after delivering the punch line, and waits for my reaction. I grin widely, because it is hard not to. I've always found it really funny.

Wally is not the first person to tell me the joke. Almost every single one of my interviewees inevitably asks me the question about fog and Daly City. There is very little variation in the way the joke is told, whether in

English or Tagalog, whether there is a pause between the question mark and the answer. There is nothing here for linguists to savor or puzzle over. In this instance, for the anthropologist, perhaps what counts most is the teller, not the tale; it is in the teller that the kind of cultural difference worth studying lies. The tale is something we all already share.

And yet, despite its silliness, despite its meteorological absurdity, the joke begins to acquire a sense of both political and semi-religious gravity: it invites us to envision the peculiarly affecting image of thousands of Filipinos depressing the rice cooker switch simultaneously, about half an hour before dinner is served, in a daily culinary ritual that comes almost as naturally as breathing. And the steam collectively rises up and out, the fog becomes a unanimous, quiet declaration of ethnic presence.

In this city, you may not always see the Pinoys. They may be hard at work at their jobs, they may be huddled in privacy behind their drawn curtains, they may be inside the warmth of their kitchens. But they are there. The fog proves it.

By anthropological standards, Daly City may not seem particularly exciting—not the street violence of Naples, or the humid rainforests of the Amazon, or the urban grit of Spanish Harlem, or the harrowing war zones of Angola—but sometimes what seems deeply ordinary to the reader can yield the most ethnographically fascinating data. The relative placidity on the surface of Daly City is matched by the pleasant orderliness of rows, by the way the candy-colored homes wriggle along the brown spines of the Colma hills. But unlike cinematic suburbia—where the trimmed hedges are mere facades for repressed anger and American adultery (and perhaps a murder or two)—Daly City has an alternate, more fixed identity: it is known, both in the Philippines and in America, as "the Pinoy capital of the United States." Filipinos live and work among Filipino restaurants, television shows, video stores, newspapers, and concerns that allow them to imagine a life in many ways indistinguishable from life "back home."

As the largest and fastest-growing ethnic minority in a city where the majority of the residents are Asian and over half are foreign-born, Filipinos constitute almost 32 percent of the population. In this suburb of San Francisco, with a total population of 103,621, about 32,720 Filipinos make their home. These population statistics reflect demographic patterns in the country as a whole: since 1965, after the removal of national origin quotas, Filipinos have made up the highest number of Asian immigrants admitted annually into the United States. By 1990, 1.4 million Filipinos were in the United States (in 2000, 1.9 million), of whom 64 percent were born overseas (Querol-Moreno, 1994).

Early in 2002 a survey research group released some rather surprising findings: 19 percent of all Filipinos, or almost one out of five, saw the Philippine situation as "hopeless" and would, given the chance, live or work abroad (cited in Pazzibugan and Batino 2002). As expected, the report provoked a flurry of responses in newspapers, some of them critical of the survey's methods (only 1,200 people were interviewed), but most of them portraying the results as a "wake-up call" regarding the dissatisfaction of the citizenry. The president, Gloria Macapagal-Arroyo, not very helpfully responded that the emphasis should have been on the 81 percent who did not want to migrate. (Twenty percent were undecided, so the number should actually have been about 60, not 81, percent.) Her finance secretary, Jose Isidro Camacho, grumbled, "It is so frustrating to work in government and to sometimes see our efforts being unappreciated" (quoted in Pazzibugan and Batino 2002, 1). This was because many Filipinos had already shown their disapproval with their feet. Whether those 19 percent, or about 8.2 million, would indeed join their (at the time) 7.4 million compatriots living and working overseas was another matter. Nonetheless, their inclination to leave indicates the crisis in which the Philippines found itself—the continuation of a long discontent that impelled people to seek their fortunes elsewhere.

Many of the people who left—specifically, those who left for the United States—have a complicated, ambivalent relationship with the country and the people they left behind. They are accused of betrayal, are tugged in different directions by familial and national obligations, experience nostalgia and guilt, and repeatedly turn between the homeland and their adopted country. Pinoys in the United States live their lives as migrants caught up, willingly and unwillingly, in a network of sometimes competing definitions of identities, connections, and loyalties.

The post-1965 generation of immigrants in Daly City and in the United States in general—again, a mostly foreign-born population, of varying citizenship statuses—raises questions about the inflexibility of citizenship and national belonging, and about what it means to be a Filipino in the United States. Daly City represents a certain class ideal that is both a product and a component of Filipino middle-class imagining. And it represents an odd, disconnected form of Filipino national belonging as well. But this ideal is fraught with the potential loss of the very markers that indicate belonging to this particular class and nation.

The Filipino community in Daly City also exemplifies the ambiguities produced by the intensification of connections between Filipinos in the United States and in the Philippines. I contend that these intensified links—and the act of migration itself—are not necessarily a direct result of colonialism, as many scholars of Filipino American studies have argued. Moreover, these transnational links, which supposedly characterize a new form of migration, do not necessarily lead to a redefined, more fluid conception of Filipino (and American) identity and belonging.

Much of the discourse about identity revolves around the concept of obligation, whether to one's relatives, one's country, one's homeland, or one's people. For the immigrant, this sense of obligation and responsibility—produced in discourse by entities both abstract and concrete, such as the state, tradition, kinship, ethnic solidarity, nationalism, and so on—may coincide with or compete against narratives of ethnicity and loyalty.

Khachig Tololyan touches on this sense of obligation in his discussion of the word *diaspora*:

> It makes more sense to think of diasporan or diasporic existence as not necessarily involving a physical return but rather a re-turn, a repeated turning to the concept and/or the reality of the homeland and other diasporan kin through memory, written and visual texts, travel, gifts and assistance. (1996, 14–15)

It is this "repeated turning" that I find in Daly City's Pinoy population. Whether manifested as political activism, assertions of ethnic pride, nostalgia, consumerism, or just vague remembering, the repeated turning is obliquely opposed to the narrative of assimilation. The tension between this remembrance and the demands of citizenship in the new homeland, the obligations in different directions, constitute a predicament for the Filipino immigrant; I examine how they negotiate—or indeed, fail to find—a balance between the two.

This book also performs a repeated turning of its own. The chapters move back and forth not just in terms of location (either in the United States or in the Philippines), but also in terms of time period. This is not necessarily a stylistic maneuver, but a reflection of the way historical events, and more importantly, competing obligations in different sites, affect Daly City residents in the temporal present. In the following pages I outline the arguments on this constantly shifting, reorienting terrain.

Outline of Chapters

For the first substantive chapter, I will use official census reports, interviews with residents, and ethnographic data to provide an overview of the history, politics, and cultural and economic demographics of Daly City. I will present an ethnographic portrait of the city's Filipino immigrant population and, on a more figurative level, the city's identity itself, utilizing the personal narratives of some of its Pinoy residents. I will argue in this and the following chapters that the rapid circulation of commodities, ideas, and images—which can be attributed to phenomena described in transnational theory—has encouraged the reproduction of a more orderly version of Philippine life set in Daly City.

The next few chapters—on the media, on nostalgia, and on obligations—will employ a kind of circularity: the phenomena of homesickness and nostalgia, I argue, are strongly associated with "nationality." These chapters will also be loosely structured around two seemingly conflicting discourses of obligation—towards the adopted country (in terms of civic responsibility), and towards the homeland (in terms of nationalism and guilt)—and their intersections with class, ethnicity, and nationality. Looking back, both temporally and spatially, involves identification with the nation; the Philippine state, in turn, employs similar idioms in interpellating its former citizens. But the process of fashioning an identity as an immigrant in a new land, I will explain, "ideally" involves a "progression" from nationality to ethnicity to "Americanization," as the parameters of belonging change. In turn, the incorporation of the immigrant into the new nation-state effects other changes, mostly perceived in terms of class status and, again, nationality.

The Philippine state tries to turn the familial obligations of Filipinos overseas into a form of service to the Filipino nation. Pinoys who live in, and may be citizens of, the United States, are enjoined to remember their homeland, not just by sending money, but by remaining loyal to that homeland as well. In real life, however, such an obligation has to be balanced with their new lives and responsibilities in America. Filipino Americans, then, bear the discursive brunt of being seen as "less Filipino" or as having "betrayed" the Philippines; this is because they are far more likely to settle permanently than are Filipino migrants to Saudi Arabia or Singapore. Although the portrayal of overseas immigrants as less culturally "whole" or "authentic" is nothing new, it is revealing to contrast this claim with their own assertions of ethnic identity (contradicting, therefore, the logic of assimilation)—as well as with the Philippine government's largely successful attempts to portray overseas contract workers as national heroes.

I explore, therefore, the contradictions between the different parameters set both by nation and by state with regard to Filipino identity. This particular debate also has to do, crucially, with class; the middle-class Filipinos who come to live in the United States are already economically set apart from those who work as domestic helpers in Hong Kong, for instance. At the same time, this identity, this longing to "remain" Filipino, is at odds with the demands and responsibilities of American citizenship, and this disjunction may affect civic participation and incorporation into the American body politic *and* involvement in civic life in the Philippines.

Chapter Three, "Looking Forward: Narratives of Obligation," examines Pinoy immigrants' attitudes toward living in America: how and why they immigrated, their perceptions of differences between the United States and the Philippines, their experiences with work, and the relevance of ethnic solidarity, among others. Rather than illustrating the flexibility and fluidity associated with transnational theory, the interviewees' narratives confirm the material hurdles and restrictions on immigration and conceptions of self. My research shows that narrowly conceived notions of Filipino immigration to the United States—whether clumsily attributed wholly to former colonial relations or to the crass allure of materialism—miss the point. What impels immigration is in fact a complicated and ambiguous combination of factors stemming from family obligations, colonial history, economic conditions, images fostered by the media, and an overall quest for prosperity.

One focus of this chapter, however, is a particular facet of the immigrant predicament that reflects the tension between competing obligations. The perceived responsibilities of citizenship (for instance, political participation) in the adopted country sometimes clash with notions of loyalty and responsibility to the homeland. Often attitudes toward national and ethnic belonging spill over into the political sphere and reveal cleavages within the Filipino community that are products of immigrant conditions—for instance, in a historic city council election, where the primary candidates were, for the first time, both of Filipino background. Community leaders have long noted the lack of electoral participation among Filipinos in Daly City; I argue that these elections in turn illustrate a perhaps fundamental cultural split within the community itself—one between the native-born and the naturalized foreign-born. This example illuminates the political and cultural dynamics of the Filipino community and, most important, raises questions about the meanings of American citizenship and civic responsibility.

How are these twin senses of belonging expressed? The situation not only invites questions about belonging, or even loyalty, to both countries, but also produces a general imagining of both places from the perspective of the other. How is this act of imagination articulated in public and private discourse—in both the mass media and in migrants' narratives about themselves? How is the Filipino nation reproduced in daily life away from the "homeland?"

These conflicting obligations—and their precisely international nature—are a result of how the immigrant identity is produced and circulated. Imagination, stimulated by the flow of commodities and the mass media, takes on a social role. The images produced by movies, television, and newspapers are also important because of their wide-ranging circulation. For instance, politicians and members of the public alike have invested much energy in the control of representation of Filipinos in both Philippine and American media. This is an indication of the importance of public discourse to everyday Filipino life. The immigrant's sense of belonging is embodied both in the repetitive, automatic acts of the ordinary, and in the categories and narratives people tell and employ.

Chapter Four, "Spreading the News: Newspapers and Transnational Belonging," is centered on an ethnographic analysis of the *Philippine News*, the most prominent of all Filipino newspapers in the United States. I discuss how the media in general, and the *Philippine News* in particular, define identification and loyalties towards a particular national form—in this case, a fictive, ideal, transnational one. In short, I focus on how the newspaper, as a product of this desire for transnationality, reflects the relationship between a Filipino identity and a Filipino American one.

The *Philippine News* primarily sees itself as responsible for shaping its community of readers and generally urging them toward political empowerment in the United States. But this orientation is accompanied by a similarly dedicated orientation toward Philippine affairs—a perfect example of transnationality, in all its ambiguity, at work. A parallel dynamic, between assimilation and the carving out of a separate ethnic identity, also operates within the newspaper. Conceptions of belonging, of generational differences, and of being a Pinoy in America are discussed and contested publicly in the articles and the letters to the editor. It is the relationship between the media and the political and cultural process that concerns me, and I contrast it with my informants' narratives.

The tension between adopted home and homeland—or, as I argue in the conclusion, the apparent lack of it—produces different and sometimes competing responsibilities. In Chapter Five, "Looking Back: Indifference, Responsibility, and the Anti-Marcos Movement in the United States," to illustrate the immigrant orientation toward the homeland, I will focus on the discourse of responsibility utilized by some members of the Filipino community in the United States during the Marcos dictatorship. This is admittedly a particularly aberrant time, but it starkly demonstrates how Pinoy political activists in the United States employed metaphors of loyalty and responsibility in an attempt to mobilize what they saw as an increasingly forgetful Filipino community that had "abandoned" its homeland and its people. The chapter also examines the competing ideologies within the opposition to Marcos in the United States, and the ways in which class complicates political positions. It also illustrates the similarities between Filipino immigrants and earlier immigrant groups in terms of overseas political organizing oriented towards the homeland.

Obligation links up, on a more encompassing level, to social class and the figure of the balikbayan, or the Filipino overseas returnee. The Filipino immigrant experience necessarily entails the concept of money, and not necessarily the colonial link. This particular "bind" is conceived as being in opposition to the concept of the nation. In Chapter Six, "Betrayal and Belonging," I have brought together various instances, drawing from both the United States and the Philippines, that illuminate the variety of ways in which class intersects with definitions of Filipino national belonging. These notions of Filipino identity and belonging are evoked to regulate the class and national inclusion/exclusion of middle-class individuals outside the country. I explore the perception that Pinoys in the United States have "lost" a certain cultural authenticity in exchange for what is perceived as a higher class status.

Nostalgia and homesickness take various social forms, and the boundaries of the nation-state are expanded and manifested through differing venues (community cultural events, the media). In Chapter Seven, "Citizenship and Nostalgia," I address the manifestations of homesickness in a place like Daly City, where the trappings of Filipinoness are already almost commonplace. Whether nostalgia is seen as uncontrollable remembrance or as a rosy fabrication of a narrative of the past—a concept analogous to nationalism's smoothing of historical bumps in the road—such narratives are manifest in the everyday, and are an intrinsic part of the experience of Filipino immigrants. This act of "turning back" contrasts with the act of naturalization, which is seen as constituting a radical change in identity, and therefore forestalling any possibility of "return" to the homeland.

The Pinoy immigrant community, like other communities, does not manifest a kind of belonging—not a new variant, but one elaborated from previous historical forms—that has merely intensified because of the faster "transnational" connections between the two countries. Rather, this is a citizenship in which migrants harbor feelings of ambivalent commitment to nation-states (and not just governments). While there migrants have similar sentiments of ambivalence about the postcolonial relationship between the United States and the Philippines, a closer examination of the issues involved reveals more practical and material reasons for immigration.

In the concluding chapter, I take a more ambiguous and ambivalent position—in considering nationalism, belonging, ethnic solidarity, and political involvement—that more aptly characterizes Filipino immigrant identity. The reality, however, as I wrote at the beginning of this chapter, is that they have already left. This is why a genuine transnationality has yet to exist; a state of existence in which one can belong to two places at once is merely a kind of transcendent hope on the part of the immigrant. Pinoys in America, who are, in interesting ways, similar to the immigrants who came before them, may still see the Philippines as home, but not as a place in which to live.

A Tentative Status

Filipino migration to the United States is of course rooted in the American colonization of the Philippines,[1] though its early history is rarely discussed as part of current immigrant experience.[2] Such a disconnection is mirrored in the history of contradictory attitudes towards the United States: resistance to U.S. occupation on one hand, embrace of American ideals on the other. Actively recruited by the American sugar industry, the first few thousand Filipinos arrived in Hawaii between 1906 and 1910 to work as laborers on sugar plantations (initially to replace Japanese and Chinese laborers who were on strike). This direct recruitment, plus agrarian unrest and the depressed economy in the Philippines, resulted in a massive influx of Filipinos, mostly from the Ilocos region, to the mainland in the succeeding years. Vividly and bleakly depicted in Carlos Bulosan's famous book *America Is in the Heart*, the Filipino immigrant population—the majority of whom were migrant farm laborers who suffered extremely harsh working conditions—would number over 30,000 by 1930.

Filipinos occupied a tentative status: they were classified as U.S. nationals since the Philippines came under the control of the American colonial regime in 1899. But "national" was an oddly liminal category, reflective of the

---

[1] Marina Espina's pioneering research has uncovered the presence of "Manilamen" in Louisiana as early as 1763 (Cordova 1983, 1–7). Scholars affiliated with the Filipino American National Historical Society have pushed the date as far back as 1587 (in Morro Bay, California), but the location and the date have been questioned (Santos 1997). Moving the historical goalposts is familiar to students of nationalism, and is understandable, given Filipinos' minority status in the United States. But such remembrances had little, if any, impact on Spaniards, Americans, or Filipinos—the latter quite unlikely to have conceived of themselves as such. In any case, I begin my discussion with the American colonial period in the Philippines.

[2] As the former candidate for the Philippine Assembly Eva Estrada Kalaw shamelessly put it, "the better Filipinos" are migrating to the United States nowadays, as opposed to "the lower-class vegetable pickers" (quoted in Denton and Villena-Denton 1986, 125).

Philippines' ambiguous status in the eyes of the colonizers. Filipinos in the United States were neither aliens nor citizens, and were therefore ineligible for naturalization like other Asians.

Hostility to Filipino migrant workers began to increase; they were becoming more militant in their labor organizing, and their growing aggressiveness, coupled with the availability of even cheaper Mexican labor, made Pinoys less and less popular. An effective way of dealing with the antagonism (and one in keeping with trends in American immigration policy) was to bar Filipinos, like other prospective immigrants from Asia, from entering the United States.[3] And the easiest way to bar Filipinos from migrating to the United States was to grant independence to the Philippines. After the U.S. Congress established the Philippines as a Commonwealth in 1934 via the Tydings-McDuffie Act, the Filipinos who were already in the United States were suddenly reclassified as aliens. Despite the fact that they became ineligible for government assistance, Filipinos continued to stay even after the passage of the Repatriation Act the same year. The U.S. government had calculated that, for $87, it would be cheaper to transport Filipinos out of the country than to support them on welfare. Despite estimates that 15,000 to 20,000 would leave (Catapusan 1936), only 2,190 availed themselves of the opportunity; the rest stayed on (Takaki 1989). Despite their travails, Filipino farm laborers preferred to stay in the United States.

After 1936 immigration slowed to a trickle, particularly during the war years (only 252 Filipinos immigrated from 1941 to 1945). But the long-delayed granting of naturalization rights, first to Filipinos in the U.S. Army in 1943, and finally to all immigrants from the Philippines in 1946, paved the way for the larger migration to come.[4] Some women arrived under the War Brides

---

[3] Much of this exclusion of Asian immigrants had already been accomplished with the passage of the Chinese Exclusion Act in 1882, the Gentlemen's Agreement (in which Japan was pressured to deny visas to prospective migrant laborers) in 1907, and the creation of a "barred zone" in 1917.

[4] Similar shifts in naturalization rights occurred for other Asian Americans: first for the Chinese, and much later, for the Japanese.

Perhaps the clearest pathway to American naturalization for Filipinos during this period was opened under colonial auspices. The 1947 R.P.-U.S. Military Bases Agreement established the presence of U.S. army bases in the Philippines to protect American interests in Asia. One of its provisions was the continued recruitment of Filipino nationals—and later, *citizens of a sovereign state*—as members of the U.S. Navy. The twist here—which was also a blatant act of employment discrimination—was that Filipinos were restricted only to steward and mess attendant positions; their reward was the opportunity to avail of American citizenship after a period of service.

The controversy still rages over the rights of World War II veterans from the Philippines. Drafted into service in 1941 as part of the United States Armed Forces in the Far East (USAFFE), Filipino soldiers were promised that they would be considered "active service" U.S. veterans. This promise was revoked in 1946 with the Rescission Act. The 1990 Immigration and Naturalization Act allowed the naturalization of about 25,000 veterans because of U.S. military service; however,

Act, but on the whole the numbers were minimal. In 1965 the new Immigration and Naturalization Act was passed, and the racial/national origin quotas of the 1924 act were abolished. Geared primarily to family unification and the admission of professional and skilled workers (in direct contrast to previous patterns), the act radically changed the composition of the Filipino immigrant population. Mostly composed, initially, of health-related professionals (specifically, nurses and medical technicians directly recruited from the Philippines), engineers, accountants, and their families, who were dissatisfied with economic and political conditions in the Philippines, the new wave of immigration increased the Filipino immigrant population fivefold, to 85,000, within the next five years (Pido 1985). From then on—each year from 1965 to the present—Filipinos made up the highest total of Asian immigrants admitted.

Initially, immigrants arrived under the third preference (professionals of "exceptional ability") and the sixth preference ("workers, skilled and unskilled, in occupations with short labor supply in the United States"); in 1975 Filipinos constituted 18.5 percent of all third-preference immigrants. But the family-reunification preference immigrants soon outpaced the professionals. From 1966 to 1975, the proportions of the two kinds of preference immigrants were about equal. A decade later (1976 to 1988), however, the occupational-preference immigrants accounted for only 20 percent of the total, whereas family-reunification preference immigrants rose to an overwhelming 80 percent (Espiritu 1995, 21).[5]

As is the case with almost every other Asian immigrant group, the numbers kept growing: during the Aquino administration in the Philippines, between 1986 and 1990, more than a quarter of a million Filipinos arrived in the United States. In 2000, the number of Pinoys in the United States was

---

they were denied medical benefits and were ineligible to be patients in Veterans Administration hospitals. (The obvious question of "patriotism" is largely unexamined here, particularly by Filipino American activists, as the only logical scenario would have the veterans fighting for the defense of "their country"—the United States.)

[5] This change can be partly explained by later policies that restricted the entry of professionals. The 1965 Immigration Act was revised in 1976: third- and sixth-preference immigrants, i.e., those who entered through occupational preference, had to have actual job offers before they could receive their visas. The Eilberg Act of 1977 further required that employers show proof of recruitment within the U.S. labor pool before hiring non-citizens (Chan 1991, 147–148). Currently 36 percent of employed Filipinos and Filipino Americans in the United States are categorized as employed in "technical, sales and administrative work," 26.6 percent in "managerial and professional work," and 16.8 percent in "the service industry." This change in the category of immigration applications resulted in a corresponding shift in the economic and educational background of the Filipino American community.

The gender ratio has also changed radically from that of the bachelor society of the '20s and '30s: in 2000 women outnumbered men by about 100,000.

officially estimated at 1.9 million; including undocumented immigrants, the number is probably closer to 2 million.[6] The 1990 population (1.4 million) was divided almost evenly among naturalized citizens (53.8 percent) and non-citizens (46.2 percent). Only 35 percent of this population was born in the United States, underscoring the relative recentness of the Filipino community (Querol-Moreno 1994). About half (51 percent) of the foreign-born Filipino population arrived before 1980, and the rest came to the United States in the following decade. This proportion of Philippine-born Filipinos in the overall population is reflected in the composition of the Pinoy community in Daly City.

The bulk of my ethnographic research was done in the mid- to late '90s, when the largest wave of immigrants after the People Power Revolution of 1986 had more or less settled into a comfortable stasis. The political upheavals of the '70s and '80s in the Philippines—reflected in a quieter (but not gentler) fashion in Filipino community politics in the United States—had given way to a sleepy peace, a calm before the chaos of post-9/11 America, recession in Asia and the United States, disastrous military interventions, and punitive immigration policies in the name of homeland security.[7] Hot-button issues like affirmative action (especially in California), voting registration campaigns, the struggle for veterans' equity, increased militarization in the Philippines, or even the continued demolition of Filipino enclaves via "gentrification" like that of San Francisco's South of Market (SoMa) area, had failed to ignite a movement outside activist realms, as can be seen in succeeding chapters. Anecdotal accounts from many of my interviewees suggest that some former Daly City residents were enjoying a measure of prosperity, cashing in on the wild Bay Area housing market, selling their Daly City homes, and moving to larger residences in the East Bay and further down the Peninsula.

It was during this particular context of contentment, if not complacency, that my research was conducted. It may seem contradictory, especially to scholars of cultural change, to study a community that, in hindsight, was going through a generally stable period in its history. But it was also an opportunity to observe, at *Philippine News*, the production of good news and bad news when there was relatively little of either, or the chance to watch ordi-

---

[6] According to Concepcion Montoya, the Philippines is the third biggest "provider of visa overstayers" in the United States, after Mexico and Haiti, with an average of 14,800 overstayers per year from 1985 to 1988 (1997, 115).

[7] See in particular the Critical Filipina and Filipino Studies Collective's report, "Resisting Homeland Security: Organizing against Unjust Removals of U.S. Filipinos" (2004), which asserts that almost 85,000 Filipino immigrants—most for mere visa violations—are targeted for arrest, detention, and removal as a direct consequence of the PATRIOT Act.

nary citizens go about their sometimes perfectly ordinary lives. One could imagine, given this scenario, a deepening of roots, a cultivation of formerly fallow land, a building of community and political coalitions without intramural distractions. Still this was a community that, after putting itself on the map of the United States by electing its first Filipino mayor, continued to dream of places back home.

Filipino/Filipino American /Pinoy

The reader will have noticed the odd absence of the phrase *Filipino American* in the history recounted above. Perhaps indicative of both the paradoxical rigidity *and* the slipperiness of the symbolic boundaries between "Filipinos" and "Filipino Americans" are the terms themselves. In this section I shall discuss some categories and use them as a starting point for addressing issues in widening spheres: from identity and national belonging to the borders between academic fields to colonialism and postcolonialism. The importance of these symbolic boundaries can be seen even on a semantic level, but government policy and ethnic identification are also at stake.

I use the term *Filipino American* with hesitation, even though it is the technically correct term; individual understandings clearly differ from state-imposed ones. *Filipino American* can refer to any of several possibilities, or a combination thereof, depending on the speaker: (1) a person of Filipino descent residing in the United States, (2) a person of Filipino descent born in the United States, (3) a person of Filipino descent who is a naturalized citizen of the United States, and (4) a person of mixed race.

Most of my Philippine-born interviewees—some are naturalized citizens, some are permanent residents, some are neither—disavowed the term as applying to themselves. Many of the people I spoke to pointedly refused to identify themselves as Filipino American, explaining that the term was more appropriate for Filipinos who were born in the United States.[8] (American-born college students embraced the term, as referring to themselves, almost without question.) For one interviewee, the term referred only to people of mixed race, such as half-Filipino, half-white. Simon Roldan, an interviewee who was born in the United States but who had lived in the Philippines until he was 21, readily identified himself as Filipino American solely because of his American citizenship. After further questioning, some interviewees were

---

[8] As Rick Bonus similarly writes, "My respondents only occasionally referred to themselves as 'Filipino Americans.' More often they used 'Filipino' . . . to distinguish themselves from those . . . born in the United States. My reason for stressing that they are 'Filipino American' speaks to my contention that they are engaged in processes that have implications for being Filipino and American at the same time" (2000, 5–6).

clearly puzzled by my insistence on categories; some, like my informant Michael Santos, simply said that they were "wala, Pilipinong nasa Amerika" (oh, nothing, a Filipino in America).

The latter categorization reflects a very particular status—one of displacement. It is the category of a person whose identity is ostensibly "intact" but who is located in a different place. For some this entails a rejection of the adjective *American*—in effect, treating the United States as merely the issuer of one's passport. Being a "Filipino in America," as opposed to being Filipino American, is a state that seems to highlight the lack of a sense of belonging: this may, in turn, signify and intensify a longing for connections to the homeland.

What accounts, then, for this reluctance to be categorized? One explanation is the relative recentness of the term *Filipino American*, born from the Asian American movement of the late '60s and used primarily (at least in the beginning) by academics and politicians.[9] Related to this odd reluctance is the term's progression (or decline) from a declaration of ethnic Americanness to a mere census category. For instance, one interviewee said that he uses the term *Filipino American* only when filling out forms—it is the box he checks off when asked about his ethnicity.[10]

Indeed, for many non-Filipinos, *Filipino* and *Filipino American* are interchangeable, the former being shorthand for the latter.[11] This usage is simply a matter of semantics, of course, but I believe it may also reveal an unconscious and unremarked slipperiness between the two categories. Not only does it reflect the increasingly immigrant component of the Asian American communities themselves, but it can also be read as manifesting the tentative nature of the ethnic identification itself. But, as my ethnographic interviews

---

[9] Indeed, the term of choice among second-generation Bay Area activists (particularly those influenced by '60s rhetoric) is "Pilipino American," following arguments that the letter "F" did not exist in the precolonial alphabet.

[10] Such identification is perhaps analogous to the clumsy "Asian Pacific Islander" (API) and "Asian Pacific American" (APA) categories, which clearly have their origins in government bureaucratese. Nonetheless, government agencies have been partly successful in forcing identification with these categories, if only for census data or funding requirements. Espiritu argues that the acceptance of the "Asian American" category is not just a result of pressure from above (which she traces to a homogenized view of Asians by white society in general), but a calculated, pan-ethnic strategy as well. Nevertheless, "the pan-Asian concept is now so well institutionalized," she writes, "that new Asian immigrants and refugees often encounter . . . pressure to consider themselves Asian Americans, regardless of whether or not they see themselves in such terms" (1992, 16). This process is arguably similar to how "Filipino American" is becoming begrudgingly accepted as the default political category.

[11] Colloquially, of course, it is simply easier to drop the *American* part of the phrase for *any* term of ethnic identification in the United States, but this is not the case here; some interviewees took pains to distinguish themselves from "Filipino Americans."

show, the boundaries between the otherwise transposable terms can be suddenly, rigidly drawn, depending on the context.

I will use the generic term *Filipino* to refer to Filipinos both in the Philippines and the United States, using *Filipino American* only to denote people who identified themselves thus (like those at the *Philippine News*) or who belong to the second generation. I choose this terminology not only for the sake of accuracy but to highlight the tensions regarding national belonging. I prefer to keep the two terms—*Filipino* and *Filipino American*—separate, but I am aware that these categories and their putative subjects/members may not necessarily coincide.[12]

And finally, a word or two about *Pinoy*. A slang term for Filipinos (*Pinay* is the feminine counterpart), *Pinoy* began to be used by Filipino labor migrants in the United States, ostensibly to differentiate themselves from Filipinos who lived in the Philippines. (I have found no concrete evidence to support this latter clause, especially if there was little to no reason to claim a specifically Filipino American identity this early in their migration history.) It is clear, however, from oral narratives, that the term was used by Filipinos to refer to themselves, as Carlos Bulosan (1973) does, in a passing reference in *America Is in The Heart* (see also Vallangca 1977). The term also began to be seen in print in the 1920s and '30s in the Philippines[13], and it gained widespread demotic currency in the 1970s, aided by a couple of hugely popular nationalist folk songs ("Tayo'y Mga Pinoy" [We Are Pinoys] by Heber Bartolome and "Ako'y Isang Pinoy" [I Am a Pinoy] by Florante). Since then it has been used by Filipinos more or less everywhere.

Whatever its origins,[14] I employ the term fairly interchangeably with *Filipino* in the text—not out of caprice or a utopian wish to elide differences, nor

---

[12] Others have discussed the term as well, notably Oscar Campomanes (1995, 147), who argues that "Filipino American" is "oxymoronic," and uses "U.S. Filipino" in its place. Lisa Lowe (1996) similarly explores the political and legal contradictions inherent in the category "Asian American," one that Dylan Rodriguez pushes to its logical limit, describing the "unnamable violence that deeply troubles the very formation of the field [of Filipino American studies] itself" (Rodriguez 2006, 146).

[13] See Carson Taylor's *History of Philippine Press* (1928), which mentions a 1926 journal called *Pinoy* from Capiz. From http://name.umdl.umich.edu/acr6448.0001.001 (last accessed January 18, 2008).

[14] Spuriously fanciful etymologies of the term have been bandied about—that it is a contraction of "P.I. [Philippine Islands], Noy" (the supposed answer of a Bicolano laborer, when asked where he came from), or that it is short for *Pilipino boy* (and therefore emphasizing a Filipino servility to American bosses), or, most dubious of all, that it is from *Pilipino* and *unggoy*, or "monkey" (the latter supposedly proving that *Pinoy* began as an ethnic slur). Monkeys and Filipinos were certainly connected in the American racial imagination as early as the turn of the twentieth century, but I have found no concrete evidence for any of the above folk etymologies, and there is no reason to believe that *Pinoy*—used liberally, after all, by Filipinos in the United States and in the

as a willful semantic gesture to avoid the contradictions and implications of *American*, but to highlight a genuinely transnational nickname for a people, and it is with those connotations of familiarity, endearment, and affection that I use it in this book.

Interviews and Narratives

My interest in studying notions of belonging is a reaction to previous studies of migration that have underscored the flow of capital and the economic and political systems that regulate the movement of people. In contrast, I focus more on the emotional dimensions of belonging as a way of foregrounding the more "irrational," human element of immigration. In keeping with my concern to represent immigrant belonging as an emotional, subjective state, reflected in people's perspectives rather than in an abstract, more material structure, I focus on discourse about the United States and the Philippines. The words and categories that interviewees use to delineate nationality and ethnicity, or to describe themselves as belonging or not belonging to particular classifications, are important.

While formal interviews comprise an important basis for my research, my book is still, primarily, an ethnographic work, the result of regular hours of participant observation and informal interviewing in different venues: shopping malls, social service offices, cafeterias, festivals, coffee shops, parks, restaurants, parking lots, and people's living rooms in and around Daly City. As part of my research, I also participated in and observed the *Philippine News* staff's daily activities, from editorial meetings to telemarketing campaigns. I also conducted interviews with staff members regarding the selection of news articles for publication, advertising, the newspaper's relationship with the Filipino community, journalistic responsibility, and the like.

From a cross-section of Pinoy immigrants from Daly City I collected almost 50 narratives about their lives in the United States. Central to these narratives are such themes as their motivations for leaving the Philippines, patterns of arrival, varying expectations of life in the United States, and searches for employment. Most of my interviewees (like the majority of Filipino immigrants) arrived as professionals, were petitioned for as members of the first-preference category (as unmarried children of American citi-

---

Philippines themselves—was ever employed derogatorily. The suffix -*oy*, in any case, should be familiar to any Tagalog speaker as used in nicknames after one drops the final letter (Nonoy, Doy, Totoy, Caloy)—diminutive, perhaps, but most certainly meant with affection. (The slang term *Flip* could have been derogatory in its origins, but it is clearly a contraction of *Filipino* and surely predates its erroneous folk etymology, i.e., that it is an acronym for "Fucking Little Island People.")

zens), or were petitioned for by their parents' siblings. I discuss my informants' stories at length, focusing on about half a dozen in particular, not just to put names and stories to what would otherwise be immigration statistics, but also to highlight the complexity of each individual's family, class background, and so on. Most of the narrative, if not direct quotations from the informants themselves, is paraphrased or directly translated from the interviews.[15]

Many of the conversations, whether prompted by me or not, revolved around identifiable themes: the informants' departures, differences between the Philippines and the United States (and, by extension, contrasts between Filipino immigrants and American-born Filipinos), work, the possibility of return, homesickness, and, in general, being Filipino in America. Generally, the themes arose from a chronological narrative: I would begin by asking how they came to immigrate to the United States, and their retellings would proceed from there. Though I prepared some questions in advance, the conversation would usually proceed of its own accord, depending on the interviewee, toward topics such as race, colonial history, sexuality, and politics. Certain questions, however, remained foremost in my mind: How were career or lifestyle decisions balanced with decisions concerning family reunification or in conflict with them? To what extent, if any, is Pinoy immigration to the United States already structured or conditioned by a colonial legacy?

I made clear at the beginning of each interview that names and other relevant identifying details would be changed in the final manuscript. I also stressed that the interview had nothing to do with my work as a reporter, and that no details of the interview would be appearing in any of my newspaper articles. I asked permission to tape the interviews, which almost all gave.

Except for people whom I worked with at the newspaper or met at various Daly City venues and events, I generally located my interviewees through snowball sampling: subjects recommended someone else who would be willing to be interviewed, and so on. They were fully informed of the nature of my research and, at the beginning, my identity as a graduate student in anthropology. Such an identity was not always feasible; monkeys and bones were understandably the first things to come to my interviewees' minds. My

---

[15] Almost all my interviews were conducted in Tagalog, but since I am a native Tagalog speaker, it is quite possible that my Tagalog blinders were on and I had simply taken for granted the possibility that all my interviewees could understand me completely. For some interviewees, particularly those who had arrived earlier, it was clear that they were uncomfortable speaking in Tagalog, preferring to answer my questions in English instead. But for the most part, the post-1965 generation of immigrants spoke some form of Taglish (a speech form composed of Tagalog and English mixed in varying quantities), and our conversations "naturally" fell into it.

reluctant adoption of the label "sociologist" did not work either, and so, a few weeks into fieldwork, my more accurate introduction of myself as a "student" sufficed.

But my position as a Filipino student asking to be taught about the Filipino immigrant community generated its own set of interesting problems. My interviewees, though not cognizant of the anthropological debates about emic and etic knowledge, were skeptical of what made them so intrinsically interesting in the first place, especially to someone who seemed like "one of them." In the first few weeks, my blundering initial question—along the lines of "When and how did you come to the U.S.?"—was mostly answered with stony silence, especially by people I was meeting for the first time. Because I was also a Filipino immigrant myself, there were times when our conversations would seem like exercises in a kind of feigning of ignorance. Repeatedly, an interviewee would begin to describe something, then stop herself and say, "But you know what I mean! You're from the Philippines too!"

It was these frustrating interruptions in the discourse, however, that provided the most interesting entry points into the discussion. What *was* I supposed to know because I was from the Philippines too? These glossed-over topics referred to cultural experiences that Filipino immigrants presumably shared—traits, phenomena, views of how the world worked, that had passed into the sometimes unarticulated realm of Filipino common sense, the specifically discursive stuff that bound together an imagined community of Filipino immigrants. And it was at these points, which happened often, that I would respond, "I think I know what you mean—but could you elaborate further?"

Questioning the Transnational

My interviews were situated in a period marked by what some scholars have heralded as a new empirical object: transnationalism. An exploratory article by Nina Glick Schiller, Linda Basch, and Cristina Blanc-Szanton (1992c) formulated perhaps the first conceptual framework for analyzing "the process by which immigrants build social fields that link together their country of origin and their country of settlement" (1). I use the term *transnational theory* to refer to the body of academic writing on the subject. "Researchers," the authors note, "had found in their own field work evidence of a new pattern of migration" (1). The scholarly consensus seemed to be that previous conceptualizations of migration were inadequate for describing the emerging phenomena. Migrants, assisted by the very visible hand of global capitalism, were creating networks that crossed state borders instead of producing dislocated experiences, and the borders of nations did not coincide anymore with their physical, state-determined territories.

What scholars call transnationalism, however, can be seen simply as a continuation of quite *old* processes; it is in that respect only a response to changing theory. In many ways, Filipinos in Daly City seem to live their lives very much according to the classic patterns of migration, according to earlier configurations of migration and settlement in the late 1800s and early 1900s. These earlier patterns are, arguably, "transnational" as well, but even then, some aspects of the theoretical model of transnationalism are simply not supported by my findings about Daly City.[16]

Many scholars of the supposedly emergent phenomenon of transnationalism have focused on immigrants primarily as rational economic and political actors.[17] This simplistic approach does not adequately describe an experience that also encompasses complicated transformations in symbolic conceptions of identity and belonging. Is it possible to conceive of multiple homelands, of different, multiple narratives of the self? In this sense of belonging, the transnational is perhaps better understood as a kind of "transnationality"—as a state, as an experience, with all its accompanying, sometimes contradictory sentiments, located among and within individuals, rather than as an organized economic system. Such a state of being is expressed, not only through migrants' practices and activities, but through their words as well, embodying a wide range of sentiment and imagination.

I take seriously Arjun Appadurai's suggestion of the relevance of studying imagination as "an organized field of social practices." Because of the mass media, he writes, "more persons in more parts of the world consider a wider set of 'possible' lives than they ever did before" (1990, 5; 1991, 197). The topic of imagination is not as odd as it seems: if the nation can be imagined (from within and without), then one can also imagine oneself "outside" it. Daly City may loom large as a potential destination within a Filipino's sphere of possibilities. The pervasiveness of emigration from the Philippines and the ubiquity of mass media have long made it possible for Filipinos to imagine alternate life stories, different possible trajectories.

---

[16] There are, of course, some crucial but related differences: the impact of rapid communication and transportation, the greater role of the media, and the wider and faster distribution of commodities. This is particularly important in relation to the circulation and stimulation of discourse and a more intense reconstitution of connections between the so-called homeland and Daly City, but it does not necessarily lead to a different sense of belonging.

[17] Indeed, much research still needs to be done. Is transnationalism, for instance, as Glick-Schiller, Basch and Blanc-Szanton ask, transmissible between generations (1992a, xiv)? Is the second generation—for which the idea of home may necessarily be different—included in transnationalism's theoretical embrace? How do gender, class, and sexuality fit within the framework? How are the ramifications of transnationalism changed when intention is considered, when people plan to stay or plan not to?

This imagining may be done in different directions—that is, both about the Philippines and about the United States, from any location—and in different tones of voice. Recent studies of migration and "the transnational" have generally overlooked emotional components—notions of home, loss, belonging, patriotism, ambivalence, nostalgia, and homesickness—and these affective elements, particularly important in understanding the emotional lives of immigrants, are articulated in social practices that reinforce or subvert national conceptions and processes. "Transnationality," however, may not necessarily be an embodied state, but primarily the (failed) object of immigrant yearning.

The possibility of migration—or, if one is in Daly City, of a "transnational" mode of existence—becomes most potent on the discursive, symbolic level. Though anchored in the everyday reality of letters, phone calls and the absence of relatives, the imagining of a different life elsewhere, or a life left behind, is also mediated through constructions of mass media. In turn, the boundaries that delimit migrants' lives, that circumscribe the cultural definitions of *here* and *there*, of *Filipino* and *non-Filipino* (or *less Filipino*), are located and established in people's memories and narratives. The language used by these moving subjects is crucial in tracing the categories that Filipinos use in the formation of a Filipino identity in the United States.

In this respect I am cautious about studying the Filipino community in Daly City as a "transnational" one. Examining the emotive aspects of immigration, particularly by listening to the narratives of Daly City residents, makes it clear that the oversimplified push-pull migration model must be abandoned. Furthermore, the familial, political, cultural, and financial connections between Daly City Pinoys and their relatives in the Philippines highlight the structural links between the two places. The features described by scholars—the supposed reconfiguration of nation and state boundaries, the growing role of high-speed media in the social imagination, and its impact on anthropology[18]—even if their theorization has been found wanting, have been instrumental in my conception of Daly City as an immigrant community.

---

[18] Other anthropologists have used a transnational framework effectively, examining both the material and subjective aspects of transmigrant life: they have looked at Hong Kong entrepreneurs in California and their strategies in accumulating cultural capital (Ong 1992), and at non-resident Indian immigrants investing in the "homeland" and their difficulties in communicating a certain "Indian-ness" to relatives and business partners in India (Lessinger 1992). Naficy (1991), in his study of Iranians in Los Angeles, examines nostalgia and its articulation in souvenirs and music videos, using psychoanalytic methods.

On Two Fields

The apparent multiple belongings of Daly City's Filipinos point to an important bridging of Asian studies with Asian American studies. Though resistance comes from both fronts, Asian studies and Asian American studies are growing closer to each other, at least in their subjects and the geography of their respective realms. Regrettably, the guarding of academic turf, together with the unpredictable politics of funding, has made it difficult to find common ground between those two obviously limited spheres of area studies. The highly politicized nature of the history of Asian American studies in particular has necessitated, unsurprisingly, a defensive inflexibility on the part of Asian American academics. This has also, unfortunately, resulted in a failure to change along with a rapidly shifting population, or to account for historical connections with Asia since the beginning of Asian immigration to the United States.

Surely the large influx of Asian immigrants into the United States after 1965 alone demands the inclusion in Asian American curricula of histories claimed by well over half of those who may now call themselves Asian Americans. In turn, scholars of and in the Philippines would do well to understand the political and cultural dynamics of the communities their former compatriots have formed. As the Philippines shapes the forms of homesickness and nostalgia for Pinoy immigrants in the United States, so does the United States occupy the social imaginary of the Filipino people. One should recognize the necessity of Filipino American studies in Philippine studies and vice versa, and the ways in which the boundaries of both fields acutely affect analytical perspectives. My ethnography is located at the much-contested junction between both fields.

The connection between the Philippines and the United States is clear, particularly in historical, economic and political structures. Some contemporary scholars have seen this link in psychic formations as well, though it is debatable. The relevance of these postcolonial links, however, may become clearer if the connections between two fields of study—Asian studies and Asian American studies—are defined further. It is perhaps understandable, then, that given the circumstances, bridging the two academic fields of Philippine studies and Filipino American studies should be met with deep suspicion. At academic conferences, warnings are raised, from time to time, that even the study of the transnational itself threatens the borders of Asian American studies.

Such worries are not entirely unfounded. Deeply embroiled in politics, funding for ethnic studies seems to be more dependent on the vagaries of university administrations than that of other more "traditional" departments and fields. Area/ethnic studies as a whole—but especially ethnic studies—are forced to justify their existence continually or be subsumed under the more "legitimate" discipline-based departments. Some of the bad blood stems from the fact that Asian American studies and ethnic studies in general, and certainly at their inception, were construed as alternative spaces for educational curricula "said to be irrelevant to the experiences of people of color" (Wei 1993, 17). Born from the Third World Strike at San Francisco State College (now University) and at the University of California at Berkeley in 1968, Asian American Studies was a direct challenge to what was seen as an educational system that promoted Eurocentric ideology. This consciously oppositional stance was directed at the academic "Establishment," as it were, and what it stood for—including, one may argue, the field of Asian studies, whose beginnings were linked with matrices of colonial knowledge and particular strains of Orientalism (Said 1978; Rafael 1994). Asian American scholars of the '60s, in particular, sought consciously to separate themselves from Asia, finding little in common (including language) with those who lived there.[19]

My work bridges the two spheres of study—not just in my investigation of identity as forged from the intersections of two places and cultures, but also in my emphasis on people whose senses of belonging are rooted in different locations. The population demographics alone—not to mention the links and networks forged between people of different countries—demand that studies of Pinoys in the United States, particularly in places like Daly City, not be automatically confined to Asian American studies and the mechanical "Americanness" the field implies, but be considered as extensions of Philippine studies as well. For the latter, the sheer number of Filipinos overseas has required a rethinking of government policies and cultural norms and an overall reconfiguration of the Philippines' identity as a nation and as a state. One must also understand how Filipinos in the Philippines view themselves and the country in relation to the unprecedented, massive absence of their friends, relatives, and neighbors. An estimated six million Filipinos were working abroad in 1994—roughly 10 percent of the total population and 22 percent of the 27-million-strong labor force (Beltran, Samonte, and Walker 1996, 19). By 2006 eight million were working abroad. Such possibilities for overseas employment, in turn, expand the horizon of options for those left behind.

---

[19] Asian American Studies is also the product of students and activists of the second (and third) generations, and could be seen as a reaction against their parents' immigrant generation. One can argue that, in many ways, the keystone works of Asian American studies and literature can be read as repudiating the parents' immigrant culture—either for its seeming backwardness or for its concession to assimilation.

2

LITTLE MANILA

~

I f you drive down California's Skyline Highway a little too fast, you might miss Daly City altogether. Bordering San Francisco to its south, Daly City, like much of suburban America, stretches its boundaries into the next town, in a diffuse mass of tract housing—varying in age, cost, architecture, and prestige—that extends from the Sunset District in San Francisco all the way down south to Foster City and beyond. What were once acres of cabbage patches and pig ranches became, from the late 1940s through the 1970s, rows upon endless rows of suburban dwellings crisscrossing the Colma hills.

Sheer numbers are only part of the reason that Daly City—or "Dah-lee City," Filipinos say jokingly, in a parody of Filipino mispronunciation—is known as "Little Manila" or "Manilatown," even though the appellations may not seem apt.[1] More Filipinos live in Los Angeles County (almost 300,000), San Diego County (over 130,000) and Honolulu County (almost

---

[1] A "real" Manilatown on Kearny Street in San Francisco, with barbershops, hotels, restaurants, and clubs—and, at its height, 10,000 Filipinos—did exist just south of Chinatown until 10 blocks' worth was swallowed up by the Financial District in the late '60s. One of the last structures to remain was the International Hotel, and the defense against the eviction of its tenants became a rallying cry for the Asian American civil rights movement in 1977. Today, the area south of Market Street—the part that has not been made into convention centers or hotels—still houses many Filipino residents. Described in 1979 as "perhaps the largest Filipino ghetto in the U.S.," the Filipino tenement houses, "sandwiched in alleys," are located next to warehouses and whorehouses (Luna 1979, S2). Many Filipino veterans—soldiers who fought with the United States Armed Forces in the Far East (USAFFE) during World War II and moved to the United States, in part, to claim veterans' benefits—also make their home in hotels in the Tenderloin district.

TABLE 2.1   DALY CITY IN COMPARISON WITH SELECTED AMERICAN CITIES

City/County	Total Population	Filipino Population	White Population	Asian Population	% Filipino
Daly City	**100,237**	**35,905**	**27,465**	**57,097**	**35.82**
San Diego County	2,941,454	130,604	2,065,987	302,392	4.44
Chula Vista	211,253	21,073	128,465	27,222	9.97
Imperial Beach	26,992	1,418	16,805	1,767	5.25
National City	54,260	9,363	190,770	10,077	17.25
Poway	48,044	1,509	39,807	3,584	3.14
San Diego	1,261,251	72,604	819,464	192,482	5.76
Chicago	2,749,283	26,968	1,004,760	134,837	0.98
Jersey City	82,789	15,481	82,789	45,827	18.70
New York City	8,214,426	68,147	3,604,789	963,295	0.83
Virginia Beach	435,619	15,321	305,596	23,881	3.51
Seattle	562,106	13,190	393,431	73,067	2.35
Los Angeles County	9,948,081	295,888	4,660,343	1,288,643	2.97
Cerritos	51,488	6,046	13,851	30,091	11.74
Glendale	192,340	8,335	139,653	25,837	4.33
Long Beach	466,718	20,517	192,800	62,090	4.40
Los Angeles	3,773,846	111,939	1,776,822	391,705	2.97
West Covina	112,809	9,154	40,639	28,051	8.11
Honolulu County	909,863	128,827	201,795	402,365	14.16
Honolulu	364,522	44,212	76,476	203,707	12.13
Waipahu	33,108	16,668	1,566	21,774	50.34

Source: U.S. Bureau of the Census 2006.

130,000)—all areas with older, more historically established Filipino communities and, consequently, the focuses of recent scholarly research (see Bonus 2000, España-Maram 2006, and Espiritu 2003). Other less prominent California cities were Filipino agricultural migrant centers in the 1920s and '30s. The population of Delano, for example, is 14.81 percent Filipino. Watsonville (1.30 percent of whose population is Filipino) was the site of major anti-Filipino riots, and Stockton (6.76 percent of whose population is Filipino), with its vibrant Little Manila, was "the heart of Filipino America" prior to World War II (Mabalon et al. 2008, 8). But it is still Daly City, with the highest concentration of Filipinos (almost 36 percent) in any midsized American city, that is called "the *adobo* capital of the U.S.A"[2] (see Table 2.1).

Certainly the "-town" suffix is more properly applicable to relatively bounded areas within bigger spaces like cities, as in San Francisco, but not to Daly City. Nor does it properly apply to Monterey Park, California, for that matter, despite its reputation as "the first suburban Chinatown" (Fong 1994). Moreover, there is no single grouping of areas or census tracts in Daly City where Filipinos reside.

[2] *Adobo* is a popular menu item made with chicken or pork and, at its most basic, stewed in vinegar and soy sauce. Despite its Hispanic/Chinese origins, *adobo* is generally thought of as the Filipino national dish.

As an account executive at *Philippine News* said, sounding like others through the years, "I had heard of Daly City even before I arrived in the United States. There are lots of Filipinos there." People in the Philippines inquiring about my research would ask, on hearing the name Daly City, "Aren't there lots of Filipinos there?" People, including a few *Philippine News* employees, expressed surprise when I told them that Filipinos constituted only a little over 30 percent of the city's population. "Is that all? I always thought that it was 60 percent. 80, even," said one. Such inflation of numbers attests to Daly City's semi-mythical status. On the East Coast, only Jersey City is perhaps commonly associated by Filipinos with a large Pinoy community. But with a concentration of only 19 percent, it does not come close to Daly City's numbers.

It is this same high concentration of Filipinos in Daly City that contributes to something of a puzzle; what explains the prominence of Daly City, despite the seeming lack of Filipino commercial centers, mainstream political importance, or a long-standing history of settlement? The answer may lie simply in demographics. At over 100,000 people, Daly City is a large enough suburb to "exist" on its own, whether politically or discursively, and not be lumped together with San Francisco. (San Diego and Los Angeles are, of course, famous for many other reasons, but Daly City is well-known, at least to Filipinos, for just one thing—its Pinoy population.)

Most crucial, however, is the role of the San Francisco Bay Area in establishing and disseminating the terms of media discourse and coverage of the Filipino community in general. *Philippine News, Filipinas*, and The Filipino Channel (TFC)—the most prominent Filipino American newspaper, magazine, and cable channel, respectively—have their corporate headquarters and most of their staff members based in the Bay Area, with the result that much local news (and by extension, Daly City news) is amplified to become *national* news.

Daly City has experienced rapid demographic change in the decades since 1970, when 86 percent of the population was listed as Caucasian (Daly City/ Colma Chamber of Commerce 1992, 3). Between 1980 and 1990, the Pinoy population in Daly City nearly doubled (Daly City/Colma Chamber of Commerce 1992, 3). By the 2000 U.S. census, Filipinos in Daly City, who comprised 32 percent of the population, outnumbered those who identified themselves as "white" (not including those of Hispanic origin) by almost 6,000 people. In 2006, according to the American Community Survey Demographic and Housing Estimates, there were 35,905 Filipinos in Daly City, or 35.82 percent of the total population. This increase in numbers is directly attributable to immigration. Of the foreign-born population in Daly City (54,213, or 52 percent of the total population), 24,627 Filipinos made up 44 percent. In other words, 3 out of 4 Filipinos in Daly City were born in the

Philippines. These numbers are consistent with the 64 percent of the Filipino population in the United States as a whole that is foreign-born.[3]

Daly City's Bay Area neighbors, however, have smaller immigrant communities in proportion to their total population. Almost 37 percent of San Francisco's residents were born overseas, for instance; South San Francisco's population was 39 percent foreign-born. Only in Southern California do we find areas with concentrations of immigrants, whether from Asia or from Latin America, comparable to that of Daly City. In Monterey Park, for instance, Chinese immigrants have reconfigured the suburban landscape (Fong 1994)[4]. Many other "traditional" American suburbs have long been experiencing a demographic shift to residents other than Anglo Americans as Daly City has.

Pinoys are spread out everywhere in the San Francisco Bay Area, except in "whiter," wealthier communities like Atherton and Menlo Park. One city's inhabitants and services spill over into the next, making the perception of concentration somewhat illusory. To Daly City's west, for instance, lies Pacifica, a seaside town where Filipinos constitute the second-largest ethnic minority group; over 16 percent of South San Francisco's population, to the south, is Filipino, making Filipinos third in population rank in the city. Filipinos live in large numbers down the Peninsula, all the way to South Bay cities like San Jose (where they are the third-largest Asian American group) and Sunnyvale. In the East Bay towns like Union City (where they make up 19 percent of the population), Hercules (where they make up 25 percent), and Pinole (11 percent Filipino, and whose public library contains an impressive Philippine collection), Filipinos have been making their mark. For instance, the presence of U.S. Navy facilities in Vallejo paved the way for a Filipino population of 22,000 (almost 20 percent of the city's total population)[5] (see Table 2.2).

---

[3] It should be made clear, however, that this proportion of native-born to foreign-born Filipinos is not so large when compared to that of other Asian groups. In 1980, for instance, 80 percent of Indians in the United States were foreign-born; the percentage was understandably higher for the Vietnamese population—as high as 90 percent (Hing 1993).

[4] Asians constituted almost 62 percent of the city's population in 2000; those who identified themselves as white were only 21 percent. The percentage of foreign-born (54 percent), however, is only a little larger than that of Daly City.

[5] By World War I, 6,000 Filipinos were working in the U.S. Navy. The 1947 Military Bases Agreement not only prolonged the existence of U.S. military bases on Philippine soil, it also continued the direct recruitment of 2,000 Filipinos a year into the U.S. Navy—even though the Philippines was fully independent at that point. In the '60s, 100,000 Filipinos applied each year; by 1970 there were more Filipinos in the U.S. Navy (14,000) than in the Philippine Navy itself (Espiritu 1995, 15).

TABLE 2.2   DALY CITY IN COMPARISON WITH SELECTED SAN FRANCISCO BAY AREA CITIES

City/County	Total Population	Filipino Population	White Population	Asian Population	% Filipino
San Francisco	744,041	36,089	394,265	236,497	4.85
Alameda County	1,457,426	77,708	666,814	357,939	5.33
Alameda	70,208	3,753	42,706	15,532	5.34
Fremont	207,356	8,403	79,520	95,139	4.05
Hayward	129,986	17,778	41,608	33,528	13.68
Oakland	377,256	5,242	128,672	58,903	1.39
Union City	62,749	12,168	15,938	34,076	19.39
Contra Costa County					
Hercules	19,488	4,877	5,453	8,327	25.02
Pinole	19,039	1,853	10,356	4,134	9.73
San Mateo County	705,499	62,572	432,364	164,038	8.87
Daly City	**100,237**	**35,905**	**27,465**	**57,097**	**35.82**
Pacifica	38,390	3,215	26,684	5,868	8.37
San Bruno	40,165	3,075	23,156	7,506	7.65
San Mateo	90,959	2,550	64,473	15,304	2.80
South San Francisco	60,552	9,987	26,671	17,510	16.49
Santa Clara County					
Milpitas	62,698	9,381	19,353	32,482	14.96
San Jose	916,220	50,782	430,286	279,350	5.54

U.S. Bureau of the Census 2006.

Little Boxes

The transformation of Daly City into "the new Manila" (Aranda 1992) is a recent phenomenon, considering the city's short history. Before the arrival of Irish immigrants, the area where Daly City stands was part of Rancho Guadalupe la Visitacion y Rodeo Viejo when California was still Mexico's northernmost province. But historians trace the political establishment of the city to the arrival of refugees from the San Francisco earthquake in 1906, when evacuees to Daly's Hill bought plots at $200 to $300 each. The former Bostonian

---

San Juan describes the situation as "an anomalous phenomenon where Filipino citizens function as mercenaries eager to serve their former colonial master" (1994, 2). But a practical guarantee of U.S. citizenship, rather than "eagerness to serve," is a more plausible explanation than San Juan's cynical analysis.

A further irony here—which belies their "eagerness to serve"—involves the actual positions Filipinos take. After World War II the Navy issued a new ruling restricting Filipinos to serving as officers' stewards and mess attendants. As Espiritu writes, "Barred from admission to other ratings, Filipino enlistees performed the work of domestics, preparing and serving the officers' meals, and caring for the officers' galley, wardroom, and living spaces. . . . Unofficially, Filipino stewards also have been ordered to perform menial chores such as walking the officers' dogs and acting as personal servants for the officers' wives" (1995, 16). This description is reminiscent of what my uncle, a steward at the Subic Bay Naval Base, called himself half-jokingly: "tsimoy ng Kano," slang for "servant to Americans."

John D. Daly, the owner of the land, broke up his San Mateo Dairy after realtors persuaded him and other landowners in the Colma Hills to sell. Threats of annexation from San Francisco put pressure on residents to seek incorporation; they then established city borders, and voters finally approved incorporation into the county in 1911.[6]

Throughout the 1920s and up to World War II, Daly City earned most of its income from flower and vegetable gardening. At times the area devoted to cabbage patches alone could reach 10,000 acres, depending on the season. Growth due to wartime industry did not make as much of an impact on Daly City as it did on other parts of the San Francisco Bay Area.[7] Within a few years, however, the massive construction of residential housing—known in local booster literature as "The Era of the Builders"—created the "little boxes on the hillside"(Malvina Reynolds, quoted in Donaldson 1969, 59) that give Daly City its distinctive quality today.

Beginning in 1948, residential buildings and strip malls were erected across the landscape.[8] The developer Henry Doelger, who had already constructed 3,000 houses in the Sunset and Richmond districts in San Francisco between 1934 and 1940, purchased 1,350 acres in what is now Daly City's Westlake district, and built 9,000 homes (San Mateo County Historic Re-

---

[6] Daly City's borders did not include Colma, which remains an unincorporated town within Daly City to this day. Colma, with an area of about two square miles, is famous for its more than 20 cemeteries—mostly the resting places of dead San Franciscans (except for Chinese, who were buried in a separate cemetery in South San Francisco), as burials were prohibited in San Francisco in 1901. Twenty percent of Colma's 1990 population was Filipino.

[7] By 1944, 26 percent of all ships deployed in the Second World War were made in the Bay Area; San Francisco alone hosted a large number of naval facilities. Vallejo, the site of the now-closed Mare Island naval complex, tripled its population during the war.

To the south of Daly City, in San Bruno, one shameful legacy of World War II in the Bay Area can be found where the Tanforan racetrack was located. During World War II, Tanforan was used as an assembly center for Japanese Americans on the way to the internment camps; all that is left of it is now one of the shoddier malls on the Peninsula.

[8] Malvina Reynolds's satirical 1963 folk song "Little Boxes," long thought to be based on Daly City and made famous in a version recorded by Pete Seeger, is not too far from more strident scholarly opinion at the time. The lyrics went:

Little boxes on the hillside,
Little boxes made of ticky tacky
Little boxes on the hillside,
Little boxes all the same.
There's a green one and a pink one
And a blue one and a yellow one
And they're all made out of ticky tacky
And they all look just the same.

Later stanzas talk of "the people in the boxes" going to college "where they were put into boxes / And they came out all the same . . ." (Quoted in Donaldson 1969, 59).

sources Advisory Board 1984). The Suburban Realty Company, owned by Carl and Fred Gellert, built a few thousand units more as well as the Serramonte Shopping Center in what is now the Serramonte district. The Zita Corporation came along in 1957, building 79 units a month in St. Francis Heights.[9] The Daly City historian Samuel Chandler writes that the area came to be seen as emblematic of "the West Coast housing mess" (Tebbel 1963, quoted in Chandler 1973, 130). Chandler reports that Daly City was criticized by journalists as "sloppy, sleazy, slovenly, and slipshod"(1973, 130) and a "look-alike, think-alike instant suburb" (1973, 107).

Many of these houses contain so-called in-law apartments—generally small units converted from garage space, and ostensibly reserved for parents who have come to live with their children. In-law apartments almost always have their own entrances and bathrooms, but they rarely fully adhere to building codes—the ceiling is too low, or insulation is thin, or there are no phone jacks in the apartment. Such units are fairly common in Daly City and in San Francisco's Sunset District. They have functioned not only as a source of extra (untaxed) income for the homeowners, but also as a first home for newly arrived immigrants or starving students.

In short, Daly City fits the cliché of the poorly planned suburb, much scorned by city planners. By the '50s, 90 percent of the population growth in metropolitan areas had occurred in the suburbs, and the idea that the suburb represented the American ideal had quickly soured—at least so far as urban planners and sociologists were concerned. Scathing commentary attacked the houses as "little more than a repository of an exceedingly wide range of artifacts" (Seeley, Sim, and Loosley 1956, 42), the typical suburbanite as "an Eisenhower Republican, seldom informed, rarely angry, and only spasmodically partisan" (Riesman 1958, 377), and the suburb dwellers' lives as "witnessing the same television performances, eating the same tasteless prefabricated foods, from the same freezers, conforming in every outward and inward respect to a common mold" (Lewis Mumford, quoted by Donaldson 1969, 70). The homogeneity of housing styles made suburbs easy targets for such criticism.

Another area of complaint has to do with the streets. Langdon notes that zoning of residences away from commercial areas has fostered "dispersed,

---

[9] Filipinos began moving into Daly City's new houses soon after; by 1980, 18 percent of Daly City's total population was Filipino. By 1989 almost half the residents in the Serramonte census tract were of Filipino origin. The demographic changes in general have been quite dramatic: in 1970 the population of Daly City was almost 87 percent white (U.S. Bureau of the Census 2003). Zip code 94015, Daly City's St. Francis district (where I lived), saw 5,940 new Filipino immigrants arrive between 1983 and 1990 (Fong 1994, 13). No census data exist specifically on Filipinos in Daly City before 1980; in 1970, not even the category of Asian American was being enumerated.

automobile-dependent suburban development," itself corresponding to the government's neglect of public transportation. He points out that public transportation would be prohibitively expensive—and inefficient—in such a scattered environment, and that small stores could not survive in such areas: "The scarcity of connections among the streets—hobbled by all those movement-stopping cul-de-sacs—would prevent potential customers from reaching them" (1994, 36). In the city of San Francisco—in the Sunset District, designed by the same planner who would later map out Daly City's Westlake district—the streets are all laid out on a grid. The streets running from north to south are numbered avenues; the names of west-to-east streets begin with every letter of the alphabet, and are in alphabetical order. In contrast, Daly City incorporates the typical street hierarchy system, where highways lead to so-called arterial roads, which lead to collector roads—"the sole access routes from the arterial roads to homes in the subdivisions," Langdon writes (1994, 29). Though there are exceptions in Daly City, collector roads are still few and far between, and—because this is a suburb, after all—there are four-way stops at almost every intersection, making automobile progress through the area slow. The curvilinear direction of the roads makes for a gentler grid pattern, where roads follow the contour of the terrain, but it also makes the street blocks longer. A little farther south, in the Serramonte district, a long median planted with trees and shrubs bisects the main arterial road, Callan Avenue. The greenery beautifies the area, but also ensures that pedestrians can cross only at the traffic lights, which are many meters apart.

In Daly City the isolation imposed by the spatial layout means there is a nearly total reliance on motorized transportation, either public or private, but mostly the latter. Riding on the San Mateo Transit bus that weaves through the Daly City streets, one constantly hears snatches of conversations in Tagalog and Ilocano. The 20J bus line winds its way through Daly City's St. Francis and Serramonte districts—both areas exemplifying the song's "little boxes on the hillside"—and stops in front of the Seton Medical Center, the largest employer in the city and, according to anecdotal evidence, responsible for the initial influx of Filipino medical technicians and nurses after it opened as St. Mary's Help Hospital in 1965.[10] The buses generally run every half hour, with almost every route taking the passenger either to the Serramonte Mall or to the Daly City Bay Area Rapid Transit, or BART, station.[11] Only playgrounds

---

[10] The hospital employs 1,500 people. The City of Daly City is the second-largest employer, with 698 people, followed by the Jefferson High School District with 657 people.

[11] The Filipino population is thrown into relief when one rides the BART. Daly City was, until 1998, the last stop on the Peninsula in a transportation system that extends as far northeast as Concord and as far southeast as Fremont. As the number of passengers (packed like sardines during rush

and parks, at least in this part of town, are within walking distance; to walk to the nearest large mall would require traveling on empty streets with long, winding blocks, or alongside busy six-lane arterial roads with unpaved sidewalks. This layout explains why the residential areas, especially in the afternoons, look oddly deserted. One hardly sees anyone walking on the sidewalks because, one realizes, there is no place to walk *to*. As with other suburbs of the same type, the houses have no front lawns; the space in front is covered with a slab of concrete serving as the driveway to the garage. At night the streets, barely illuminated by streetlights powerless to pierce the thick fog, are lined with cars in addition to those already parked in garages.

Just a few miles further north, however, the landscape changes. The section of Daly City that shares a border with San Francisco is busier, more crowded. More vehicles clog the streets. This area is also somewhat more rundown, as the buildings are older by about two decades than those in the rest of the city. In this neighborhood, residential and commercial areas are close to each other; unaffected by the more rigorous zoning in the suburban tracts further south, car dealerships abut schools and Filipino video stores. Because rents are lower here, according to my interviewees, many Filipinos live here at or near the Top of the Hill on their first move to Daly City (usually after San Francisco).[12]

Living like Filipinos

For many people the center of Pinoy activity is the Serramonte Shopping Center, where, amidst McDonald's, B. Dalton's, and Mervyn's, Filipinos of practically every demographic background congregate. Every day, veterans and senior citizens—most are men, and many look very formal in their coats and ties and slicked-back, sometimes dyed, hair—sit on the wooden mall benches in the food court, reading newspapers, gossiping, queueing up for lotto tickets. The men move from table to table, greeting each other. Few pretend to drink coffee or eat a slice of pizza to justify their presence; almost everyone is empty-handed and simply talking to one another. There are other non-Filipino senior citizens as well—some are Irish, most Italian—but they keep to themselves, and do not seem to know the Filipinos. One informant in his twenties, Fred Corral, told me: "I can see myself looking like them in the

---

hour) starts thinning out on a trip, say, from the Embarcadero in San Francisco to Daly City, it becomes noticeable that many of the commuters left are Filipino or Latino.

[12] The incredibly popular Filipino fast food restaurant chain Jollibee opened its first U.S. branch in the Top of the Hill district in 1998 and was instantly deluged with customers; there was a minimum hour-long wait for food in the first few months of its opening, with lines stretching around the block.

future, man. Hanging out at Serramonte, wearing a baseball cap, eating a hotdog." Filipino American teenagers, wandering the mall in packs, wearing baggy pants and their caps on backwards, represent another generation. Most of the senior citizens take the early buses to get here, arriving as the mall opens at 10:00 A.M. Many of the teenagers ride the bus; some drive souped-up Hondas and Acuras.

When I take Filipino visitors to Serramonte Mall they usually express some surprise, if not shock, at the number of Filipinos milling around. I experienced the same thing when I was new to Daly City. Coming from a remote central New York town like Ithaca, I rarely saw Filipinos in the street, and, except for the occasional Filipino Cultural Night, certainly not *en masse*. One of my interviewees, Wally Curameng, was "very much surprised" to discover that there was a Goldilocks restaurant in Daly City, and that Serramonte was "like Shoemart" (Goldilocks and Shoemart are hugely lucrative restaurant and department-store chains in the Philippines). He added: "[It's like] 4 out of 10 is Filipino, 4 out of 10 [in the] crowd is Filipino. [So] I was surprised." Kiko Novero told me, "when I first got here, I said, oh my gosh, ang daming Pilipino [there are so many Filipinos]. And I was really happy about it, I was like, oh my gosh, I can make friends."

These reactions to Serramonte Mall suggest that Pinoys are not *supposed* to be here, especially not in such large numbers. The mall would never be mistaken for one in the Philippines, for there are still many Caucasians wandering about. But our initial surprise upon seeing so many Filipinos makes Daly City unique in the United States. In Hong Kong's Statue Square, many domestic helpers congregate during the weekends, and the experience is similar. Though there are certainly more Filipinos in Los Angeles, for instance, the sheer numbers of people in that city works against the sense of disjunction. In Daly City, Pinoys are literally everywhere.

Except for the food, Serramonte Mall is not much different from suburban shopping malls throughout the country, selling books (B. Dalton's), computer software (Waldensoftware), "specialty apparel" (Victoria's Secret, President Tuxedo, and a new addition, a nursing wear store), chocolate (See's Candies), shoes (15 stores, including Payless and Foot Locker), housewares (Lechter's, Stroud's Linen), clothes (Structure, Lerner New York, Forever 21, etc.), music (Sam Goody, Camelot Music, etc.), glasses (Site for Sore Eyes), and videos (Suncoast Picture Company, Blockbuster). There are also other standard mall stores such as jewelry stores, The Body Shop, Perfumania, Radio Shack, General Nutrition Center, and Kits Cameras.[13] Only 2 of the 130

---

[13] That most ubiquitous of all mall stores, The Gap, closed in early 1996; the rumor, according to Filipinos in the food court, was that it had closed because of "excessive shoplifting." True or not, I

businesses are specifically Filipino—Manila Sunset, a restaurant in the food court serving standard (and greasy) Filipino food, and the relatively new Tatak Pilipino, a souvenir store.

As is sadly characteristic of inadequate suburban planning, Daly City lacks a community center. Serramonte Mall (and for others, a bowling alley on the corner of San Pedro and Mission) serves that function. The mall is where many of the Filipino senior citizens and teenagers hang out by day in the summer. This absence of a place for people to congregate has as much to do with the weather as with poor city and environmental planning. Parks, for instance, are cold and windswept, even on sunny days. People do not linger after Little League games. In the evenings the local Barnes and Noble bookstore, which has a cafe with seats in the lobby, is packed with young students and adults—chatting, mostly, but also reading and doing homework. It is, as far as I can tell, the only equivalent of a small cafe in the entire city.

It is possible to live like a Filipino—at least as regards consumption—even in such a seemingly bland environment. For the Filipino consumer, a wide range of choices exists; Filipino restaurants abound in Daly City, from the ritzier Tito Rey, with a strict dress code, to the many *turo-turo*[14] style eating places where one can find quick Filipino fare from *adobo* to *sinigang na isda* (stewed fish in tamarind soup). Branches of the Philippine originals are everywhere in evidence: Max Fried Chicken, Barrio Fiesta, and Goldilocks. Chips, crackers, and candy imported from the Philippines, as well as locally made Filipino meat products, are widely available in Asian food stores, including the occasional Filipino market. The United States headquarters of the *Iglesia ni Cristo*, the politically influential Philippine religious organization, is within walking distance of Serramonte Mall, across the vast parking lots. Video rental stores display movie posters featuring popular Filipino actors pasted up on their windows.[15] Through a cable network, The Filipino Channel, residents can have sitcoms and news from the Philippines beamed into their living rooms every day. Half a dozen Filipino newspapers and magazines, from free, limited-circulation tabloids to glossy four-color publications, circulate in the Bay Area and keep the community informed

---

have witnessed (on three separate occasions) shoplifters, pursued by store clerks or security guards, rush out of a store, out of the mall building, and into an idling car parked by the entrance.

[14] *Turo-turo* literally means "point-point," a reference to cafeteria-style eateries where the customer points to the food she wants to eat.

[15] Before video, there were theaters that would show Filipino movies (as advertisements in *Philippine News* showed). Teddy Encinas remembers theaters in the southern part of San Francisco (the Apollo on Geneva, another on Mission), as well as a Filipino AM-radio station in the '70s.

about happenings affecting Filipinos both in the United States and in the Philippines.

Numerous Filipino organizations in the Bay Area have been established around various focal points, from occupations and ethno-linguistic origins to religious affiliations and school alumni organizations. The back pages of Filipino newspapers are full of advertisements from remittance companies, travel agencies, food catering services, immigration counseling services, and other businesses aimed exclusively at the Filipino community. Popular musical performers from the Philippines hold concerts in San Francisco every year.

There are no simple explanations for how Daly City grew to attract so many Pinoy residents. Daly City is not unique, and other Bay Area suburbs have experienced a large influx of Filipinos as well. In jest, some informants have attributed Daly City's popularity to its not-so-apparent similarity to Baguio City, a major tourist spot in the northern Philippines.[16] Some interviewees have also attributed the influx to the Seton Medical Center, which actively recruited nurses and medical technicians from the Philippines soon after its opening. (When asked why he thought there was such a large Filipino population in Daly City, Wally Curameng ventured, "Maybe because this is closer to the airport?" and laughed.)

Most likely, however, Daly City's proximity to San Francisco was the deciding factor; many Pinoy residents of Daly City had lived in San Francisco upon their arrival, then moved to the suburbs once they could afford a bigger house. This was, as some informants suggested, part of what they imagined life in America to be. But housing prices on the Peninsula started increasing in the early 1980s with the rapid increase of Silicon Valley money further south. As the former Daly City mayor Michael Guingona said,

> You came here [to Daly City] 'cause back then, the housing was affordable, and . . . it was close enough to work, and nobody bothered you, and the schools were good, they still are, but what happened later on in the '80s was that people came here, rented here, and saved their money and moved to places like Vallejo, Hercules, Pinole, in the East Bay.

The housing prices in the East Bay were, and still are, lower than on the Peninsula. But the relatively higher income of the earlier group of post-1965

---

[16] Baguio City, located in the mountains of Benguet Province, was a former colonial hill station, with much of its infrastructure built by the American colonial administration. It is now a popular tourist destination mostly because of its climate—the temperature is 10 degrees cooler than Manila's. The presence of fog, rare in a tropical country, is what elicits comparisons to Daly City.

immigrants, and the fact that many moved as nuclear family units, explained the practicality of larger-sized suburban houses in places like Daly City.

Chain migration based on family reunification grew in the latter half of the '70s, when Daly City started to become known as a mostly Filipino suburb.[17] A few years after arrival—the length of time depending on their immigration status—immigrants would petition for their parents or siblings, who in turn would send for their own immediate relatives. "You know the clannish type of our culture," said one of my informants. "They always want to be with the same group, with their families. . . . They are following their relatives and friends of course. . . . It's a kind of security blanket."

One of my interviewees, Michael Santos, arrived with his two sisters in the United States in September 1993. They lived with his maternal uncle in Daly City for six months. As he said this, he quickly added, "Of course, when you arrive here, you still don't have—of course, Filipinos, we're a close-knit family, even at your uncle's, you still won't be able to afford to rent an apartment, of course, we still didn't have jobs, we were newcomers, three of us arrived."[18] Many of my interviewees, particularly those who arrived in the '80s and later, did the same; they lived with their relatives until they found jobs that could support the rental of a separate apartment or house.

Michael's family's entry into the United States typified the classic textbook chain migration pattern. Michael's eldest sister, who lived in Los Angeles, petitioned for their mother, who arrived in 1984. She then waited until 1989, when she had become a citizen, to petition for Michael and his siblings as first-preference immigrants. Their mother later moved to San Francisco to be with her brother. Their airfare was sent in a chain of sorts: at the very beginning, the sister first sent airfare to their mother. Because she was a senior citizen, the mother was able to receive Social Supplementary Income, which she saved and later sent to her other children for airfare. The children then pooled their resources—appliances, savings, separation pay—in order to supplement the airfare: "hindi kami nag-depende sa kanila [we didn't depend on them] totally."

---

[17] In August 1975 the *Ladies' Home Journal*, in contrast to critics of the suburbs, selected the increasingly Filipino-populated district of Westlake in Daly City as one of the "best 15 suburbs" in America. The *Philippine News*'s characteristically proud reaction: "[This] serves at best to prove that Filipinos, in freedom and when left in charge of their own lives and destinies, not only remain the friendly, likable, hospitable, generous, physically and spiritually clean people they traditionally are but that even in the most advanced and sophisticated of communities, Filipinos inevitably rise to the highest social, cultural and economic levels attainable" (Garcia 1975).

[18] In his own words: "Siyempre, pagkadating mo dito, wala ka pa namang—siyempre, mga Pilipino, close-knit family tayo, maski sa uncle mo, hindi pa naman kami makaka-afford mag-rent nang apartment, siyempre, wala pa kaming trabaho, newcomers kami, tatlo kaming dumating."

The presence of relatives, and the expectations of seeing fellow Filipinos in the new home, helped ease their transition into American life. Santos told me that "kilala na [sa Pilipinas] ang San Francisco 'tsaka Daly City na maraming Pilipino" (it's already known in the Philippines that San Francisco and Daly City have many Filipinos). Kiko Novero[19] and his siblings already "expected," before emigration, that there would be many Filipinos in Daly City, from letters his family had received from his wife's relatives. The Filipino community proved to be enough of a draw for Novero. He and his family moved to a bigger home in Belmont in 1993, but Novero still works and goes to school in Daly City, primarily "because it's all gonna be Filipinos." He recently had the opportunity to be promoted to manager of the men's fragrance counter at a department store in San Mateo, but he preferred to stay at the department store's branch at Serramonte instead. "I feel like I belong here. Everyone that passes . . . I know them." Not everyone, however, "knows" Daly City.

An "Invisible" Ethnic Enclave

Daly City is not recognized, or recognizable, by so-called mainstream white America as an ethnic enclave, despite the proliferating number of Filipino-oriented businesses and its image to Filipinos both in the United States and in the Philippines as the foremost Filipino enclave. This phenomenon already contradicts Daly City's long-held characterization as merely a "bedroom community," with almost 19 percent of its residents working in San Francisco in 1990. But exclusively Filipino groceries are few and small; the huge (and very visible) Asian supermarkets like Ranch 99 and Pacific Super are owned by Taiwanese and Vietnamese. Daly City certainly has a substantial number of Filipino-oriented establishments; in 1998, there were at least 11 restaurants, 1 beauty salon, 2 currency exchanges, 3 remittance companies, 3 bakeries, 4 video stores, and 8 grocery stores. They are, however, spread throughout the city, with the exception of a small clutch of stores on Mission Street near the San Francisco border.

Daly City is not immediately identifiable in the same manner as Chinatowns in, for instance, San Francisco or Oakland, or other cities where the majority are Asians, like Monterey Park in California. Driving through Daly

---

[19] Kiko Novero was perhaps my youngest interviewee; he arrived in 1989, two days after he graduated from high school in the Philippines at 16. His immigration to the United States was much like Santos's: Novero's elder brother was born in the United States when their father was getting his master's degree at Syracuse University. When he was of age, he decided to come to the United States, and he eventually petitioned for his parents, who then petitioned for Kiko. His sisters came first; Kiko, one of nine children, came with one of his brothers.

City, the casual observer is not likely to recognize it as "Little Manila." She or he will see no flags in the windows, no infrastructure projects sponsored by Filipino organizations as in the Philippines, no real "strip" of Filipino businesses. This seeming absence of Filipino characteristics accounts for the sense of dislocation I described earlier; Daly City seems an odd place at first glance to be the Filipino capital of the United States. It is in extreme contrast to a place like the San Gabriel Valley east of Los Angeles. When driving through cities like Monterey Park, Rosemead, Alhambra, or Hacienda Heights, our casual observer has no doubt about the ethnicity of their residents: she or he sees billboards and signs in Chinese everywhere, and Asian restaurants and groceries end to end on each block. No such signs exist in Daly City.

One might infer from this—and some scholars and community leaders have done so—that Filipinos lack a sense of ethnic solidarity. Their seeming inability to coalesce into distinct ethnic neighborhoods has long been seen even by Filipinos themselves, some dating back to American colonial times, as evidence of a set of naturalized cultural traits: divisive regionalism, or the so-called "crab mentality." "If a contest were held," the sociologist Antonio Pido writes, "to determine which among the racial groups [sic] in the United States had the most intraracial conflicts and factionalism, the Pilipinos could easily win" (1985, 107).[20] Pido is partly right in his assertion that "what makes the Pilipino organizational divisiveness unique is that it is almost always based on leadership personalities, personal, familial, regional/linguistic linkages, or highly personalized gemeinschaft type networks, rather than ideological or structural differences" (1985, 105). Even if he accurately characterizes the infighting that plagues some Filipino organizations, such intraethnic squabbling is by no means unique to Filipino Americans.

Regionalism and people's corresponding traits have long been discussed and framed in sociological terms—as early as the 1903 Census of the Philippines and earlier. Their enshrinement in popular culture was perhaps most facilitated by the famous opening chapter of Teodoro Agoncillo and Milagros Guerrero's high school textbook, *History of the Filipino People*. They wrote:

[The Filipino] does not think in terms of national boundaries but in regional oneness. This feeling is an extension of the closeness of family ties. . . .

---

[20] San Juan adds, "We Filipinos don't have any real identification of ourselves as belonging to a nation because that nation of all the classes and sectors in the Philippines is non-existent" (1994: 11). I disagree: that nation, and belonging to it, does of course exist, but it is severely riven by class.

So strong is this regionalistic feeling that the Filipino of one region looks down upon his countryman of another region. This strong regionalistic feeling may be traced to the Spanish administrators who pursued a policy of "divide and conquer." (1987, 12–13)[21]

They argue further that regionalism has led to political disunity, an argument much like scholars and community leaders' assertions concerning Filipino immigrants in the United States. This argument then raises the question of whether Filipinos were really "Filipinos" before they left the Philippines—that is, whether a national, Filipino identity is, in general, subordinate to a regional identity.

Community leaders and academics have seized upon the proliferation of Filipino hometown associations and the like in the United States as evidence of the impossibility of political and "national" unity. Adding to this seeming insurmountability is the very specificity of these organizations. The focal unit of membership is not a region or a province but something as minuscule as a hometown—or even occupations within home provinces or cities: dentists from Pangasinan or lawyers from Cebu, for example. The evidence points overwhelmingly to the predominance of regional identity over a "national" form. But is the presence of regional organizations and associations really proof of the persistence of regionalism? Is it more pronounced in the United States, as Bonus hints, because it mitigates the immigrants' "common . . . dislocation and misery" (2000, 103)? Or do the associations merely fill the need for a kind of linguistic companionship, and not necessarily an identity predicated on "anti-national," separatist leanings?

"Dislocation and misery" explains in part the way Pinoy immigrants "keep to themselves," as one interviewee after another told me. This form of retreat was not exactly a calculated reaction to racism, but more an initial reaction to the unsettling nature of immigration.[22] One "naturally" searches

---

[21] It is unclear here what the Spanish administrators were supposed to be "dividing," at least in the early part of the Spanish colonial period; *las Islas Filipinas* was in many ways still a mere collection of islands until independence, and arguably afterward.

[22] I had repeatedly asked interviewees—sometimes directly in reference to racism, sometimes when discussing their social networks—about their relationships with people of different races and ethnicities. But despite their references to undocumented "Mexican" immigrants—they were almost always cited as the opposite of apparently law-abiding Filipinos—and interviewees' comments that one needed to learn how to get along with whites, there was little sense that they had meaningful interethnic or interracial interactions. (Indeed, the latter was seen as a source of suspicion, particularly among parents fretting about their American-born children.) One could, for instance, visit the Serramonte Mall food court at any time of the day and observe, as one would in many American high school cafeterias, the Filipinos, the Italians, and the Chinese sitting at separate tables.

TABLE 2.3   AMERICAN COMMUNITY SURVEY 2006 DEMOGRAPHIC
ESTIMATES FOR DALY CITY

	Total	%
Total population	100,237	
One race	97,345	97.1
White	27,465	27.4
Black or African American	2,937	2.9
American Indian and Alaska Native	560	0.6
Asian	57,097	57.0
Asian Indian	1,144	
Chinese	13,316	
Filipino	35,905	
Japanese	726	
Korean	514	
Vietnamese	2,150	
Other Asian	3,342	
Native Hawaiian and Other Pacific Islander	1,472	1.5
Some other race	7,814	7.8
Two or more races	2,892	2.9
Hispanic or Latino (of any race)	22,557	22.5

U.S. Bureau of the Census 2006.

for the company of one's own, and for family-reunification immigrants, such a safety net—or "security blanket," as it was described above—is already in place. This phenomenon results in one of the paradoxes of Daly City: how, in a multiracial and multiethnic community (see Table 2.3), where people share residential and business space with others of different backgrounds, Filipinos mostly mingle and network within the same immigrant circles. While I did not explicitly ask my interviewees about this, one got the sense—especially from various community activities I attended—that they socialized with very few non-Filipinos. But this phenomenon also occurs because the demographics of the city allow this self-enforced "seclusion" to take place.

Neither of these explanations allow for the complexity of identity formation, particularly within the immigrant context. A regional identity does not exclude an overarching national identity as well; one can be Ilocano and Filipino at the same time, depending on the context, or depending on who

---

Racism, on the other hand, was a different story, if similarly inflected. As with many recent English-speaking immigrants (and indeed, an increasing number of my second-generation Asian American college students who grew up in the Bay Area), or, for that matter, many Americans in general, racism was almost always understood only on the level of a "hate crime," i.e., a physical or verbal act of violence. My interviewees had to stop and think for a while before recalling an incident to relate. Many of them could not. Institutional, systemic discrimination was beyond their purview, and was something relegated to the distant past.

is doing the asking. Indeed, it is arguable that external forces—the U.S. government bureaucracy, the media, Asian American activism, and so on—have fostered, or at least eased, a transition of sorts to a broader Pinoy identity.

This is not to say, however, that this progression to a national identity had not already occurred on Philippine soil. I am simply taking care here to stress that immigration throws continuous processes of identity formation into relief, much in the same way that Taglish is further used and circulated in the United States as a continuation of usage in the Philippines. There is, of course, much historical precedent for such a transition from regionalism to a form of nationalism; Dino Cinel (1982) writes that regionalism became economically disadvantageous for Italian immigrants to the United States, and that it became more important to emphasize Italian national interests if they wanted to progress financially. This transition away from regionalism was facilitated as well by the rise of Italian nationalism prior to World War I. Charles Tilly goes further and argues that this regionalism was not necessarily something transplanted and "carried across the Atlantic like so many pieces of luggage" (1990, 85). Neapolitans and Sicilians, in his view, became Italians in the United States—in a process similar, certainly, to the formation of an Asian (American) political and cultural identity.

Nevertheless, discussions of Filipino immigrants harp on their apparent inability to unite, and attribute the apparent absence of an "ethnic enclave" to this presumed disunity. The absence of a Filipino "center" may have to do more with neighborhood regulations and zoning laws than "Filipino culture." Daly City, like many suburbs, restricts commercial establishments to certain designated areas; chain supermarkets generally already occupy these locations. More to the point are other historical factors shaping immigration patterns: the immigrants of the first wave (roughly, from 1900 to 1941, though the peak of Filipino migrant labor immigration was in the '20s and '30s) were mostly men in temporary plantation camps who would move from town to town, following the harvest of various crops. In contrast, the Chinese, for instance, arrived in California about half a century earlier; after the Gold Rush and the construction of the Transcontinental Railroad, they established themselves in urban Chinatowns. Like the Chinese, pre–World War II Filipino men were confined to a bachelor society. The high men-to-women ratio ensured that few families would be established or reconsolidated on American shores; the lack of families in turn impeded the growth of a more stable community in general until several decades later. Stuck in an ethnic-labor market (as employees of laundries and restaurants), many Chinese had no choice but to settle in an ethnic enclave. Filipinos, with their better command of English, had a somewhat wider choice of jobs working for white employers (though these were almost always limited to menial positions in the service industries).

Although efforts to build communities succeeded to some degree in places such as Stockton, California, Filipinos by and large faced legal or financial obstacles—especially in the midst of the Great Depression—to establishing infrastructure. For instance, only one Filipino grocery store existed in Los Angeles in 1933; by 1953, the city had only six (Takaki 1989, 336). Many Filipinos congregated in ethnic enclaves created with other ethnic groups; some of the pivotal scenes in Bulosan's 1943 memoir/novel *America Is in the Heart* (1973), for instance, take place in Chinese-owned gambling joints and restaurants—the few places where Filipinos were allowed.

By the '60s and '70s, because of the 1965 Immigration Act, many Filipino immigrants already had jobs (and sometimes even housing) waiting for them in the United States when they arrived; this meant less reliance on ethnic or family networks and less possibility that the incoming immigrant would need to seek the company of her own kind. The alien land laws passed in the western states in the '20s had already been repealed; racial covenants aside, no legal barriers prevented Filipinos from owning property.

I have enumerated above some historical and economic factors that may explain the apparent absence of an ethnic enclave for Filipino Americans. Structural and migration patterns notwithstanding, however, the delineation of place boundaries more often than not comes from outside, and the relative absence of Filipinos in the American mainstream, whether political or cultural, explains Daly City's similar invisibility. For instance, Filipino cuisine, despite its distinctiveness, has not made significant impressions on the mainstream American palate, and questions of authenticity—visiting Daly City for "real" Filipino food, for instance—do not crop up.[23]

As Doreen Massey writes, the identity of a place "derives . . . precisely from the specificity of its interactions with 'the outside'" (1992, 13). Perhaps one indication of Filipino invisibility is the weekly mini-museum exhibit

---

[23] The absence of Filipinos from the mainstream merits more discussion than the few factors I mentioned concerning Daly City. But rather than attributing this absence to purely "cultural" rationalizations—regionalism, lack of ambition, a greater tendency to assimilate—I offer more historical/structural considerations: the relatively recent arrival of Filipinos (as compared to the Chinese and the Japanese), and the historical amnesia surrounding the American colonization of the Philippines.

As for Filipino food, the current propensity for fusion cuisine has not included Filipino dishes, even though the Philippines has certainly not lacked a tradition of haute cuisine. Is it perhaps not "distinctive" enough to the mainstream palate? Are some dishes seen as mere imitations of recipes that Chinese restaurants can cook better? Is it the lack of marketing? Is it the unapologetically oily preparation, or the lack of vegetable dishes—in short, a stubborn refusal to concede to low-fat eating of any sort?

held by the History Guild of Daly City/Colma: the section devoted to Filipinos consists of a piece of cardboard attached to the side of a library shelf, where newspaper clippings on Filipino immigration and the Filipino mayor are pasted. (The bulk of the exhibit is photographs from the 1910s and '20s, and aerial shots of the evolving suburb in the '50s.) Daly City has, however, trumpeted itself in brochures sent to business owners and prospective job applicants, among others, as "one of the most ethnically diverse cities in the nation".[24]

Also explaining the invisibility of Filipinos is the matter of how Filipinos physically inscribe themselves onto the landscape. Signs written in Chinese or Vietnamese in Monterey Park and Alhambra, or distinctive architecture in San Francisco's Chinatown, contribute to a general inscription of difference that mark them as ethnic enclaves, whereas Daly City, as I have indicated, simply blurs into the homogenized suburban mass. Signs on Pinoy establishments are without fail written in English; the rare Tagalog (i.e., "foreign") word refers either to a Philippine town or to food.

Perhaps the closest thing to a Pinoy commercial enclave is St. Francis Square, in the heart of the St. Francis district. Surrounded by tract houses in all directions, St. Francis has three Filipino restaurants: Kadok's, Lech Go (a reference to their specialty, roasted suckling pig, or *lechon*), and Tito Rey. The first two are small cafeteria-style restaurants with five or six tables each and meals lined up behind a glass counter, the latter a more formal establishment with lounge-style performances, which is a frequent venue for office and organization parties and political meetings. Johnny Air Cargo, one of the more successful parcel service companies specializing in U.S.-Philippines shipping and remittance transfer, also has its Daly City office here.

Gerry's, also located in St. Francis Square, is a darkly lit, somewhat faded establishment that is packed with an odd range of goods, and at first glance it is not apparent what the store is supposed to be. Behind a long glass cabinet at the entrance are shelves filled with boxes of *barong Tagalogs* and *sayas*

---

[24] As the former mayor Michael Guingona put it in an interview with me: "There's like up to a hundred and eight countries represented in Daly City, and at any given time you can hear . . . all the different dialects, here in Daly City 'cause we're so well-represented by everybody in the community. . . . In fact, one of our mottoes is the 'Community of Many Cultures.' I mean, you know, if you can't learn to get along, live with your neighbor, this ain't the place to live."

Perhaps a more relevant question would be why the existence of an ethnic enclave is necessary to validate Filipino American culture. It may be argued that Americans from immigrant backgrounds can point to their respective enclaves—as business centers or tourist attractions—with pride for their heritage. Filipino Americans, in turn, can only gesture weakly at a suburb like Daly City. But this is to neglect the historical factors that led to the ghettoization of immigrants in the first place. As I mentioned above, San Francisco's Chinatown may have been a place of refuge for its Chinese residents, but its slum conditions illustrate that the Chinese were not allowed to live anywhere outside of Chinatown in the first place.

(Philippine formal wear), all selling for about $25 each. On the left side of the store are video racks, both up front and at the back. Bleached blue by the sun, the Regal Films posters on the glass window outside tells the shopper of the newest video titles for rent. The videos are mostly new titles from the Philippines, but there are also vintage ones from the late '70s and early '80s. Off to the side is what seems to be a fairly extensive collection of American pornographic videotapes. More glass cabinets in the center of the room hold little rosaries and other Catholic accessories; a statuette of the Santo Niño, wrapped in plastic, stood on a cabinet. (In a later visit to Gerry's, there were more statues of the Virgin Mary, in various sizes, for sale.) On the right side of the store, the wall is completely covered with handbags—leather, faux leather, woven. The long glass cabinet that runs the length of the wall is packed with boxes of American running shoes. (Upon closer inspection the shoes all turn out to have been made in the Philippines.) Next to the shoes are boxes of rice cookers and Japanese-made "airpots," or large thermoses for holding soup, coffee, or hot water. There are no grocery items for sale, presumably because they are available in the big Pacific Super grocery store next door.

My informal inventory tells me that Gerry's offers for sale items that one would find in a store that carries somewhat pricey sundries in a town in the Philippine provinces. Gerry's occupies a Filipino immigrant niche, selling products associated only with the Philippines, or that are difficult to find in the United States. This store caters to other recently arrived or first-generation Asian immigrants as well. The rice cookers and thermoses, though easy to find in Chinatown shops, are inexpensive household appliances that nicely round out the middle-class immigrant lifestyle.

I stress this particular immigrant quality of the possibilities of consumption because I believe it says a good deal about the Pinoy community's orientation toward the Philippines itself. Many of the Filipino and Filipino-owned businesses in Daly City are overwhelmingly geared to making and fostering a "transnational" connection between the Philippines and the United States, whether through the transfer of remittances, the shipment of balikbayan boxes, or the purchase of imported goods. In that respect these processes of consumption facilitate a constant movement, both literal and symbolic, between the two places. This movement, in turn, furthers the social process of nostalgia and keeps it operating in Daly City.

The rather barren and grimy Philippine Grocery, on Washington and Hill (cut off from the Filipinos in the Westlake district by Interstate 280), serves the same immigrant niche. Although the stock on its shelves looks untouched, the well-stocked meat and fish counter seems quite popular. It displays mostly "exotic" cuts of meat—ham hocks, some pig's blood, chicken innards—mostly things one can't find at Lucky's, a couple of blocks to the east. The stock is almost indistinguishable from that of Pacific Super, or Ranch 99—the same imported Indonesian, Malaysian, or Hong Kong brands. Therefore one gets the same kind of *patis*, or candies (Storck, White Rabbit, etc.), crackers and chips (Nagaraya, Clover, Sunflower), dried mangoes, folded-up Anahaw balikbayan boxes, and so on, that the bigger stores already have. This is probably why the stock looks dusty. The most popular part of the store is the *turo-turo* food section as you come in, with *asado, afritada, dinuguan*, and big slabs of *tikoy* and *maja blanca* in a counter window— Philippine meat dishes and dessert favorites all served up cafeteria-style. When I visited a little after noon, some six or seven people who had clearly gone out of their way to have lunch here still waited in line.

Other kinds of stores may clarify their immigrant orientation further. Tatak Pilipino (*tatak* means "mark" or "seal," but can also mean "brand") in Serramonte Mall, is one such store. The space is compact, with items on display almost up to the ceiling. As you enter, you are practically assaulted by the variety of items: Pidro T-shirts, postcards, key chains, university patches, Christmas lanterns. On the left is an aisle full of religious figurines, and the aisle next to it has folded *barong tagalog*s and *saya*s. In the center, just behind the cash register, are gossip weeklies; behind it are various handicrafts (the barrel man, a wooden jeepney, dolls in Philippine costumes, a wooden *sungka* game board). The rightmost section of the store is occupied by music CDs (the usual, plus a lot of ballroom dancing), VCDs, a handful of DVDs, and a large selection of karaoke VCDs. All along the back wall are coffee table books, a good number of history books (mostly Ambeth Ocampo's), dictionaries, cookbooks, and so on.

A store like the Philippine Grocery will always have regular customers because of the food; during the times I visited, people were always shopping, even at odd hours. Tatak Pilipino, on the other hand, was almost always empty, partly because of the more expensive items for sale. But what they sold in the store was a particular version of Filipino culture: the kind that catered to tourists. Except for the CDs, many of the items were of the kind to be found in the "Filipiniana" sections of Manila department stores—handicrafts that were bought as souvenirs for tourists, or as presents to non-Filipinos. These goods, in effect, were not just Filipino. They *represented* Filipino culture, and were, in turn, the kinds of items that I would see in Filipino living rooms in Daly City, along with giant wooden spoons and paintings of the Last Supper. Tatak Pilipino's goods were certainly emblematic of Filipino culture, and perhaps purchased because of the stirrings of nostalgia or the demands of ethnic pride. I believe, however, that they also represent a kind of distanced, abstracted consumption, which I will discuss further when we look at homesickness and citizenship.

I have sketched a perhaps typical ethnic community, one formed by the confluence of particular historical and economic circumstances. The relative invisibility of the Pinoy community in Daly City can be attributed to housing and migration patterns already established in the '20s and '30s; the class status and career trajectories of the post-'65 immigrants have also prevented the establishment of a traditional urban enclave. The community is intensely attuned to the homeland, giving it a strong immigrant orientation that has only intensified with the movement of ideas and capital in this so-called transnational period. But it is also this seeming invisibility which animates my project: how does the fog of this American suburb apparently conceal—and why this concealment?—the lives of people who comprise a third of its residents.

As noted earlier, members of the Filipino community in Daly City are marked by a repeated turning, their focus towards the homeland accompanied by a complementary and contradictory turn to their adoptive home even before their arrival. What is the Filipino immigrants' orientation toward the United States? What are their expectations, their obligations towards family, their attitudes towards work, the function and disappointments of ethnic solidarity, and the practice (and non-practice) of immigrant politics? Let us take a closer look.

3

LOOKING FORWARD

~

Narratives of Obligation

When he was 11, Wally Curameng[1] dreamed of coming to America. His cousins, who were his earliest childhood playmates, immigrated to the United States. "Even then," he told me, "I was already excited to come here to the States because my cousins, they'd write, they'd send pictures—it's like this in the United States, it's great in the States, like that. But I said to myself, I decided to ignore it because I knew I had no chance to come here." Curameng's father had been a Boy Scout and one of the Philippines' representatives to worldwide Scout gatherings, or Jamborees, in Washington and Canada. Wally felt "envious," "because when [my father] was only a boy, he was already able to travel abroad." He continually asked his father to sponsor him, but several Jamborees went on without his being able to go. By Curameng's third year of high school, his brother had joined the U.S. Marines and, two years later, petitioned for their mother in 1977. Nine years later Wally left the Philippines, a day before the so-called People Power Revolution in 1986, which saw the relatively peaceful ouster of President Ferdinand Marcos and the end of his dictatorship.

For Curameng and other interviewees, immigration to the United States presented itself as a more than tangible possibility for a future life. Nurtured

---

[1] I interviewed Wally and his wife Debbie Patron in their in-law apartment in Daly City one afternoon in May 1996. The interview itself took much longer than I had expected; after the first hour they insisted that we continue—"since these were things we never get to talk about," said Patron.

by his imaginings, life in the United States came to take on an alternate existence for Curameng, as a place beyond his reach and yet so close at the same time. To imagine oneself somewhere else is a powerful motivator, and for some Daly City Pinoy residents, the possibility of going to the United States gave structure to their lives in the Philippines.

In the United States, a sense of doubleness haunts the lives of Filipino immigrants, much as it did earlier immigrant communities. Irish, Taiwanese, Greek, Korean, and Polish immigrants have enthusiastically supported nationalist and independence movements, making their homelands a palpable presence in their daily lives. But this doubleness also clearly manifests itself in the Philippines, from which it derives its origins; there, an American life was a distinct, and not even particularly distant, possibility.

Tololyan's concept of "repeated turning," mentioned in Chapter One, entails several directions. The image may not necessarily be benign—it summons up the conflicted picture of someone pulled in multiple directions by obligations and desires—but it captures succinctly the immigrants' experience of living their lives in a "transnational" fashion. Filipinos in the United States are continually reminded, through various avenues and in different degrees, that there is a similar but different existence, a "home," somewhere else. Such reminding—from everyday conversations to official state exhortations—is by no means novel, but it is intensified by the advances in communication associated with the present age. The question, however, is whether such reminding is actually heeded. Memories are unwillingly pulled up to the surface only at inopportune (or unfortunate) moments. Otherwise "home" constantly remains in the background, summoned only as nostalgic, apolitical manifestations.

A constant theme running through my interviews is ambivalence. It is reflected in the wide-ranging and sometimes contradictory motivations given for immigration, and in the mixed feelings about staying or leaving—and perhaps is seen as well in the diversity of the Filipino community. The repeated turning can be thought of as a form of ambivalence: one looks "forward" and looks "back," as if unsure of one's place—or, more concretely, as if uncertain of one's decision to immigrate.

In the succeeding chapters I divide this repeated turning artificially; this chapter and the next deal with the United States and the following two are focused on the Philippines. I say "artificially" because such distinctions are not necessarily compartmentalized easily—even, for instance, in the pages of the *Philippine News*. Both places intertwine, depending on the vagaries of memory and the trajectories of possible futures.

Coming to America: Responding to Obligation

The possibility of moving to America has given structure to the immigrants' expectations, and it affects their present decisions. For at least two of my interviewees, not much thought was given to continuing their careers (or indeed, the possibility that one still had to work). Curameng, for instance, started becoming lazy, by his own admission, after the immigration petition process began. He never got to finish his degree in Fine Arts at the University of the Philippines in Diliman, as he left for the United States early in his final semester.

> My feeling was like I was not taking my studies seriously. It was as if I was expecting, when I get to the States, when I go to the States, I would just be taking it easy, you know. But then, I write to my brother often, and my brother said, if your goal is just to get to the States, that's not a good vision, he said. At least, he said, finish college first. He said, it's not that easy in the States. He told me. Which is true, when I got here, I realized, if you have no education, it's not that easy here [hindi basta-basta rito].

It was not easy, indeed. When Curameng was younger, he thought the United States would be "very clean" and that "all people are nice, they're hospitable, they're willing to take you, hug you, and you know, sit next to you, eat with you." His expectations about the United States were quite different from what he later encountered; a brush with racial discrimination in the U.S. Army and a series of low-skilled jobs with no chances for promotion made him realize how naïve (as he admitted) his preconceptions were.

Curameng was most excited about seeing his relatives again: "I would go to their houses, makikita mo 'yung nasa picture, tapos nakikita mo na, in real life, 'yung actual, hindi na picture" (I would go to their houses, you would see what was in the picture, then you would see, in real life, the actual, not a picture anymore). For him, as for other interviewees, the United States was chiefly constructed and mediated through images, whether produced by mass media or through the intimacy of personal photographs. Indeed, he did not talk about his relatives in particular, but about the photographs of his relatives—or, to be more specific, about the houses and their contents. "It's like this in the United States," he said, quoting his cousins talking about the photographs. It is almost as if the background, or the contents ("'yung nasa picture") were more important than his relatives—who did, after all, already exist for him previously. For Curameng, arriving, and being there in the United States, acted as a kind of validation—or the end of a journey of sorts—that *finally* he could view the image in "real life." To be in the presence of an idealized image—or rather, to be in the presence of the real—was reason enough. In a sense, it was a form of wish fulfillment: the wish to visit the United States and the wish to see the image materialize were both fulfilled.

I am tempted to link his statement to a kind of materialism. Perhaps to him it was the possibility of gaining access to those places (and goods) pictured in the photographs that was more important. The association of immigration and materialism is well entrenched in discourse among Filipinos, as we will see in the next chapter. But this semantic relationship can be better illustrated by considering the example of Kiko Novero, for whom his parents (or rather, the *absence* of his parents) were explicitly linked with money and access to higher status in the form of material goods from the United States.

Novero's parents arrived seven years before he did, in 1982, and lived in Daly City, in the St. Francis district. His father, with a degree in plant science, had worked for a multinational research institute in the Philippines; his mother worked as an editor in the same place. Upon their arrival in the United States, they found themselves working in far less prestigious occupations. Novero's mother took on proofreading jobs. His father sold encyclopedias and vacuum cleaners door to door; at one point he was working at Circuit City, an appliance store. "But after a while he got tired, 'cause he was standing all day, for a 50, 60, almost 60-year-old man, it's like, it was really hard." But as Novero put it, his father was "trying to support two households, one here and one in the Philippines." At the time of the interview his father was working as an exterminator, inspecting and treating houses for termites.

Kiko Novero went through high school during the seven years that his parents lived far away.

> It was really hard. Well actually, at that time I thought it was really good because, omigosh, all this new-found freedom, I could do any-thing I want to, which of course in the long run is bad, right? You have too much freedom, you get to do things—like before I would just, like, cut school, and play video games—like you know Atari? Remember? I would be sort of into that, I would just go home, and basically—so yeah, there was that freedom, to do anything you want, basically . . .

Though he would talk to his parents often—sometimes twice a week, and his mother wrote often as well—the freedom he had gained exacted an incalculable toll on the family in general. Novero's eldest brother ended up raising him and his siblings—"basically my parents just, like, sent the money, and he just, like, budgeted, disbursed it among us."

The separation made him markedly different from his school classmates in other ways. He distinctly remembered that his parents would send him shoes, for instance—which, Novero disappointedly found out later, were bought from the Salvation Army—but "in the Philippines it was such a big deal . . . and when you wear them in the Philippines, gosh, you're so different." Such an inscription of difference set him apart from his friends and increased his status in the eyes of his classmates. This also made him look forward to his impending departure for the United States: "In a way I was very excited, because, omigosh, America, all this idea of fast cars, beautiful women. And then just getting everything you wanted, basically, the American dream."

His parents' absence returned, in effect, in the form of cultural (and economic) capital. But this capital, embodied in difference, did not symbolize for him his parents' largesse (or love), but something else:

> So I guess it made me think of, just led me to go, gosh, when you're in the States you can have all this stuff. But I don't know if that was right or not, 'cause I think that is also a big problem that Filipinos face, 'cause when they first come here, they have this idea that they're gonna have all this material stuff, but in reality, most of this stuff that you get, it's not really yours because you loan them.

Novero was referring here to purchasing items on credit (thus they are "on loan"). What the shoes represented was not just a strengthening of emotional ties between parents and child (this is, indeed, subordinated), but the idealization of the United States as a site of modernity and a source of material goods and capital. Although the depiction of the United States as a site of limitless consumption—"when you're in the States you can have all this stuff"—is nothing new, it is reinforced here by its more intimate connection to the interviewees' respective domestic spheres.

Such intertwining of the family—or, in this case, an absence in the family—with money is by no means a new phenomenon. But for the Philippines, it has taken on an overwhelmingly broader dimension with the state's reliance on overseas remittances. Having a family member overseas confers, in a sometimes wildly varying degree from that of those without, higher financial status or stability, if only in the form of high-status goods. Of course, this response is not limited to immigrants to the United States.

Many Daly City residents choose to migrate in a quest for financial stability. Nevertheless, it is clear from my interviews that there are more complex reasons—though in a sense the strongest reason is the simplest of all in the post-'65 context: family reunification. But the statistics mentioned earlier—by the late '80s, for instance, almost 80 percent of all Pinoy immigrants arrived through non-quota, family-reunification channels—gloss over people's individual and sometimes conflicted reasons for leaving.

Like Curameng's, Teddy Encinas's family had prior connections with the United States, long before the 1965 immigration law changes.[2] Encinas's father had worked in the U.S. Embassy in the Philippines, continuing a long history of employment in the U.S. government that began during World War II. It was because of his father's close associations with Americans, Encinas explained, that his father began wanting to immigrate to the United States; he himself had gone back and forth between the Philippines and the United States even before they had immigrated. In addition, his mother had worked as a secretary for an American colonel before World War II. Such connections, however, were not necessary. It was the pull of familial obligation—facilitated by the revised immigration laws' guiding principle of family reunification—that ultimately became the deciding factor for many recent Daly City residents to migrate.

Unlike many of my more recently arrived interviewees, the longtime Daly City resident Nancy Navarro[3] was the person who did most of the petitioning for her family members (though she lived with an uncle when she

---

[2] I had met Teddy at a get-together for regulars on the Internet newsgroup soc.culture.filipino. The party, held at a friend's house, was meant for the newsgroup's Bay Area–based posters to meet each other face to face, as opposed to just on the Net. My friend introduced Teddy to me as someone from Daly City who would be willing to be interviewed.

The interview took place at the Barnes and Noble coffee shop in Colma. It was, as he pointed out correctly, one of the only places open late in the Daly City area where one could talk. We were the oldest people in the coffee shop: the place was full of teenagers chatting and doing their homework. Encinas, like many other Filipinos, is approaching middle age at a slow pace.

Encinas arrived in the United States around 1968 or 1969, when he was 12. His parents separated when they were still in the Philippines, and then his father wanted to emigrate. Teddy didn't. He wanted to stay in the Philippines instead, in Paranaque, Manila. His father and siblings then left him in the Philippines, where he fell in with a "bad crowd." This prompted his desire finally to join his family in the United States—or, more likely, his father's decision to petition for him.

[3] Navarro was sent to the United States at the age of 19 by an international women's organization of which she was a secretary in the '60s. But now she thinks the circumstances were a little more complicated than that: she thinks they wanted her to stay. "Because the Philippines was getting harder in the '60s. Life was getting harder. But of course, they don't tell us those things. Especially the women, they don't tell the girls."

Her father, who inherited property, had advanced her uncle money; upon sale of the uncle's property, her family did not receive as much money as they expected. "So, effectively, his brother here owed him money. So, that was the agreement. I learned about this later on, not at the time." She thinks this was the reason her uncle bought her a car upon her arrival. "So I guess sending me here, and [my uncle] going to take care of me, was a collection, kabayaran [payment]."

Arriving in San Francisco in 1967 was, to put it mildly, a shock. "I was very out of place," she said. As she related: "I came from St. Scho [short for St. Scholastica College, an elite Catholic girls' school in Manila], and you know, we were wearing this bouffant hairdo, very high—like a helmet? And then we wore makeup, we wore high heels, we wore stockings."

first arrived). She met her husband, Noel, while in school. He was an American citizen who had entered as a third-preference immigrant to work as a chemical engineer. They later married, and she received her green card two weeks after he petitioned for her permanent resident status.

Both of them had immigrated to the United States alone, and it was difficult for their siblings to decide whether to follow them or not. She explained that they were fairly well employed, as administrators and journalists—"but you see, there are seven of us, and so we wanted a family together. Gusto namin magkakasama kami [We wanted to be all together]." Now all the members of her family, including her husband's, all live in the States. Her 83-year-old mother had migrated to the United States as well, and lived 45 minutes away in Pleasanton at the time of our interview.

Because Nancy and Noel were the first to arrive, they were able to take care of each of their siblings who immigrated later. Navarro's brother stayed with them in their house for a year, until he had earned enough money to rent an apartment of his own. The other sisters followed suit, staying for two to six months. "It was so much easier for the next batches to come, really, because they already have a house and food, whereas the first ones who came—para bang ano [it is as if] you're foraging for everything, you're starting everything. So it was much harder for the first ones who came." Here she addresses the burden of the first generation, with regard to family reunification; they, in effect, paved the way for others. Such an arrangement does not necessarily create resentment, but it does highlight the familial obligations that prevail before and well after immigration.

Jun Bautista's story helps to illustrate the pull of family obligations. He came to the United States when his mother-in-law petitioned for his wife. He had been in the country only seven months when I interviewed him in June 1996. (Mike Santos, who knew them in connection with his social-service agency, referred him to me.) All four members of his family—he, his wife, and their two daughters—arrived at the same time. His wife also came with her sister's family—in effect, a whole extended family immigrated together. He still remembers the day he received the approval letter in November 1994. A year later, they were in America.

Bautista told me explicitly at the beginning of the interview that immigrating was not of his choosing, and that he came only because of his wife. "Nadamay lang kami"[4] (we were only included accidentally), he explained. Then he backtracked and clarified by saying that he was holding a better po-

---

[4] *Damay* means "sympathy," but his use in the passive voice (*nadamay*) here is closer in meaning to "involved (accidentally, or tangentially) as an accomplice in a crime." Most important, it connotes passivity—migration as a response to an opportunity presenting itself.

sition in Manila. But it was too difficult for the family to be separated, so he gave up his job. Migration was not something he had thought about, because both he and his wife had good jobs. But his mother-in-law had petitioned for her daughter more than a decade ago.

His wife was working in the import-export division of a Japanese company based in the Philippines, but she decided to retire early. As Bautista explained, they were already quite settled when the petition was suddenly, unexpectedly, approved. His wife had never actively hoped for its approval, he said. But the decision was made. The Bautistas decided to give up a career and a stable life in the Philippines for a chance—at something—in the United States.

For Kiko Novero, moving to the United States and reuniting with his parents was a similarly ambivalent act. The fact that he had dreamed about going to the United States did not exactly translate into overjoyed feelings upon his arrival. When he first arrived, he related, "[he] was always crying, [and] always sad." Though he "[didn't] get affected by music so easily," music that he listened to in the Philippines (whether the music was Filipino or not) would instantly remind him of "fond memories," and he would become sad. More important, part of this depression also came from the fact that his parents were "always gone," a reference to his teen years in the Philippines. "So in a sense the relationship that's supposed to have been built during your teen years—it's like, I don't have that bond. . . ." He continued:

> What happened with me was when I first came here—the center of my life at that point, which was basically my friends, like I lost them. So I'm now here with my parents. . . . I really didn't have that big of a bond, and you would say, sure, they've always been providing for you but in essence they don't really know you and you don't really know them. That's how it felt . . .

Novero's words speak eloquently of the emotional loss in the family created by immigration.

I believe that the change in migration patterns from occupational-preference immigrants to family-reunification preference immigrants has altered the purpose of migration—or rather, altered the *willingness* of immigrants to migrate.[5] In effect, the petition, within the new configuration that the shift in immigration dynamics has produced, serves more as an invitation,

---

[5] As I discuss in the next chapter, this demographic shift has also inadvertently led to lower employment as a whole among the Filipino immigrant community. With that, of course, comes a shift in class as well, something reflected in interviewees' characterization of different immigrant waves.

or even a command, than as something actively pursued. The filing of a petition, of course, is all accomplished in the United States; the approval of the petition comes as a call from abroad to which people must respond.

For those with careers, the moment the petition was approved came as an interruption. What would appear to be a momentous event in the course of one's life seems to have just crept up on my interviewees. Some even seem to have been taken by surprise—and some were passive in the face of such an opportunity. As Mike Santos put it,

> Well, the petition arrived, so there [Eh, dumating ang petition, di ayun]. We said, we waited for so long, and it's so hard to get a visa, so we accepted it. . . . So although we already had good jobs in the Philippines, of course there was nothing you could do, there was your chance, you were going to start on the same level [siyempre wala kang magagawa, nandoon ang chance mo, mag-uumpisa kayong pare-parehas].

"There was nothing you could do," Santos said. His passivity in the face of the call to immigrate did not stem specifically from an obligation to reunite with his family, as one might think would be the case. Rather, for him, there was his chance, presenting itself. The possibility of prosperity—especially combined with the somewhat naive notion that everyone would be "start[ing] on the same level"—was compelling enough for Santos to leave his job and his homeland behind and head out for the (familiar) unknown.

As Jun Bautista said, immigration was not of their choosing.[6] The ambivalence expressed in the statements underscores the complexity of reasons for migration; immigrants are neither fully rational economic actors cannily calculating their options, nor always willing practitioners of filial piety, ready to reunite with their relatives. Many Filipinos, from politicians and scholars to the so-called common *tao* (people), readily acknowledge kinship and its attendant responsibilities as central to living, and understanding, Philippine life. The bonds of familial sentiment are seen to override all obligations. Arguably, however, family reunification may not be the principal motive here, but merely the primary means of immigrating.[7]

This does not mean, however, that Pinoys migrate without weighing their options. The general principle is still that immigrants want better opportu-

---

[6] Some people wholeheartedly welcomed the chance to migrate. Curameng, for instance, did not have any regrets about leaving the Philippines; he alluded to experiences, "personal things" he left behind that he did not like. "So when I thought of leaving the Philippines, I said, okay, you can stay there. Something like that. I'm not coming back. That was my feeling."

[7] In this respect Filipinos differ from other earlier immigrants—they were from neither the peasantry nor the politically persecuted.

nities in regard to career advancement and stability, and that immigration through family reunification may be the most straightforward legal means of entering the United States. This is so despite the fact that many of my interviewees were fairly well ensconced in their careers (the politician Alice Bulos, for instance, was the chair of the sociology department at the University of Santo Tomas, where she had already been teaching for 22 years) at the time of migration. Hardly any were unemployed, much less below the poverty line—and as I discuss in the next chapter, immigration and citizenship requirements generally limit potential migrants to the middle class and lower middle class in any case.

Work

Expectations of frustration and unemployment coexisted uncomfortably with Curameng and Novero's anticipations of easy living in the United States. But this is not necessarily a paradox, for it coincides discursively with the standard narrative of immigrant sacrifice. Filipino immigrants, though ambivalently pulled in different directions, are aware of the difficulties that await them upon arrival.

Mike Santos's story is typical in the amount of "catching up" he had to do as a family-reunification preference immigrant. He majored in industrial psychology at a university in Manila and graduated in 1983. But the employment opportunities in his field were limited, and he ended up doing clerical work in a Baguio mining company's corporate office in Manila for six years. Upon his arrival in the United States, Santos first went to a temporary agency, which sent him to his first job, attaching brand labels to Levi's jeans for $6.50 an hour at a factory on the Embarcadero in San Francisco. Two weeks of drudgery was too much for him to bear—eight hours was too long for him, he said—and the bosses directly in charge of him, he related, were Filipinos who, he implied, were either of lower classes in the Philippines or unfit for managerial positions.) Santos then decided to go to school: "The hard part here, you have no skills, especially if you're an immigrant, of course the competition, you know, there's also discrimination, and [for] immigrants, your competition are those from here." He enrolled for a year at the Filipino Learning Center in San Francisco, studying computers, to update his skills from the Philippines.

A stint volunteering for the Salvation Army followed, assisting Filipinos at a senior citizen activities center in the SoMa neighborhood of San Francisco. He had a tight schedule, volunteering in the morning and going to classes from 6:30 to 10:30 in the evening. At the same time Santos entered a college work-study program, where he worked part time as an administrative assistant. An actual paying job at the Salvation Army opened up in

Berkeley—where Santos began to work as a tutoring and mentoring program assistant for $7 an hour—which he did simultaneously with his work-study *and* school. Santos followed this schedule every week for a year. His classes helped him upgrade his skills, as he put it, until he was hired as data management technician at a university research project. This led to his current job as a social worker for the Filipino division of a non-profit organization geared toward Asian American youth.

Teddy Encinas tells a similar story. After high school he enrolled at the City College of San Francisco, where he took college courses and worked full time as an assistant supervisor for a data-coding company for two years. His and his sister's savings allowed them to put their younger sister through school. "If I look back to it, I know the sufferings." He paused for a moment and continued soberly. "I was telling my son, I don't have time to sleep, I don't have time to do my homework, I don't have time to eat. I was poor. I'd buy six large French fries from McDonald's—one bag—I eat in the morning, and throughout the day, I eat it." He smiled. "Because that was cheap, I was a starving student, I'm working, I'm paying for the apartment with my sister. . . . So French fries, even during class or after class, I'd do my homework between classes, or if I have a free period, I'd go to the student union and take a nap." He laughed out loud. After the day of school came work from 4:30 until 12:00 midnight.

Such a work schedule, sustained almost throughout his career, clearly had its impact on his and his spouse's lives. He recounted that he was in church one time, noticing many Filipino children in the congregation. He then told me, "I wish I had more kids," but "back then, we were trying to survive as a family." He described his dilemma. "What is difficult about Filipinos here, either you choose to"—he paused for a moment—"we chose to do either way, either we have a family or we progress in our careers. I changed careers. . . . I went to school for what I'm doing right now. And that's also a sacrifice, three and a half years, going to night school and working full time. So I lost—you know, the chance to have another kid . . . it's another sacrifice. . . ." Encinas looked wistful. "So as time went on . . . we grew older too."

Encinas considered himself "one of the lucky ones": he was able to move to Daly City and raise his family there. At the time of my interview, he had been working with the same computer network company for over 12 years, and his wife was an ophthalmologist. But success stories were not universal. Unlike Mike Santos, his siblings—both with college degrees and working for firms in the Philippines—were unable to transfer their skills in the Philippines to the United States. One sister worked as an airport screener at San Francisco International Airport; another was a cashier at Office Depot.

Bautista related to me his difficulties in obtaining jobs. He was originally from La Union; his wife was "a pure Manila girl" whom he met when he moved there as a child. As a regional sales manager for a veterinary medicine company, he said, he was able to speak and understand every Philippine language as a result of his travels throughout the country. His last assignment before he left was in Mindanao. "I travel from Cavite, Catanduanes, Palawan. All of those places, all the way up to Virac. When I arrived here, I travel by"—and he chuckles—"Muni and SamTrans" (the bus systems in San Francisco and San Mateo County)—poking fun at his more limited mobility in the United States.

At the time of the interview he worked 40 hours a week as a parking attendant in San Francisco's Presidio Heights. He added that there is a difference between what is called a "subsistency job" and a "career job." He hoped to continue working in sales, so he is still looking for other job opportunities. But "opportunity in America," Bautista said, is "only for the young." Even if they say there is equal opportunity, he added, there is always discrimination, whatever happens.

Unlike other Filipino immigrants I interviewed, the Bautistas had little time for sightseeing—Fisherman's Wharf and Lombard Street were all they could really remember from San Francisco. They had had to jump right into a full-scale job search. "The moment we arrived," he said, recalling their arrival, "we were immediately taught how to ride the bus and make phone calls so that we would not get lost." His daughters quickly applied for driver's licenses, even if they had no car to drive. "So we were already ready, at an early stage. Fight" (Kaya, handa ka'gad, eh, maaga pa. Laban).

Bautista's youngest daughter was able to go to school immediately after their arrival. The difference in schooling, however, was frustrating to the daughters. Their friends back in the Philippines, Maria said, were already about to graduate from college and enter the work force. The eldest daughter wished she could graduate from college, but instead she was already working and "achieving." (She had to be a California resident for 366 days before she could avail herself of lower state-resident college tuition fees, so she had to work her first year in the country.) A month after her arrival (on Christmas Day, she remembered with regret), she began working in customer service at Honeybaked Ham.

Underemployment has become a chronic problem among Filipino immigrants. Many white-collar workers have ended up unable to transfer their skills and education to the United States, and they work on the lower rungs of the service sector. Santos lamented the fact that academic degrees earned in the Philippines were not recognized in the United States, except for those from the University of the Philippines.[8] Indeed, even before he left for the United States, he had already been warned by his officemates about the job situation here. "Their impression, probably, when you get there, what you really aspire to, you will not achieve." Santos thought of an example. "They warned that you will become a gasoline boy—but you don't need one because everything's automated here, you won't see any gasoline boys." That is, even the lowest form of employment his former officemates could conceive of was a job that, according to Santos, did not even exist in the United States. Career opportunities, or—to be more precise—the possibility of better ones, are a primary impetus in migration. They were also cited by my interviewees as the main difference between the Philippines and the United States. But the difficulties in uprooting oneself had to do with the same reason—one's career—as well as leaving one's friends and relatives behind.

Mike Santos had certainly been hoping to come to the United States,

> but when the time came that we were really about to leave, we kind of felt that we didn't want to, because we were already stable in the Philippines. I mean, we didn't have a very big salary, but of course the company, friends, your friends back there, you left your relatives, your loved ones. Kind of when the time came that you really wanted to leave, when you were about to leave, you were kind of hesitating—what if, will I be able to survive—I said, okay, we'll just see. If life is good there, we'll stay there, but if not, we'll return—that was what we were thinking, we said. Well, we've been here two years. We said, okay, life is hard, but we're being persistent.

What the United States offered was a possibility to improve one's life, a possibility that even outweighed an already stable career in the Philippines. For Santos, his decision to migrate is not permanent; it is merely one option among others, a calculated, rational risk. In this respect he is no different from many other immigrants throughout history; some of those who did not migrate as refugees surely kept open the possibility of return. But in most

---

[8] In actuality, it depended on the people hiring; as we will see later, degrees from universities other than the University of the Philippines (UP) and Ateneo were recognized at, for instance, the Pacific Bell telephone company. Surely in many quarters a degree from UP did not matter much either.

Nancy Navarro's brother was a chemical engineer who could not find work in the United States; at the time, his degree from the University of Santo Tomas (UST) was not recognized. After six months of fruitless searching, he was finally employed as a janitor at Pacific Bell, until one engineer apparently noticed him and said, according to Navarro, "He did not talk like a janitor. He did not even dress like one." The engineer ended up sponsoring him, and from then on, UST graduates were accredited at Pacific Bell.

cases, Filipinos did not—or could not—return. After the passage of the 1935 Repatriation Act that gave Filipinos free passage back to the Philippines—a slightly more benign form of deportation—only a little over 2,000 Filipinos availed of the offer. Such rates of return, even now, do not fulfill the fluid terms of what Aihwa Ong (1999) calls "flexible citizenship." Such "flexibility," however, is relegated to the realm of metaphor once it comes up against the rigidity of borders and immigration checkpoints; the Hong Kong entrepreneurial elite about which Ong writes can surely afford to cross such boundaries more easily. The countless obstacles Daly City Filipinos experience in attempting to enter the United States, much less attain citizenship, attest to the inflexibility of immigration regulations and the categories they produce.

Bautista's family still has not decided whether or not they will be staying in the United States permanently. Of course, they have just arrived. "Siyempre medyo high ka pa rin" (Of course we're still kind of high), he said. He was still enthusiastic, and he was not losing hope, he added. "Sinasabi ko lang, hindi pa namin kayang sagutin 'yung tanong na iyon" (All I'm saying, we still can't answer that question).His prospects back in the Philippines were not very bright anyhow, he said: the purchasing power of the peso was decreasing more and more, and the government in power was mostly ineffectual. Government projects, Bautista said, were begun and never carried out to the finish, unlike in the United States, where they were really implemented, with disciplined people who followed the rules.[9]

It is the sense of increased stability that Wally Curameng, for one, appreciated in the United States. In any case, salaries were different; here, Curameng said, "the amount that you exert is being paid off." The Philippines was a different story altogether: "There you scrape and scrape to make a living, your salary is still small. At least here, you can see, you earn what you do." Later he offered a conjecture about why the possibility that a Filipino in the United States would move back to the Philippines seemed slim: "Because he already adapted to the way of life in the States, that you can buy everything with your charge card." Here, he said, you can "just work and you get your paycheck every few days, you can buy things that you like." His wife, Debbie Patron, added, "There's a feeling that there's guarantees of prosperity here, as opposed to back home, with everything up in the air." Curameng agreed.

---

[9] For Ellen Bautista, Jun's daughter, the principal difference between the two countries was the amount of social services available in the United States—for instance, the programs for immigrants, or for health awareness. She contrasted the "bureaucratic system" in the Philippines with the kinds of benefits in the United States "There are benefits that people do not even know exist," she said.

"Because there's nothing solid that's waiting for me, a particular job or like a retirement home waiting for me," he said.

The "guarantee of prosperity"—as well as the increased ability to buy and consume, period—that the United States seems to offer is reflected in Nancy Navarro's comments as well, as she talked about some friends from the Philippines:

> You know, we just had visitors from the Philippines, and they worked for Levi's in the Philippines, they do very well. But when I asked them—because they're already doing well in the Philippines—except for the director, he said that he's not willing to come here. Because he's already the head, and I guess he has a maid, a driver, everything. But the others who were in the marketing, in the finance, and doing well also, making a lot of money—if given a chance, they would also come here. And that sort of bothered me—it means, if life is great there, they still want to leave [ibig sabihin, kahit mahusay na ang buhay do'n, gusto pa rin nilang umalis], get out of the country. It bothered me—it is as if, does that mean that if the Philippines gets better like Singapore, wouldn't we all wanna go back there? Wouldn't we all wanna go back to where we came from? Or if it became like a Singapore, would we want to stay in the Philippines? So what does this mean? Is the life in the Philippines so bad that we all want to leave?

But as one might expect, prosperity is by no means guaranteed. As I will discuss more fully in the next chapter, the Filipino immigrant community has seen the growth of a "declassed" population in the last decade or more. The dream of financial success remains elusive, but there are quicker, seemingly easier methods of attaining it. For instance, Teddy Encinas explained his regular purchase of lotto tickets by talking about his perceived class status: "I'm still working class here, a lot of Filipinos are hard workers, the Filipinos here. Wealthy Filipinos are rare, unless you're a doctor. A lot of Filipinos here, especially in Daly City, they're working class."

Another Generation

The differences in the "guarantees of prosperity" are of course not the only points of contrast between the Philippines and the United States, according to my interviewees. What interests me is how these differences are inscribed, and where they are located. Without prompting, interviewees would talk about the differences between occupational opportunities, or between the

two governments. But most interestingly, many of them cited "cultural" differences between Filipinos and Filipino Americans (i.e., those Philippine-born
and American-born) to illustrate the comparison between the two countries.
This appeared to highlight the ways in which each group was seen to embody
its respective "nation"; at the same time, their citing of those differences
underscored the separate spheres in which my informants saw themselves
as opposed to Filipino Americans. The fact that these differences provided
structure for their expectations and encounters with Filipino Americans is
significant, for it points to a clear distinction between the two in discourse.
(Indeed, this distinction is glossed over when "the Filipino community" is
referred to by the term *Filipino Americans*; as I explained in the first chapter, most of my Daly City interviewees eschewed the label as applying to
them.)

Cultural differences between immigrant and native-born, particularly
when seen in relation to language, constitute the kernel of the immigrant
predicament: to maintain a complicated balance between Filipino and American identities. Far from being relegated to mere theory, these perceived differences have quite tangible consequences in the "real world" as they spill
into the realm of politics. The differences also call into question the possibility of ethnic solidarity. The differences are also significant because they point
to another level of ambivalence about belonging in America.

Wally Curameng invoked differences when he started speaking about
Filipino Americans, but his conversation took a different direction, and revolved instead around his insecurities as a Filipino immigrant. Interestingly,
these insecurities centered on getting along with Filipino Americans: "My
feeling was, these Filipinos, they speak good English, then they dress okay,
but my feeling was, I couldn't get along with them. Why? Because we were
both Filipinos anyway. But of course they were raised differently, already
Americanized." The cultural difference was reflected in his romantic choices
as well: "I was looking for a Filipina that I could get along with [na makakasundo ko], so I was looking at someone raised like me, who was raised in the
Philippines. But I didn't realize that when I met her, it could be done, I could
get along with them." His wife, Debbie Patron, is Filipino American; he met
her while attending a press event.

Nonetheless, Curameng saw major differences between him and Filipinos raised in the United States. "The things that they like, and the things that
we [referring to himself and me] like—I like—are different." He found Patron to be "more aggressive" in "dating rituals," for one thing, and told me
how he "chickened out" and didn't call her after the first night they slept
together. (She suddenly appeared at his office, demanding to know why he
hadn't called. Since then they have been married to each other.)

WC: It's just that my feeling was, I'm too Filipino, something like that, to be going with a Filipina raised here.

BV: But was it really that different? Were the backgrounds insurmountable?

WC: I don't know, it was like my feeling was, I blocked it immediately. I don't think I can get along with someone raised here. Or have a relationship with someone raised here. If yes, as friends, something like that, that was possible. Maybe that's part of adjusting, trying to learn the culture, I think that's part of it.

He explained that his attitude may have come from when his Filipino American cousins would visit the Philippines and how he "couldn't grasp what made them tick." Part of it also was his feeling that "if you say or do something, they might laugh at you."

WC: Yeah. How you look sometimes, how you move, the things that you like—a pop star that you like, it so happens that American-raised teenagers didn't like it, something like that. It was as if I felt that every step that I do should be appreciated by them, in order for me to fit in that group.

DEBBIE PATRON (DP): You had to be some sort of ideal, to match their ideal, for you to feel comfortable. So you're thinking, whatever's Americanized, so up there.

WC: I think, it's also—that affected me too, because in the Philippines in order for you to fit in a group or a barkada [peer group], you need to be—for you to fit in with them, their traits you have to follow too—like haircuts, things like that, how you wear your shirt compared to those nerds. It was as if I always feel that if I act nerdy, or act too Filipino, American-raised teenagers wouldn't take me as a member of the group. Accept me as a barkada. But I was wrong, I was wrong. Until I met Debbie.

Now, he says, he is more "confident," for he has realized that "American-raised Filipinos are also interested in Filipinos." "Especially now," he said, "there are more and more American-raised Filipinos, they wanna trace their roots. But then I wasn't thinking of that, when we first met. It turns out there are American-born Filipinos that are willing to learn their culture."

Curameng's remarkable feeling of inferiority in the face of Filipino Americans was consistent with the high regard in which he held American modernity; he saw himself as embodying Filipino inferiority in the face of the American gaze. His feeling of not belonging was finally offset by his realization that he had something of value, something cultural worth possessing, something the Americans, as it were, did not have. But possession of this kind of cultural capital is not the relevant point here; what is important is that it signals Curameng's recognition of himself in the United States, that he and other Americans did indeed have something in common.

Nancy Navarro gave a typical example—typical, at least, of my interviewees—of the differences between young Filipinos in the Philippines and those in the United States. Changes in the "complexion" of the more recent immigrants have led to young Filipino immigrants who are "easily swayed," she said.[10] They "acquire all the bad habits of the Americans . . . the environment takes over, and then peer pressure is very strong, and then the desire to belong is very strong." Navarro followed up with a discussion of safe sex and the "wrong," supposedly anti-abstinence, message that it sends, that "it's okay to have sex." The old fears, she explained, have been removed, particularly "because the state is a very, very generous father."

Part of the reason for this "lack of morality," she explained, was the growing number of latchkey kids, because of Filipino parents who hold more than one job. "The kids are being raised by television. And what kinds of things do they watch on television? So it's not easy for young people here." For Navarro, the combination of so-called American values and the exigencies of immigrant life (with parents in two jobs) has led to more delinquency among the youth, which constitutes the difference (however imagined) from teenagers in the Philippines. Such perceived differences are carried over to Filipino media representations of Filipinos in the United States, as we shall see in Chapter Five.

Language and the Immigrant Predicament

Perhaps the most important of the differences between Filipinos and Filipino Americans, however, was constantly brought up my interviewees: it had to do with language. This factor, in fact, would crop up as well in the media portrayal of Filipino Americans, as will become apparent in the next chapter.[11] I use the example of language to illustrate the "immigrant predicament,"

---

[10] Although Navarro probably meant "aspect" or "character" when she said "complexion," it is certainly possible that there was a hint of a racial/class element to her description as well.

[11] One puzzling point about language was what was *not* talked about. Whenever the subject of language was raised—and indeed one can see this in Filipino American newspapers as well—it almost always had to do with the difference between English and Tagalog, or with the inability of the second generation to speak Tagalog. That is, there was little discussion of other Filipino languages in my interviews or in official discourse; cultural presentations (dancing, singing, and the like), local Bay Area television programs, community-sponsored events like Fiesta Filipina,

or, to put it simply, the age-old conflict between tradition and assimilation. The concept of assimilation and its criteria, for instance, is not merely limited to sociological theory; the fact that some of the interviewees actually used the word *assimilate* shows how deeply the sociological term has permeated everyday discourse.

My interview with Alice Bulos— a cofounder of the Filipino American Women's Network and the Filipino American Democratic Caucus, and a presidential appointee to the Federal Council on Aging—took a different direction from all the others. Bulos was, for starters, a public figure, a long-active political spokesperson for the Filipino community in the Bay Area. Her curriculum vitae, in the general sense of the word, already preceded her. Our interview took place in the living room of her house, punctuated throughout by numerous phone calls and her granddaughter playing in the hallway. Bulos is perhaps as stereotypically opposite to the image of a powerful community activist and politician as possible. A diminutive woman in her sixties, with graying hair and a disarming, maternal demeanor, Bulos looked very much like the grandmother she indeed is. (The homemade brownies she brought out for me made it difficult to dispel that image as well.) But the interview began, unsurprisingly, with a straight recounting of her achievements—the mark of a public figure used to talking about her life.

Alice Bulos had brought up the topic of language, though she was initially talking about being Filipino in the United States. She had asked me about my relatives, and where I was from. Then she added, "Buti at hindi mo nakakalimutan, 'yung iba diyan sasabihin nagpunta lang dito, ay naku hindi na ko marunong mag-Tagalog. Naku, nawala na ang Tagalog niya" (It's a good thing that you're not forgetting [Tagalog], some people here have just arrived, and they say they don't know how to speak Tagalog anymore. Oh my, she/he has already lost her/his Tagalog.). Her grandchildren, she said, refused to learn (or speak) Tagalog, though they could understand it.[12] She continued:

---

and so on are generally conducted in a transplanted Manila version of Taglish. Although it is clear that the activities of regional organizations and associations are conducted in Filipino languages other than Tagalog, I am tempted to argue that Taglish functions as a kind of unofficial lingua franca in the United States—but one that merely supplements the use of English, as *Philippine News* does, to communicate to Filipinos from different regions and generations. (Many newspaper and television advertisements in the Filipino American media (and indeed, in the Philippines as well) routinely use Taglish in ad copy.)

[12] Teddy Encinas and his wife speak to their son mostly in English, but their son understands and speaks a little Tagalog. When Encinas scolds him, he said, he scolds him in Tagalog, so his son knows he's angry. Mike Santos also told me that his one-year-old niece could understand Tagalog. "Kasi inisip namin, lalaki din siya rito, Ingles rin ang kalalakihan niya, so better na maintindihan

Now look at what has happened, our Filipino Americans here, maybe their parents were really so afraid that one would say you are not American, you are not like this, and then they refused to let them speak Tagalog, they don't want to speak Tagalog. They were speaking English, so now, most are estranged [Iinglis-inglis sila, e di ngayon, nag-estranged itong karamihan]. These lawyers, Filipino Americans. So what is happening with them? They are learning Filipino. They're enrolled in some of these colleges because they want to learn Filipino.

Bulos was referring to the stereotypical first-generation practice of teaching children exclusively in English to facilitate assimilation.[13] For her, one has to strike a balance within one's Filipino American identity, a balance between being American and preserving "one's heritage." Language was a primary indicator of identity, and so was food. She related that her youngest grandchild was more American "in orientation" because she ate salads and burgers. "But the other one, that's the one who always eats rice. But this one," she said, pointing to the girl sitting in another corner of the living room, "eats sandwiches more."

You need to become American, assimilate, that's fine. You have to assimilate. I am also against those very nationalistic kind of Filipino. By the way, why did you come here if you are not going to assimilate? But the assimilation is okay, but don't forget your heritage. . . . You really have to maybe establish your identity. You've got to. Because if you don't recognize your identity you will be lost. Because if you establish your identity—I'm a Filipino American—develop your power and develop your community, to be involved and to be visible, then that is your victory.

She added later: "On the onset I know that I have to make an adjustment. That I cannot really be too nationalistic, quote and unquote, but rather, I am in a new society, a new country, and you really have to adapt, and make adjustments to the conditions at your new society and your new country."

---

niya ang Tagalog. Di ba?" (Because we thought, she'll be growing up here anyway, she'll be growing up in English, so it's better that she understand Tagalog [as well]. Right?)

[13] Immigrants from various backgrounds have written much on this topic. For Filipinos, see Espiritu (1995); see also Bonus (2000, 53), who relates that Filipino parents in San Diego would speak to their children in English to prevent the youngsters from being mistreated in school.

As Bulos tells her children, "Don't be ashamed of your heritage. You're still a Filipino, they will never, never accept you into the mainstream. Although you don't have an accent because you were born here, but that does not really make any difference, you are still a Pilipino American." For Bulos, a Tagalog accent is a concrete signifier of the origins of first-generation Filipino immigrants. "Ayaw nilang masabi na meron silang accent. Sabi ko, pag nawalan kayo nang accent, hindi kayo Pilipino" (They don't want it said that they have an accent. I say, when you lose your accent, you are not Filipino).

The balance between the old and new countries, however, is only secondary when it comes to politicization:

> I always believe that the issues in this American society you must really know. The issues in the Philippines are not really the issues that will concern ourselves as Americans specifically. But don't forget that we have relatives over there, don't forget the country of our origin. And there is a saying, I love my country. But once you have already relinquished your allegiance, it means you are double already, isn't it? You are here in America and so take all the opportunities to at least progress in this community, this society. Sometimes we fail to do that.

Bulos recognized, however, that there are major differences within the Filipino community in the United States—some are "still" permanent residents, she points out. This explains why political empowerment has been "so difficult": their loyalty is to the Philippines, she said. But interestingly, her explanation constantly contradicts itself, moving from one thought to another ("You have to assimilate," "Don't forget your heritage," "The issues in the Philippines . . . [do not] concern [us] as Americans," "Don't forget the country of your origin."). Her reminder to her children further qualifies her thoughts—that her children may not have a Filipino accent (again, inscribing difference in language), but that they will "never [be] accept[ed] into the mainstream." Her speech mirrors, in effect, the repeated turning of the Pinoy immigrant from forgetting to remembrance, from one orientation, from one country, to another.

Bulos speaks in the seasoned language of the politician, used to making prescriptive pronouncements. But she does touch on what is seen as the fundamental responsibility (or, if you will, predicament) of the Filipino immigrant, at least as formulated by politicians and activists: to create a balance between "assimilating" and being "nationalistic" (a term, interestingly, that Bulos used only to refer to feelings toward the Philippines). In this respect her ideas are close in disposition to those enshrined in semi-official discourse (the ethnic media); as we shall see in the chapter on *Philippine News*, these contradictory impulses and orientations are appealed to and, paradoxically, simultaneously repudiated.

Repeated turning becomes more possible (and more frequent) in the present. At the same time, however, the demands of Asian American politics have made it imperative to commit to "developing your community," as Bulos put it (arguably more now than ever before). That is, the growing political empowerment of Asian Americans in recent years has necessitated a shift in focus from homeland politics to strictly "American" issues—a shift made difficult by the immigrant composition of the population. Bulos's frustrations with Filipinos who are largely oriented towards the Philippines and how their orientation stunts political growth in the United States can be seen here.

Perhaps my interviewees' unease regarding Filipino Americans—Bulos's contradictory advice (which perfectly captured the Filipino immigrant's opposing obligations), Curameng's apprehension, Navarro's disapproval, and the cinematic representations I will discuss in Chapter Five—stem from an ambivalence similar to the one experienced upon immigration. The figure of the Filipino American is the embodiment of a desire for modernity—or more to the point, a kind of assimilation. Handlin writes:

> The young wore their nativity like a badge that marked their superiority over their immigrant elders. It was this superiority that gave the second generation its role as mediator between the culture of the home and the culture of the wider society. . . .
>
> Accepting that role, the immigrants nevertheless resented it. It reversed the proper order of things. (2002, 226)

Although the conflict between parents and native-born children can obviously be characterized as generational, it has also been depicted as precisely cultural. And although the conflict may revolve around issues of morality, it seems to me to represent a form of envy as well. The Filipino Americans can speak English better than the older generation, and they are more familiar with America's foods, customs, popular culture, morals— in short, more American than the first-generation immigrants will ever be. Immigrants can therefore live vicariously through the second generation's successful "assimilation." At the same time, however, the assimilated also symbolize a loss of Filipino identity. This characterization (as having lost Filipinoness) also affects, and afflicts, the Filipino immigrants themselves.

Electoral Politics in Daly City

Immigrant orientations, whether to the Philippines or to the United States, can be seen generally as responses to calls of obligation as well. The 1993 Daly City elections for City Council are a concrete example of the perceived differences between Filipino immigrants and Filipino Americans, and they show how these perceptions spill over into practice—in this case, political behavior.

The 1993 election happens to be historic—it was certainly described that way at the time by local politicians and the media—because it was the first time a person of Filipino background was elected to serve on the Daly City council. Michael Guingona, an attorney for the San Francisco Public Defender's office, was elected to the City Council in June 1993. Through a rotating mayorship, he became mayor in November 1995, becoming the first Filipino American mayor of the city. His election campaign was one of the most closely watched, and most contentious, in recent Daly City history. It also became the most divisive issue among the Pinoy community in Daly City since the Marcos regime.

The election split along American-born and Philippine-born lines: Guingona's primary opponent was Mario Panoringan, an insurance agent and immigrant from Pangasinan. What was to be, at least ideally, an opportunity to demonstrate ethnic solidarity and the collective strength of the Filipino community disintegrated into infighting. As Vic Torres, in a magazine article reporting on the campaign, put it, "The latter [the Philippine-born] resent the former's 'lack of Filipinoness,' while second generation Fil-Ams recoil from the immigrants' political culture ('the unorthodox way agendas are set and meetings are run')" (1993: 15). Contributing to the conflict was Guingona's political strategy "of not projecting [himself] as a 'Filipino' candidate that was only concerned with the Filipino community." Torres adds that Guingona's positioning opened him up to charges that he was failing "to address the issues of the Filipino community," and not a few members of the community urged him to withdraw from the race. The strife typified the dilemma in which many "ethnic" politicians find themselves: appealing to white mainstream voters while addressing the concerns of their own ethnic communities without being accused of "selling out."

Earnest and boyishly enthusiastic, Guingona epitomized the young (he had just turned thirty at the time) Asian American politician. He had succeeded in an election victory in Daly City where many others since the early '80s had failed.[14] Previously the City Council had deadlocked on choosing an

---

[14] Guingona had also run in 1992, when he placed fourth out of ten candidates running for two council seats. Five of those candidates were Filipinos.

appointment for an empty Council seat, and so a call for a special election was made. Filipino community leaders had formed a committee to decide on a "compromise candidate," but when the committee meeting broke down, Guingona and Panoringan announced their separate candidacies almost immediately.

I interviewed Guingona in August 1994, a little more than a year after he was voted into office. When asked about his campaign strategy, he replied, "You can't win an election in Daly City on a Filipino platform, you just can't do it. I don't think it's even proper to run an election like that." Panoringan, he said, "had nothing but Filipino fundraisers." "I couldn't ask people for money and I couldn't ask them to give me money because I was Filipino," he added. He explained further:

> My background as a person that walks a line between being Filipino and being American, was one that was a very natural line, a line that I've walked in my personal and professional life forever. Filipinos think you're too white. White people think you're too Filipino. I mean, at this point, I really didn't give a shit, I knew who I was, and they took me for who I was rather than the color of my skin or my ethnicity.

But it was precisely his ethnicity that became the main target for criticism; some of his harshest critics, he said, had come from the Filipino community itself.

> Filipinos in Daly City tend to be fragmented, and there was a feeling back then of the old guard versus the new guard and, of course, I was not part of the old guard, I mean, the main criticisms that I would get from the Filipino community is he doesn't speak Tagalog, how does he know about what our needs are, da da da da, all this crap about not knowing what the needs of the community are.

"I think that what sold people more on me," Guingona added, "was I was young and I was a local." He could knock on people's doors, he said, and know them by name, and who their relatives were. Guingona arrived in the United States as a child in 1965. He remembers "being one of two Filipinos in [his] kindergarten class." Only some years later, when he was in fifth grade, did other Filipinos started arriving in large numbers in Daly City.

> They couldn't argue with 29 years of community. They could say 20 [years], they could say "I was born in 1945 in Paranaque, came here

when I was seven." No. They all said, you know, "I came here after I got married, I raised my children here," you know, that's you know, that's basically what they're like. All came in the '70s with their wives, that kind of thing. So, you know, I didn't want to play it to the Filipino community. It just doesn't, it just doesn't sound right. Not only that, but from a tactical standpoint, it wasn't a smart thing to do. I, I needed to win, I didn't need to make the Filipino community happy, I needed to win, I needed as many people to vote for me as possible. Did it cost me votes? I'm sure it did.[15]

Guingona's more direct wooing of the (white) majority paid off. As Alice Bulos, a veteran of Bay Area politics, said of Guingona's campaign strategy,

What the Filipinos do not know is that they need to be perceived by the mainstream as electable. Acceptable. Like Mike Guingona. Why? Filipino American. Born here. I am not saying that the other Filipinos who came here are not qualified; they are qualified. But there is another degree that you have to understand to be elected, and that is electability. Will the whites vote for you. That is the question. And they did, for Guingona. . . . And he was born here, with his articulation and everything, that's still important. I'm not saying that the individual with such an accent is no good. . . . But the question is, you have to ask yourself whether the mainstream will really see that there is an individual who is born there from the Philippines can really qualify as their representative. So that is their thinking. I'm not saying that these Filipinos coming from the Philippines are not qualified, they are very, very qualified.

She added, however, "he must really do his homework more, more. Because although he is accepted by the mainstream, still he has to look back at his base population, his own community."

Filipino political leaders worried that the two candidates would split the ethnic vote—though as Guingona put it, "that whole split-the-vote argument really doesn't hold water. It does hold water if you assume the electorate votes purely on ethnicity. That's not true," Guingona added, criticizing the notion of ethnic solidarity and the so-called ethnic vote. Several interviewees even told me Panoringan's accent was "too thick," for one, and did not appeal to white voters, as Bulos pointed out above. Panoringan's fatal reliance on the

---

[15] As Guingona explained further: "That was one of [my] appeals. I wasn't this carpetbagger asshole who just moved in yesterday. I've been here."

ethnic vote was said to be a holdover from the way politics was run in the Philippines—"there are no white people in the Philippines, for one thing," Guingona said.

> Um, I didn't wanna run it the way—look, if it were successful, maybe I woulda thought about it, but the fact of the matter is, when Filipinos started running here in 1982, '84, unsuccessful every time. Why? Because they would not, did not wish to broaden their base, they thought they could do it on sheer numbers alone: "There's enough of us here, we can do it, we don't need to play the white community."

In the end, Guingona won with 38 percent of the vote, and Panoringan came away with 28 percent. One thousand Filipinos who had registered to vote failed to show up at election time (Torres 1993, 16). Guingona was voted by the Council to act as mayor in 1995, and he served his term until November 1998. During that period he started the Daly City–Quezon City Sister City Committee and appointed Filipinos to the Parks and Recreation Department and the Planning Commission.[16] In December 2001 he was again elected mayor and has served in the City Council up to the present.

Why did a thousand Filipinos register but not vote? There is a certain irony here about courting the ethnic vote when political participation seems to be thin on the surface. Still, counting on the ethnic vote is particularly salient in places with sizable numbers of Filipinos like Daly City. That particular kind of numbers rhetoric—where candidates and community leaders cite the sheer numbers of Pinoys as support, if not proof, of their electability—I witnessed at a voter registration drive in 1998. Sponsored by the Filipino Empowerment Movement, a Daly City–based collective of Filipino leaders in San Mateo County, the "Get out the Vote" project aimed to add to the 4,000 registered Filipino voters in Daly City. This was quite a small number, compared to the more than 30,000 Filipinos in the city alone, especially

---

[16] Guingona was the target of criticism in October 1997 when he unexpectedly terminated one of his Filipino appointees (coincidentally, Philippine-born) to the Planning Commission. Cesar Alegria, the appointee, had unofficially announced his interest in running against Guingona in the next year's council elections, and he believed this was the reason for his firing. Claiming that he wanted to diversify the commission ethnically, Guingona replaced Alegria with a Hispanic American woman. Letters from Filipino Daly City residents protesting Alegria's termination threatened to polarize the community again; Mitos Santisteban, the president of the Filipino American Council of San Mateo, stated that Guingona's action had "a negative impact on our struggle to politically empower the Filipino American community." The incident fizzled out after Alegria ran for City Council the next year but lost.

considering that only about half of those 4,000 had actually voted in the previous elections.[17]

The meeting, more of a press conference than a rally, was held in the organization's tiny office at the Westlake Shopping Center. Five members of the press were present, including one non-Filipino representative from the Chinese-owned *Asian Week*; the rest were other local Filipino American activists and three of the seven other Filipinos running in Bay Area elections that coming November. But the meeting, instead of focusing on disseminating election awareness, quickly turned into candidates stumping for themselves—much to the visible chagrin of the moderator.

One reason for voter apathy, claimed the movement organizers, was that Filipinos were worried about being called for jury duty. The organizers countered that jury duty rosters came from the Department of Motor Vehicles, and not from voter registration lists. Another apparent cause was that Filipinos did not know where their local polling places were; the organizers then recommended the use of the absentee ballot for that very reason. Cesar Alegria (who at that point had not yet announced his candidacy), one of the leaders of the Filipino Empowerment Movement, said that many times during their door-to-door campaign they had found only one registered voter per household.

The main reason for voting, according to the movement's pamphlet, was that "only 11,000 votes will [be needed to] elect Filipinos in [*sic*] the City Council." Citing the large Filipino population in Daly City, the pamphlet went on to say that "we can have: 2 to 4 Pinoys in the City Council, more Pinoys appointed to the different commissions . . ."—subscribing to the belief that Filipino voters would elect only Filipino candidates, and that those candidates, in turn, would appoint Filipinos to commissions. (The furor over Alegria's later termination, discussed in note 16, obviously proceeded from this belief.) Repeatedly referring to Filipinos as "Sleeping Giants of California," the pamphlet, written both in English and Tagalog, enjoined readers, "Gising Na, Kabayan sa Daly City."[18]

The "strength-in-numbers" method should have worked in principle, though perhaps not for the right reasons. But overwhelming the polls was a possibility that could happen only in places like Daly City with a large Pinoy

---

[17] Asian Americans have, in general, been turning out to vote in relatively large numbers, despite the popularly held belief that Asians do not vote. In 1994, 39 percent of U.S. citizens of Asian background voted, in comparison to 50 percent of whites and 38 percent of blacks (U.S. Bureau of the Census 1996).

[18] *Gising na* is in the imperative mood, and means "wake up." *Kabayan* is somewhat trickier to translate: it can be taken to mean "fellow townsmate," but primarily "fellow countryman/woman". In any case it is unclear, and lends itself to multiple interpretations.

community. Such cities, of course, were few in the United States. That the method failed is testimony to two things: a deep division within Daly City and a naive belief in ethnic solidarity. The failure also points to a kind of self-fulfilling prophecy: this lack of solidarity, whether manifested in regionalism or in the so-called crab mentality, is constantly employed and cited for its power in explaining Filipino failure in general. Such hoary artifacts of colonial discourse are unfortunately seen more as causes than as symptoms, and are far too deeply embedded in both scholarly and popular thought.

That the Daly City elections would split between locals and immigrants was, in hindsight, not much of a surprise.[19] What was more revealing was that it involved both Filipino groups, and that the perceived difference between the two became as much of an issue as it did. What made the Daly City elections unique in that sense were the specifically *cultural* matters on which the candidates were judged, and on which the campaign hinged. The Guingona-Panoringan race for City Council brought culture-specific issues to the fore; indeed, their platforms hardly differed from one another's, or their opponents'. Language became the primary indicator for cultural difference, and it was used as a measure of whether the candidate could "truly understand" the community.

There are no specific data, unfortunately, for how Filipinos, whether foreign-born or not, voted in the 1993 elections. The discourse on the elections reflected the particular structure of the Filipino community. It was a community that was predominantly foreign-born, and its members clearly considered an American-born Filipino—indeed, one who consciously defined himself as an American "native"—as not "one of them." The campaign involved a scrutiny of the candidates' "Filipinoness" even as they were to represent the Filipino community in America. In the end, the American-born candidate won—shunned by some Filipino immigrants because of his "Americanness," which ironically was perhaps the reason for his successful

---

[19] In the late '70s and early '80s, Filipino teenage "gangs" were split along immigrant and native-born lines as well. Teddy Encinas related that Filipino gangs were prevalent when he was in high school; rivalries were created between "FOBs"—"Fresh Off the Boat," updated since to "Fresh Off Boeings"—and the "ABCs" or "ABFs," which Encinas said meant "American-born child" or "American-born Filipino." Gangs were also grouped according to their high school (Balboa High School, for instance, had its own gangs, which opposed those of other schools), or district, or ethnicity (Filipinos versus Mexicans). "Sometimes you see each other in the park, people would just stare at each other, then they'd start beating each other up. Just like the Philippines. Shooting, that was also prevalent." Encinas recalled a riot between Mexicans and Filipinos at Mission High School in the late '70s. The police were called in and the school had to be closed. But sometimes the ethnic lines were disregarded; Samoans, he said, fought along with the Filipinos. Debbie Patron, who had worked with immigrant teenagers to help them make the transition into their new high schools, said that "[the gangs] didn't see themselves as Filipinos killing Filipinos."

crossover into the so-called mainstream (read: white) voter consciousness, and his ultimate victory.

Most important, the election and the voting campaign pointed to a remarkable political apathy among Daly City's Filipino residents. Getting people to vote is by no means a problem unique to Filipinos, of course. But it is rendered more glaring in a place like Daly City, where the frustrations of Filipino community leaders run high. From January until the primaries in June 1998, the empowerment movement managed to get a meager 200 to 500 new Filipino voters to register—a far cry from the 7,000 projected new voters. (A bemused Alegria later attributed the low numbers to the climatic phenomenon El Niño.)

The apathy can be explained, externally, by past factors: that Filipinos, historically denied opportunities for political participation (as a direct result of discriminatory citizenship policies), have ended up shying away from the political process. The "liberal" explanation would be that the powers-that-be benefit from keeping Filipinos and other minorities politically marginal so they will remain, as Rick Bonus writes, a passive labor force (2000). But it is likely as well, particularly for this immigrant population, that voter apathy is produced by previous political experiences (or lack of them) in the Philippines. In my interviews, Daly City residents cited the endemic corruption and the frustrating local and national politics of the Philippines as one of the main differences between it and the United States and as one of the main reasons for their departure.

But one could also argue that the election campaign and its results—and the lack of political participation in general—are illustrative of immigrant ambivalence. The Filipino immigrant recognizes herself in both fellow immigrant and Filipino American—Panoringan, with his accent, as the telltale linguistic mark of immigrant status, and the latter as a figure of both cultural loss and successful assimilation. Non-participation in local politics can be read as being not merely apathy, but an act of conscious deferral, a refusal to engage oneself in American affairs—for doing so would require a deeper, perhaps even more emotional commitment to an American belonging.

On Ethnic Solidarity

What I find interesting as well about the elections and the voting campaign is the invocation of ethnic solidarity as a rallying point. My interviewees, by and large, cited the *absence* of solidarity, to their surprise, as one of the major differences between the Philippines and the United States. Mark Santos, for instance, had given the presence of the Pinoy population as reasons for his family's move to Daly City—but, emotionally, it was not as they expected:

I guess we would always say, it's better to live in a community where you feel you belong. As I said, here there are many Filipinos. But I did not expect that even if there were Filipinos here, it's still not as it is back home, not like back home. Isn't it true, even if you don't know them, even if they're Filipino, not even once do they greet each other, even if you see them you don't greet each other. And then the tendency is, those Filipinos who grew up here, their, you know, is different, of course they're more, you know, they don't really, you know, unless they just arrived too.[20]

Santos is specifically comparing the capacity for friendliness, or hospitality, of Filipinos in the Philippines and of those in the United States. But he is addressing a cultural gap between Filipinos and Filipino Americans as well, which is alluded to here. He reacted to Daly City's failure to meet his expectations; despite the fact that there are many Filipinos, Daly City is still "not like back home." He later adds that San Francisco was different—"At least in San Francisco, companionship among Filipinos was good there, the community there, the neighbors, as compared to here. Here it isn't, people keep to themselves [kanya-kanya]."

Nancy Navarro put it differently, talking about the Filipino community in the late '60s:

Because there were still few Filipinos then, whenever you see a Filipino, you were so happy. Everybody's so happy because there was a Filipino, it's like, you're still only on one [side of the] street, hi, hi, how are you doing, when did you arrive here, let's help each other. It's as if you all knew each other because there were so few of you. The moment you see a Filipino—hey, are you Filipino? And everybody was helping one

---

[20] In his words:

Siguro palaging nasasabi rin namin, mas magandang tumira sa community where you feel you belong, 'yun nga rito maraming Pilipino, pero I did not expect na kahit walang Pilipino dito, hindi pa rin ganong ka-ano sa atin, hindi kagaya sa atin—di ba, hindi mo naman kakilala, kahit Pilipino, kahit minsan hindi man sila nagbabatian, kahit makita mo hindi kayo nagbabatian. Tapos ang tendency pa, itong mga Pilipino na laki dito, iba ang ano nila, siyempre mas ano sila, hindi sila masyadong mag-aano, unless bagong dating din.

The Tagalog word *ano* means "what," but Santos uses it throughout his interview as a speech mannerism somewhat akin to "you know." He elides crucial words in his comments, the meanings of which I can only guess at: friendly? approachable? The fact that I did not ask him to clarify may perhaps correspond to a similar understanding on my part, i.e., I knew—or thought I knew—what he meant. *Atin* means "our," and I have loosely translated into "back home" what literally means "our place."

another at that time. Now it's somewhat different. I think there's so many of us now. I think it's different, the situation is different now—when you see a Filipino you don't say hi anymore. Before, anybody who even looked close to a Filipino, it's like you right away greet them, talk to each other, you compare notes—hey, have you found a job yet, you know, hey, what are you doing. There was bonding then. Because there were few of the Filipinos. You were happy to see another Filipino. Now, there are some Filipinos [who say], hmmph, there are already so many Filipinos [*laughs*], right? It was before a joy to see another Filipino, 'cause there was not too many. There were still a few then.

Navarro very concretely illustrates her excitement at seeing the rare fellow Filipino during the initial influx of migrants, to which she attributes a closer "bonding." This bonding may be attributed, at least on the surface, to how immigrant minorities may seek each other out—certainly this was my case as a student in central New York. But this novelty seems to have worn off once immigration started increasing in the next two decades. Navarro attributes a certain disdain to some Filipinos who scoff at the increasing numbers of fellow Filipinos in Daly City—whether this scorn is based on class or a sentiment of privilege for having arrived in the United States earlier than others is unclear. (It is unclear as well whether she was, in fact, referring to herself.) Still, it is worth bearing in mind that a kind of intimacy (or exclusivity) was thought to prevail during those early years of immigration. Though it is tempting to ascribe the perceived loss of intimacy to the stereotypical anomie of the suburbs, it is probably simpler to explain it in light of a rise in the Filipino population coupled with the exigencies of work.

I had asked Santos, for instance, whether he was happy living in the United States. He said he was, particularly where job opportunities were concerned. He qualified his enthusiasm, however, by recognizing that not everyone who came here could get the job he wanted. He then continued with a discussion of Filipinos at work back in the Philippines and in the United States:

> MS: And if I compare [them], the only thing here I don't—I liked my job in the Philippines, because of course it was a good company, the benefits were good, all in all, my boss was Filipino, even if you had a little problem, you know, the tension, the stress at the office, that won't disappear, but you can be with them,[21] because Filipi-

---

[21] I will return to this point—"you can be with them"—later in this chapter when I discuss ethnic solidarity, an inexact homology to *pakikisama*, which I will discuss further in the next chapter.

nos here are different. The Filipino here, I've kind of noticed that the crab mentality where they pull each other down is correct, who is better than the other, like that. If you are working with fellow Filipinos, which is why I told myself, if I will be given the opportunity I would not want to work with fellow Filipinos, I'd rather work with whites or blacks, they're kinder—well, not really kinder, but on a professional basis they're more, um, the Filipino—

BV: They're not more professionalized—

MS: —when you talk to each other, okay, when you've already turned your back, they say all these things, like that, damaging reputations, like that, pulling each other down, you know, who is better than the other, that's what I don't like about Filipinos. I thought I was expecting that Filipinos who—Filipinos like you who are also from—immigrants also that came from here, who were also able to find jobs, that's their attitude. But those who grew up here . . . they're not like that. Not that I'm generalizing, but they're mostly like that. Especially when you know Filipinos, that's what they do, then they come here, go to school, it's as if their feeling is that they're too—it's as if they "look down on" those who are newly arrived [parang dina-down nila 'yung mga bagong dating].

The phrase *crab mentality*, or *talangka mentality*, is relatively recent. Briefly, it likens Filipinos to crabs in a pot, clawing and scrambling over each other—indeed, one pulling the other down—to get to the top.[22] "Crab mentality" is constantly evoked to describe Filipinos, and it is labeled an "inherent" Filipino trait. (Columnists for *Philippine News* write about the topic at least once a year.) It is surely applied to Pinoys both in the Philippines and in the United States—indeed, variations on the theme exist among Latino communities as well—but it is often used by Filipinos in the United States to describe themselves. Santos's observation that crab mentality was confirmed for him when he met Filipinos here bears this out.

Santos answered my prompting (whether he was satisfied with living in the United States) primarily in terms of the difference between Filipinos in both places. Filipino immigrants, he said, looked down on their fellow immigrants who arrived more recently. Back in the Philippines, he said, there would be the usual tension in the workplace, but not the kind of tension produced by fellow immigrants trying to outdo each other. Bautista answered

---

[22] The popular metaphor—whether collected from interviewees or reproduced as pop psychology/sociology in newspapers and scholarly works—is also discussed in Espiritu (1995, 114) and Jamero (1997, 300).

the question in a similar manner, saying that his family did not expect that Filipinos here would be "so different." As his daughter explained, at work it was fellow Filipinos who were your main competition. (Bautista added, however, that it was Filipinos who helped him find a job, through referrals.)

Many of my interviewees, when describing popular discourse on "crab mentality," gave the sense that ethnic solidarity seemed to disappear upon transplantation into a new place. This response recalls Sarah J. Mahler's investigation of "the myth of ethnic solidarity," in which she asserts that tales of fellow ethnic immigrants exploiting each other are generally downplayed. She argues further that such a breakdown of ethnic solidarity—though obviously memories of the solidarity "back home" could be tinged with nostalgia—necessarily ensues from the financial obligations immigrants have to bear.

In her ethnography on El Salvadoran immigrants on Long Island, Mahler exhaustively details how obligations toward the families left behind are the main reason for the necessity to make income stretch further; surplus income that would otherwise be saved (for better living quarters, luxury items, or having children, in Teddy Encinas's case) is funneled directly to relatives or used to repay debts incurred during migration. This additional burden, she argues, ultimately strains "the quality of social relationships" (Mahler 1995, 98)—a constant theme in the interviews I conducted as well.

Mahler's ethnography is a response to what she perceived as a romanticization of ethnic solidarity in migration studies. But this was itself a reaction to what previous scholars saw as a negative portrayal of immigrants as a whole: they were seen as not just exploitative of their own countrymen and countrywomen, but as disease-ridden, illiterate, criminal-minded, and generally unassimilable as well. But in all this pathology lies a germ of truth. Oscar Handlin, for instance, writes about European immigrants, "In the pursuit of this fleeting success, the peasant broke with his past. His constant task here was to transform income, no matter how small, into capital. . . . To create capital in America meant a miserly scrimping at the expense of day-to-day consumption. It meant also a slighting of traditional obligations, the exploitation rather than the succor of neighbors" (2002, 84). This "reversal of roles," for Handlin, came about from a "radical shift in attitudes" that occurred during migration; values like "neighborliness, obedience, respect, and status" (2002, 55) were thrown by the wayside. "The loyal dutiful man, faithful to tradition . . . was reduced to the indignity of hired labor, while shrewd, selfish, unscrupulous upstarts thrived" (2002, 73), he writes further. His sometimes overwrought prose does not differ much from my interviewees' accounts.

Despite the accusations of a lack of ethnic solidarity, it is clear that the presence of Filipinos, whether relatives or strangers, constitutes the great draw for potential Daly City Filipino residents. That is, Daly City's very identity as a "Pinoy capital" is perceived as providing the same kind of "comfort" and belonging as the immigrant ethnic enclave of tradition. Indeed, for the newly arrived immigrant, the presence of the familiar, not to mention helpful relatives, can ease the transition into an otherwise disorienting situation. In this case "the familiar" is also based on a clear assumption of ethnic solidarity: that Filipinos away from "home" would "naturally" band together and help each other—indeed, at the very least, they would greet each other.

But as my interviewees with Filipino Daly City residents make clear, expectations of ethnic solidarity are shattered upon arrival in the United States. Solidarity is anticipated, even obligatory, but the constant pressures of immigrant life squeeze out ethnic solidarity as a priority. Immigrants feel the tensions between these conflicting obligations—whether toward the state, the family, the nation, or their ethnic confreres. Calls to stand together with fellow Filipinos are circulated and amplified through semi-official channels, such as the pages of the *Philippine News*. How the newspaper produces and negotiates these tensions is the subject of the next chapter.

4

SPREADING THE NEWS

~

Newspapers and Transnational Belonging

If the desire for transnationality is embedded in Filipino immigrant lives, it is perhaps most prominently displayed in the pages of a newspaper. The *Philippine News*, a Filipino weekly newspaper based in South San Francisco, California, is the most politically influential of all Filipino newspapers in the United States and also one of the oldest. It is the most widely circulated and the most prominent Filipino newspaper in America today. For that reason alone, the *Philippine News* illuminates the political and cultural dynamics of the Filipino immigrant community and offers a better understanding of the ways in which Filipino immigrant obligations intersect and oppose each other in public discourse.

The *Philippine News*, perhaps more than other Filipino American newspapers, claims to speak for the Filipino community. By the mid-'90s, it had earned this right, because of its long history of opposition to the Marcos regime. Such pronouncements are, of course, true for most newspapers in general: editorial opinions, however personal, are still gauged with the reading audience in mind, and one expects an overlapping of interests, if not beliefs, between the audience and the articles. A newspaper is, after all, a product that is sold; any sharp deviation from the interests of its audience—let us call it its reading community here, as each newspaper arguably has its own—would imperil its sales. It also has to be able to present itself to advertisers as able to deliver a particular community and audience. The power of the newspaper is in its ability to engage, even sporadically unite, its community of readers; in this strength lies a certain responsibility. The newspaper's influence, if not its prestige, is heightened simply because the ideas contained within it are circulated and consumed simultaneously and en masse by the members of a community.

The circumstances are a little different for the ethnic press in America. The very fact of *Philippine News*'s identity as an ethnic newspaper already marks it as outside the mainstream; the interests of the newspaper—the events it covers, the people it features—will not necessarily coincide with those of the *San Francisco Chronicle*, for instance. Although not exactly oppositional, this minority stance, both literally and figuratively, carves out a particular space. It *excludes* those from the mainstream who are not interested (and who would not "get it") and, most important, it *includes* its readers in a community of fellow ethnics with, presumably, similar interests, concerns, ambitions, and desires. As people who are, in varying degrees, "displaced" from their "homeland," this reading community is already bound together, however tenuously, as a community of sentiment as well. The newspaper therefore shapes this reading community and, by extension, the ethnic community, by giving voice to its concerns and disseminating them across the continent.

Because of its minority status, *Philippine News* sees itself as responsible for influencing its community of readers and urging them toward political empowerment in the United States—therefore, it emphasizes welfare and immigrant issues, veterans' rights, affirmative action, and the like. (Ironically— as we shall see—this emphasis puts *Philippine News* in the same sphere of "advocacy journalism" as that of leftist newspapers in the Philippines.) This is not a new phenomenon, for the Filipino newspapers of the 1930s like *The Philippines Mail* (and earlier publications, set up by *pensionados*, Filipino students sent to the United States by the Philippine government for education, like the *Filipino Students' Magazine* from 1905 and *The Filipino* from 1906) have long advocated political issues such as Philippine independence or justice for Filipino farm workers. It is clear, however, that *Philippine News*'s political advocacy is largely connected with, and emboldened by, the rise of the Asian American movement—that is, the forging of a uniquely Filipino American identity. With that comes a general politicized awareness that Filipinos in the United States may be denied certain opportunities, or that they are treated unfairly.

But the ethnic press also performs another traditional function: it is a clear sign of stability. Somewhat like cemeteries, ethnic newspapers signify that a particular ethnic group has claimed a place in its adopted country, rooted itself, and established a sizable community. Reporting the community's achievements (and social events as well) can be seen as a way of entering conventional American society—that is, the community is no longer the isolated and backward ethnic enclave of yore. In a sense, it signifies a kind of assimilation: that the community has in fact "made it" and is a step closer to the mainstream, attaining an American middle-class prosperity.[1] One of the odd things about *Philippine News* is the tension between its desire to demonstrate immigrant success (and therefore buy into the Horatio Alger/model minority myths) and its avowed responsibility to uncover and publicize social injustice and consequently to press for empowerment. It exhibits the tension between community advocacy and the striving for a middle-class–based, mainstream recognition.

To complicate matters further (and make them more interesting), this tension is accompanied by a strong, if not dominating, orientation toward current events in the Philippines—a good example of transnationality, in all its ambiguity, at work. *Philippine News* rightly calls itself a newspaper for Filipinos in North America, but its front-page coverage is at most times indistinguishable from that of a Philippine newspaper. In this regard the newspaper embodies, produces, encourages, and circulates a transnational perspective. The newspaper's contents reflect its community of readers' "repeated turning" at the same time that it reproduces transnationality in its pages. In that sense, the newspaper fashions a particular image of both the Philippine and the American nation-states and their boundaries. *Philippine News* also exemplifies public discourse about the Philippines and Filipino nationalism; with its articles, editorials, and letters to the editor, the newspaper is a rich forum for nationwide public debate on what it means to be Filipino in the United States.

It is because of the national context of the newspaper's readership and debate, and the explicitly transnational scope of its concerns, that I break away from the traditional village-bound ethnography. *Philippine News*, though based in Daly City's neighbor to the south, South San Francisco, is arguably as much an integral part of understanding Daly City's Filipino community as it is a prism for looking at Filipinos in the United States as a whole. In this and succeeding chapters, I examine the diffuse sites (and different historical periods, particularly in the next chapter) where discourse by and about Filipino immigrants are produced, keeping in mind that this "multilocality" is also partially reflected in the way these immigrants live their everyday lives. Emily Ignacio's study of a Filipino Usenet group (2005), for instance, is an excellent example of research, rich in practically ethnographic detail, on a "deterritorialized" community not bound to physical location.

---

[1] This also raises the question of the newspaper's audience, which I shall discuss later; it is as if the ethnic newspaper were produced with an "imaginary" outside reader (read: Euro-American?) from the "mainstream" in mind.

My project also follows in the footsteps of anthropologists in the last two decades who have laid the theoretical groundwork for multisited research. The growing interconnectedness among "cultures" worldwide was translated into a scholarly imperative: these connections had to be similarly reflected in ethnographic methods. Indeed, "growing interconnectedness" is misleading, for, as Renato Rosaldo argues, anthropology's historical insistence on studying specific demarcated areas obscured those ties in the first place (1989, 209). George Marcus, in an attempt to represent the larger systemic context of his subjects, has suggested a focus on multiple locales in ethnographic writing rather than the artificially bounded community (1986, 1992), and it is in the spirit of these scholars that I blur some physical (and temporal) boundaries as well.

The Paper

The *Philippine News* first saw print as the U.S. edition of the *Manila Chronicle* in August 1961—printed, as its founder and former owner Alex Esclamado is fond of writing, "from the garage of [the Esclamados'] little home in San Francisco's Sunset District" (*Philippine News* 1996b, S4). Until 1997, the weekly newspaper was owned and headed by Esclamado, a lawyer from Padre Burgos, Leyte, and a former assistant to the *Chronicle* publisher Eugenio Lopez Sr., along with his wife, Lourdes, a daughter of the late ex-congressman Ramon Mitra Sr.[2]

Before his law studies, Esclamado was instrumental in the organization of the National Reserve Officer's Training Corps (ROTC) Council under President Ramon Magsaysay. Esclamado, a mayor's son, was a graduate of the Far Eastern University in Manila; later, he would become a history and law professor at the same institution.

In the late '50s, Ramon Mitra, Esclamado's father-in-law, was the executive vice president of Eugenio Lopez's media corporation. Through family connections, Esclamado was hired as a union-busting personnel manager of the *Manila Chronicle* and the television station ABS-CBN. His success with "solving the problem with the union" (Vallangca 1987, 130) prompted Lopez to send Esclamado to the Hastings Law School in San Francisco for postgraduate studies in corporate law and taxation. Carrying a foreign correspondent visa (in the guise of the *Chronicle*'s chief U.S. reporter), Esclamado arrived in 1959 with his wife and family.

---

[2] Illustrative of how the Esclamados literally and figuratively belonged to an earlier generation is the fact that the "Juniors" of each family (i.e., the Lopezes and Mitras) became more economically prominent than their parents.

But his dissatisfaction with his law studies (and guilt, he writes, about being in the United States under an "I" visa instead of a regular "F" student visa) led Esclamado to set up a newspaper—specifically, a U.S. edition of the *Chronicle*. The Lopezes initially were opposed to it, claiming that it was "not economically feasible." But Esclamado persisted, producing an initial print run of 5,000 copies and driving to various California centers of Filipino migrants—San Francisco, Delano, Stockton, Sacramento—to sell subscriptions. At that time, only two pages were devoted to news items from the United States, mostly community event announcements; the rest (about 10 pages) were reprinted directly from *Chronicle* articles on the Philippines.

An argument, however, between Esclamado and Lopez (the former relates that Lopez told him "Your newspaper is interfering [with] our relationship. I had better kill it") led to the birth of a new newspaper; under orders from his father, Eugenio (Geny) Lopez, Jr., then stopped sending Esclamado the *Chronicle* masters. *Philippine News* finally started publishing under its own name in 1967 (Vallangca 1987, 128–131). Five years later, in 1972, there was little difference between the newspaper then and its current version. Even advertisements were quite similar—car dealerships with Filipino salesmen, travel agencies, restaurants, remittance agencies—suggesting that the types of businesses catering specifically to the Filipino immigrant community were already well established.

By 1975, *Philippine News* was reporting a circulation of 20,240 (among a population of about half a million). The newspaper expanded further in the early part of 1976 by splitting into six separate editions: San Francisco, Los Angeles, Chicago/Toronto, New York/Washington, DC, Seattle/Vancouver, and Honolulu. Each edition varied from the others only in the contents of the Metro section and the advertisements. Advertising rates, for instance, differ according to whether the advertisements run nationally or only in local editions. More than 25 years later, by 2002, the newspaper had the largest circulation of any Filipino American publication—over 20,000 copies per issue. With six regional editions (San Francisco/San Jose, Los Angeles/San Diego, New York/New Jersey, Chicago, Hawaii, and Canada) plus a national edition, the *Philippine News* is still the only Filipino American newspaper to be distributed nationwide.

The newspaper's layout has changed substantially since the 1970s when, at the height of *Philippine News*'s anti-Marcos (and anti-communist) campaigns, a lead article would occupy almost the entire front page. Its late-'90s incarnation was reminiscent of *USA Today*: brightly colored, with every inch packed with headlines and photographs. Advertisements (usually for cargo companies) were a recent addition to the front page as well, taking up either side of the title and the margin at the bottom of the page.

In the late '90s, the newspaper was divided into two sections: the mostly unvarying "A" section (generally 10 to 12 pages, sometimes more depending on the number of full-page ads) and the "B," or Metro (now Region) section, whose contents changed depending on the newspaper's edition. As in other newspapers, the most important articles were located on the first two pages. More advertisements and the regular immigration columns took up the next two pages. Pages 4 and 5 are always reserved for the Opinion section, with the main editorials, an editorial cartoon, Rodel Rodis's column "Telltale Signs", a slowly shrinking section of letters to the editor, and reprinted columns from the *Philippine Daily Inquirer*. The rest of the "A" section comprised so-called jump pages, where front-page articles are continued, and articles that failed to make the front-page cut appear.

The PhilNews Network

Located in a drab industrial park full of warehouses and one-story buildings, the newspaper office in the mid-'90s was distinguishable from other offices in the neighborhood only by a Philippine News sign on the lawn and a Philippine flag in the lobby. Inside, you were greeted by a reception desk facing some office chairs and a sad ficus before you were led into the rest of the *Philippine News* headquarters. The biggest, most plushly appointed office was to your right as you entered; this was Esclamado's inner sanctum, complete with leather chair and deep wood paneling. The building itself looked nothing like the stereotypical newspaper pit of the movies, with reporters tapping away at their typewriters, cigarette smoke filling the upper half of the room up to the ceiling. Here, each member of the editorial staff, as well as the two account executives, had a separate office, windowless except for large glass panels facing the hallway.

The interns sat along with the telemarketers in a large room with desks. Oil paintings of Philippine scenes (fiestas, rice fields, sunsets, and the like) hung on the walls, but the hallways were mostly decorated, wall-to-wall, with framed issues of the newspaper—mostly from the '70s, featuring anti-Marcos headlines. The size of the staff and the building facilitated interaction between the employees: I had very little sense that there was much of a bureaucratic tangle in terms of communication. Interoffice memoranda seemed kept to a minimum, as Esclamado himself generally went from office door to office door, speaking to the staff in person.

I worked as an editorial intern at *Philippine News* from July 1995 to December 1996; after that, I continued to work as a freelance writer up to July 1998. I had written to Esclamado, introducing myself as a graduate student of anthropology doing research in Daly City. I explained that an internship at the newspaper would enable me to make more contacts in the Bay Area Filipino community. At the same time, an ethnography of the Filipino community in Daly City would be incomplete without examining the newspaper's political and cultural influence. I specifically intended to include a chapter discussing *Philippine News*, its place in exemplifying public discourse about Filipinos' lives in the United States, and the production of the newspaper itself. A week later I was contacted by the managing editor, and we figured out the details of my internship. I was to be a volunteer intern, proofreading and writing articles; I could participate in, and take notes on, editorial meetings and various activities dealing with the newspaper.

My initial responsibilities were to proofread and rewrite articles from Philippine newspapers. Nevertheless, the managing editor needed a writing sample; my first assignment was to cover a press conference held by Asian American advocates of affirmative action. After that, stories and sometimes editorials on affirmative action and education were assigned to me, the student. But the range of topics I was assigned to write about was as varied as *Philippine News*'s coverage itself: Olympians in Atlanta, the politician mother of the comedian Rob Schneider (she was running for reelection to the Pacifica, California, school board), the Asian AIDS Project, a leadership conference in Silicon Valley, a foiled robbery attempt on one of *Philippine News*'s vice presidents, and a distributor of fake fish sauce in South San Francisco.

It seemed at first that events assigned to me almost always took place after office hours—press conferences, building dedications, convocations honoring various Filipinos in public service. This I initially attributed to the staff's unwillingness to work after office hours and the lack of correspondents in general; it was only belatedly that I realized that people had *real* eight-hour jobs and could not always attend such extra-office events. Otherwise, covering events provided the only break in the weekly routine at the newspaper; a majority of the articles were written with information gathered over the phone. (I do not mean that editorial staffers rarely went out to cover events; just that on the days I was present, the entire staff would always be in the office because they had to make the production deadlines.)

As an intern I was required to be present on only two days, Monday and Friday, although events I had to cover usually took place midweek. These were called "crunch days" because the newspaper had to be "put to bed," or finished, by the end of Monday. (The Metro section, then, had to be put to bed earlier, on Wednesday, long before the deadlines for the National section the following Monday.) The copies were sent out on Tuesday—when the editorial staff would hold a postmortem meeting on that week's issue—and would be in West Coast mailboxes by Wednesday (subscribers on the East Coast receive their copies on Thursdays).

Upon my arrival on Friday mornings, I received my assignments (except for events I might have had to cover mid-week). They varied in complexity. Sometimes they were mere rewrites of *Inquirer* articles or press releases. At other times I had to do research on, for instance, laws regarding tax exemption of non-profit organizations, or write a chronology of events concerning affirmative action and Filipinos. But a typical day would start with a lead from my managing editor; the rest of the day was spent tracking down people for their perspectives, hoping to reach them before their lunch breaks. Attesting to the relative absence of Pinoys in local politics was the fact that there were always only a small handful of people from whom to request comments. For any given issue of the newspaper there was always a good chance that, for instance, Alice Bulos or Dennis Normandy (two prominent Filipino American politicians in the Bay Area) would be called for a sound bite.

As part of the "PhilNews Network" (the newspaper's term for its readers, correspondents and various community leaders), I was one of many correspondents in the San Francisco bureau. Each bureau is staffed by anywhere from one to three correspondents; articles contributed by the bureau correspondents were typically included in the National section of the newspaper. But because the senior editorial staff members, and the highest number of correspondents, were based in the San Francisco Bay Area, *Philippine News* has, not surprisingly, exhibited a bias toward happenings on the West Coast. This emphasis was an issue of general concern at editorial meetings, but the readers did not seem to mind—all in all, a testimony to the popularity of the CommLink (short for Community Link) section. Several times staffers would have to scramble to find an interviewee in the Midwest or the East Coast, and would end up quoting an officer of a random Filipino organization in Florida or Maryland.

Most crucial to the bureaus, however, were the account executives, whose role was to find clients to advertise regionally. Most of the advertisements with national contracts (that is, ads that were published in all the regional editions) were handled by the two senior account executives in South San Francisco. Typically the national advertisements were for larger multinational corporations, such as AT&T, MCI, and Philippine Airlines. The full-page national advertisements usually arrived in the form of "mats," ready to be photographed for the printing press; smaller advertisements, with the use of stock clip art, were designed and laid out by the production department itself in consultation with the client.

Local advertisements ran in both sections (rates depended on size and placement within the paper), but usually in only one regional edition; they ran the gamut from ads for immigration lawyers, palm readers, and "Oriental" food stores to Manila condominiums, remittance agencies, and banks.

Many of these ads were specifically geared to Filipino immigrants. The largest category, employment ads, sought nurses (the largest subcategory), engineers, medical technicians, home health care workers, hotel and restaurant managers—in short, people in the very same fields in which most Filipinos in the United States are employed. Running a close second and third were advertisements for cargo shipping firms (particularly for balikbayan boxes) and long distance telephone companies; car dealerships, restaurants, immigration lawyers, travel agencies, and remittance agencies made up the rest.

Sometimes advertising clients would request "editorial support." This would typically mean the publication of a press release (there was no strict written protocol about this), but on some occasions the account executives, with permission from the managing editor, would ask me or another junior staff writer to write a full-blown article about a new restaurant or casino. In any case, I was not asked to write slanted reviews or anything unethical; anyone could read between the lines and discern the familiar wording of a press release. "Editorial support" meant an objective article (usually placed deep in the Metro section) about the product, business, or service, along with mostly self-congratulatory sound bites from the advertising client's spokesperson.

A sizable portion of the office was allocated to the production section, where the layout and graphic design of the newspaper took place. That required large light boxes where the pages were laid out, article by article. The production staff consisted of two typesetters,[3] a production manager, an art director, and a production and distribution assistant primarily in charge of getting the layouts to the printing press and sending the issues out to newsstands and subscribers. Layout of the newspaper itself, however, was divided among all the staffers, including both editorial and production staff; each writer was in charge of laying out his own section, with the managing editor responsible for the front page. Mondays during paste-up was the liveliest period of the week; everyone, from the production staff to the account executives, would congregate in the production section and chat.

The informal familiarity that reigned in earlier years changed after the signing of the "Espiritu-Esclamado Memorandum of Agreement," as the newspaper referred to the change in financial administration and ownership. But uncomfortable belt-tightening measures were already being instituted even prior to the newspaper's sale, as seen in this excerpt from my notes of November 1995:

---

[3] Before the wider use of Windows computers in the office by 1997, staffers would type their articles in a DOS word-processing program, print them out, and have the typesetters retype the articles into Adobe PageMaker. This repetition made the whole production process extremely laborious, and not a few times typesetters would complain of carpal tunnel syndrome.

The staff had gathered in the telemarketing section; people are quiet, not speaking. I heard the rumor this morning that the scheduled meeting was to be about the newspaper's finances. Esclamado—nattily dressed, as usual, in a gray three-piece suit—begins by suggesting ways the newspaper can save money, by saving electricity, for instance. Luly Esclamado, his wife, interrupts by saying that "sometimes radios are left on even though there's no one in the office"—a direct reference to the managing editor, who leaves the radio tuned to the classical music station. "Or paper clips," the managing editor points out, after a bit of a pause. She explains that we take paper clips for granted.

Esclamado then announces that there may be a cutback on personnel, and the silence is awful. It occurs to me that the staffers may have already known layoffs were coming, which explains the tension in the air—people shuffling their feet, looking at the floor. Esclamado continues by mentioning the printing costs—"500 a week," he says, but I'm not entirely sure what he is referring to. The production manager suggests, in halting English, that the employees can buy stock in *Philippine News*, citing the case of an employee-owned business like United Airlines. The business writer agrees. Esclamado responds: "That's a fantastic idea. Both of you can be in charge of studying that option." He says something about maybe there'd be better morale among the staff if they actually owned the company. Then he adds that maybe the production manager and the accountant could head the committee to investigate the feasibility of such a move; he is joking, and he laughs, and people laugh with him, but Mrs. E doesn't say anything as she usually does.

"Even on Tuesdays," Esclamado says, "I am here until 9:45." (Tuesdays were the slowest days of the week.) "I wake up with *Philippine News* and go to bed with *Philippine News*," he continues. He says he calls up the accountant at 2:00 in the morning just to ask about the financial situation. "I am not making money from *Philippine News*," he says.

He then asks the staff if they like the office. There are nods and weak assents all around. One of the secretaries mentions that the parking lot is getting cramped and forcing people to double-park; "I'm afraid of bumping the car," she says. Esclamado reiterates that the office requires electricity and water to run, and that "we spend for cleaning the bathroom and carpet" as well.

Winding up, Mr. E asks the crowd, "Can we do it?" and asks again, "Can we do it?" and people respond feebly, "Yes." He asks again, saying something about the staff being really demoralized, and there's a louder yes this time. The crowd breaks up (it's now 5:30) and everyone disappears back to their rooms. The meeting ends.

The next day I discover that the business writer "has been let go." [The business writer, Lito Gutierrez, was rehired as editor-in-chief to oversee a fully revitalized newspaper in July 2002, but was again fired five years later.] The people I speak to keep saying, "and it's so close to Christmas, too."

A little less than four months later, Esclamado sold 51 percent of Philippine News's stocks to a corporation owned by the former Philippine minister of finance Edgardo Espiritu. Both the hierarchy and the composition of the staff changed radically during my tenure at *Philippine News*. In March 1996, after Espiritu assumed the majority ownership of the newspaper, the financial and administrative responsibilities were transferred to him and his associates, while Esclamado retained his position as the publisher in charge of editorial content.[4] Two new vice presidents oversaw circulation, sales, advertising, and subscriptions, adding to the administrative staff present in the office (one general manager [formerly Luly Esclamado], one display advertising coordinator, one classified advertising coordinator, one circulation manager, one Management Information Systems manager, and an accountant). A Webmaster was hired and quickly fired after the newspaper's Web site failed to generate any new subscriptions; another intern became a full-time staff writer and editor after being fired by the previous administration. In another case, a writer and her husband were dismissed after it was discovered that she was providing leads to a rival newspaper.

Despite its status as a national newspaper and the existence of several far-flung bureaus, the *Philippine News* was firmly based in one place. All final editing, production (layout, or "paste-up," scanning, even the writing of advertisement copy), printing, and distribution were done in South San Francisco. As I mentioned, this arrangement has led to a preferential slant towards West Coast news; the New York/New Jersey edition, for instance, would still have mostly California news in the national news sections. This was, of course, because the newspaper was not large enough, in the mid-'90s, to maintain proper news bureaus elsewhere (as opposed to a couple of correspondents and advertising executives).[5]

---

[4] In August 1997 Espiritu purchased the whole newspaper and promoted the long-suffering managing editor to editor-in-chief. A few years later she became publisher as well.

[5] In any case, not all bureau correspondents were required to submit articles each week, as they were generally contacted only when needed to follow up a lead or to cover a specific event happen-

The West Coast location legitimized California as the center of Pinoy news, as the site where noteworthy events were made. The Filipino community's decision-makers, its celebrities, and its organizations mostly, it seemed, came from California. It bears repeating, however, that there has been a long history of Filipino immigration to the West Coast; the size of the Filipino community in California alone would entail more newsworthy activity. But because "local news" was consistently treated as "national news," the effect produced was to portray California—and in particular, the San Francisco Bay Area—as more important than the rest of the country. Such a discursive critical mass, circulated around the country, asserts and reasserts the notion that the Bay Area (or at least California) represents the pulse of the Pinoy community.[6]

The strength of the dominant ethnic newspaper is related to how such a place as Daly City became "the Pinoy capital." Daly City itself has little history or intrinsic significance—no naval bases, no Manilatowns from the '30s, no migrant farming communities, no old sugar plantation workers' houses. But by virtue of its location in the San Francisco Bay Area (and its proximity to San Francisco), it is already swept up, by mere association, in the depiction of California as central to the Filipino community.

The editorial staffers covered many Bay Area events firsthand. Articles on the Philippines itself were a different matter. During the period of my fieldwork—at least before March 1996—articles were rewritten from Filipino newspapers, which arrived Wednesday afternoons in a weekly air shipment from the Philippines. On Thursdays the managing editor skimmed through the newspapers and selected the important news issues.

The news budget, separated into "North America" and "Philippines"— only for the practical purpose of identifying each article's sources—was drawn up by Friday. Articles were listed with their provisional headlines, "kickers" (or subheads), and the assigned writer underneath; the only difference between U.S. and Philippine news was the listing of the source and date at the end of the article.[7] The writer then photocopied the articles from the

---

ing in their area. At times almost half the major news articles on the front page ended up being written by the editorial staff, with interviews conducted over the telephone.

[6] This result was, of course, dependent on the kind of newspaper: the short-lived *Ningas Cogon*, for instance (no pun intended—*ningas-kugon* is a Tagalog idiomatic expression meaning "fleeting," referring to projects abandoned as quickly as they were begun), had a keen sense of place as a New York City–based Filipino newspaper. Possessing a more literary bent, the weekly newspaper published impressionistic essays of Filipinos in Manhattan.

[7] A typical news budget would have about 12 to 16 articles, assigned to 4 or 5 writers. A typical article entry would look like this:

MARINDUQUE FLOODS RENDER 3,500 HOMELESS

Filipino newspapers and rewrote them, usually substantially. The writer, of course, received no byline for the rewrites, though all it took to receive credit was "one phone call"—in effect, a quick quotation, usually from a Filipino public official or expert in the United States—and a byline would be printed. Otherwise, the rewritten articles were peppered with phrases like "According to published sources in Manila" or "Philippine News sources in Manila said" as ways of attribution; direct quotations were credited as "according to the *Manila Times*," for example.

Though the Philippine articles had long been augmented by articles from the Associated Press (to which *Philippine News* had an Internet subscription), the procedures changed in March 1996 after Espiritu became the newspaper's part owner. Because Espiritu also owned the Manila-based *Business Daily* (and was a major stockholder in the highly esteemed *Philippine Daily Inquirer*) a system was then set up simply to reprint the former's news articles. Things went slowly at first—the *Business Daily* would e-mail everything from horoscopes to record album reviews—but gradually the reprints supplanted the rewrites. Since then, articles on the Philippines have been reprinted from the *Philippine Daily Inquirer*; opinion columns and editorial cartoons were also taken from the *Inquirer* until the recent hiring of an in-house artist. In this way the *Philippine News*'s operating procedures echo those of its days with the *Manila Chronicle*.

Only once or twice did I have to make an overseas call to the Philippines to confirm data or get the latest news in an attempt to scoop rival newspapers. In short, the newspaper's coverage of overseas news events, at least before Espiritu's management, was almost completely dependent on other Filipino newspapers, with no real direct link between *Philippine News* and the Philippines. This situation was understandable, as *Philippine News* was large enough not to have to be affiliated with Philippine newspapers, but small enough to not be able to afford employing correspondents in the Philippines. The rewrites and reprints were therefore not a result of laziness on the newspaper's part, but merely a logistical and financial necessity.

But the fact that Filipino news was always second hand never deterred the newspaper from making the homeland the focus of its articles and editorials.

---

* Mining dam seepage inundates 700 families around Boac_____st 3/28
* State of calamity declared in province_____pdi 3/28
BY BENITO

"st" and "pdi" refer to the *Philippine Star* and the *Philippine Daily Inquirer*, respectively, as the sources for the rewrites. Budgets were usually drawn up only for front-page articles; articles for Hometown News, Business, and other sections were passed directly to Production. The Showbiz section, however, was written by the wife of one of the senior account executives (herself from an acting family in the Philippines), who condensed it from gossip magazines included in the weekly shipment.

It is tempting to read a sense of disengagement in such procedures—that news from the Philippines was both experienced and published vicariously, as it were. Perhaps this double distancing unwittingly characterizes the Filipino community in more ways than one. But Philippine news was not exactly published automatically; as we will see, editorial considerations directly affected the flavor of the articles selected for publication.

Good News/Bad News

On Friday afternoons at 4:00, the editorial meeting would begin; unless he was away on a trip, Esclamado presided over the hour-long meeting in the windowless conference room. Generally only the editorial staff—the managing editor, the associate editor (who also handled the Lifestyle section), the staff writer (who also coedited the CommLink section), and, on some occasions, the two interns, me included—were present at the editorial meetings.[8] The managing editor would then run through the so-called news budget, article by article; their respective writers would interject every now and then to amplify a point.

At the end of the briefing, articles were ranked by importance, although the head itself was sometimes contested: the managing editor, for instance, would protest, every now and then, that "puro masamang balita na naman" (it's all bad news again). The proposed issue of May 22–28, 1996, for instance was condemned as "depressing" (as Katherine Po, one of the writers, put it): massive election fraud in the Philippine senatorial polls, a murder-suicide by an Austrian and his wife in the Philippines, a Filipino doctor in Tacoma indicted for running a social security scam, and a Filipina accusing her Vietnam-veteran husband of domestic abuse. Those were voted the top stories of the week; the election fraud story (which I had written—or rather, rewritten) and the Tacoma doctor article were going to be on the front page above the fold. But the editorial meeting came to an uncomfortable standstill, just as others were about to push back their chairs and leave. The managing editor, looking down at the news budget, said to no one in particular, "Palagi na lang bad news" (It's always bad news).

---

[8] I was never invited to the business/administrative meetings, possibly because finances were discussed; the only information I received directly from the administrators about the newspaper's business as a whole was through official announcements at staff meetings, which did not happen often. In fact, these announcements only happened four or five times while I was working there—two of those occasions at office parties. The anniversary of *Philippine News* was one such occasion; another was Esclamado's birthday, when he ordered *pansit* (noodles) and fried chicken for the entire staff.

"We can't always have positive news if there isn't any positive news," replied the assistant editor. But this exchange prompted some reshuffling anyway: A sidebar article on a campaign against domestic violence, which was originally planned for the front page, ended up being demoted to the inside, next to the other domestic abuse story. Instead, a comparatively obscure story on Filipino American students from a high school in Nogales, California (they had won a statewide inventors' competition, and were on their way to the national finals), was moved from page 5 onto the front page, in the interest of "balanced" news.

Definitions of *good news* or *bad news* were not generally contested. "Bad news" was prevalent: any Pinoy in the United States involved in, or a victim of, crime; people with immigration problems; natural disasters; the usual corruption of Philippine politics. "Good news" was rarer and almost automatically splashed on the front page: the appointment of a Filipino to a political position, an economic upswing in the Philippines, the casting of a Filipino in a Hollywood television show. Indeed, any kind of entrance into the American mainstream, whether in entertainment, politics, or business, was always deemed newsworthy, regardless of the relative obscurity of the achievement (commissioner in a small suburb, bit part in a sitcom, etc.). To a certain extent any fellow Filipino "making it big," making a "breakthrough," or recognized by the (white) majority was cause for celebration.[9] Thus the significance of good news and bad news: a Filipino's victory was a victory for all Filipinos, both in the United States and in the Philippines. At the same time, any crime committed by a Filipino (especially in the United States) is similarly perceived, with a sense of shame, as a smear on every Filipino's reputation. And so bad news creates a paradox: despite the journalistic maxim that "bad news sells," negative news items were perceived to foster a poor image of Pinoys in the United States—one that would not look good to the "mainstream." Therefore, the images produced were fraught with a deeper significance; they were seen as metonymic incidents and figures, symbolizing not only the Filipino American community but also everyone of Filipino descent.

This balancing act between good and bad news conjures up the image of an "imaginary" outside reader and raises the question whether an ethnic

---

[9] The magazine *Filipinas*'s covers and articles throughout its history perhaps best demonstrate this phenomenon. At the beginning of its publication, the requisite Filipino and Filipino American celebrities (the actress Lea Salonga, the writer Jessica Hagedorn, the businesswoman Loida Nicolas-Lewis) were emblazoned on the magazine's covers. Now, whereas the writing has become more focused and politically analytical of late, the well of Filipino American personalities has dried up in comparison, and the magazine publishes features on small-scale entrepreneurs and writers of high school plays.

newspaper is perhaps more sensitive to someone looking over its shoulder, as it were. This minority position forces the newspaper to be both politically challenging to the status quo and desiring of approval from the mainstream. The anxiety over bad news stems not simply from any insecurity or sensitivity on the community's part, but from the well-founded fear that such incidents (whether concerning Pinoy gangs, embezzlers, or wife-abusers) may be erroneously taken—by the outside, mainstream reader—as typical of the people. There is still an undercurrent here of putting on a positive news facade for the society at large.

But there was little debate on whether there was a balance between North American news and Philippine news; by the late 1990s, more and more reprints from the *Inquirer* were being published in the newspaper. More than half of the *Philippine News*'s front page articles were devoted to events in the Philippines; the sections dealing with business, sports, and show business, and even its opinion columns, were almost exclusively taken from Filipino newspapers. At no point was this apparent imbalance brought up in editorial meetings during my internship. Discussions revolved around such topics as the suitability of certain articles for publication, the content of specific articles, or the importance of one article over the other with regard to the head. Potential worries such as "too much Philippine news" or "too much American news" were never voiced; as I read it, both were seen as equally important. As do other ethnic newspapers, *Philippine News* straddles nations and borders. Headlines from both the Philippines and the United States jostle for attention on its front page, creating an almost seamless display of events. The front page demonstrated a smooth transnationality, a direct product of the editorial process itself.

This presentation of events both reflects and constitutes the reading audience's repeated turning toward both locations. But the boundaries of those locations are certainly not truly flexible. For instance, the immigration lawyer Lourdes Tancinco's weekly columns, in which she dispensed immigration advice to readers who addressed her as "Dear Atty. Lou"—or the frequency of articles on the subject, for that matter—made it quite clear that political boundaries have not been undone by late capitalism. The newspaper's readers, like my interviewees, were acutely (if sometimes mistakenly) aware of the complexities of immigration law; the subject of immigration, and the sometimes unbridgeable gulf between the two countries, were matters of constant discourse and debate.

But in general, this attention to Filipino American concerns did not prevent *Philippine News* from creating a distinct focus on affairs in the Philippines itself. At times, however, the consensus did not prevail. An excerpt from my field notes reveals some of the decision-making that occurs.

Monday, 8/6/1996. "Recap meeting." The original banner head is about the passage of a resolution in the House of Representatives to honor Filipino World War II vets: "U.S. Congress a Step Closer to Recognizing WWII Veterans." Esclamado looks at the news budget. He is adamant that this only signifies "recognition," and is not yet the long-awaited bill. "Maybe we should rephrase the kicker with 'awaiting Bill Clinton's proclamation,'" he suggests.

The managing editor disagrees: she wants the emphasis on the vets' activity, and reminds Esclamado that there are two Congress stories (one story is about an "English-only" law; the other, about the welfare reform bill and its "disastrous" impact on legal immigrants) this week.

The production manager enters the meeting room, asking permission from Esclamado to take off another half-page from one of the jumps, though Esclamado has already given up half of his Spotlight [his regular column]. The managing editor frets about the lack of space. Esclamado learns that one of the graphic designers has taken half the day off, not a wise move on a "crunch day." "Why, is he looking for a job, too?" he says sarcastically. [He was.] The production manager says, "He said it was an emergency," and Esclamado is angry that the graphic designer had not spoken to him first. "I want to find out if it's really an emergency," he says, shaking his head. The staffers stare at their budgets, shuffling their pages. The production manager says that the designer had already spoken to one of the vice presidents anyway.

Esclamado returns to the budget. It's a big news week: Sarah Balabagan, the maid sentenced to death in the United Arab Emirates, arrived in the Philippines. A rewritten story of mine—a Filipino boxer wins the Olympic silver—is also on the front page. So is a photograph of PhilNews at a trade show in New York. A report on increasing rates of anti-Asian violence has also been released. Then Esclamado discovers the Imelda Marcos story. It seems that Imelda has told the Philippine Senate that former U.S. Ambassador Stephen Bosworth stole gold certificates hidden underneath Ferdinand Marcos's pajamas and that the certificates disappeared when they arrived in Hawaii.

"My God! That's the best!" cries Esclamado. "That's the best admission she's ever made!" he said, referring to Imelda's tacit admission of ownership of billions of dollars in gold. "Do you know how long *Philippine News* has been pursuing this?" He looks around the table. "My God," he says again, running his palm over his forehead and scalp. "Do you know how much this means to me?" he asks, pointing to the line in the budget. The managing editor says yes, but unwillingly, because the banner has been written, and the article itself is merely a reprint from Associated Press.

Esclamado plans an emergency meeting to "give [the PN vice president] the courtesy" of informing him what's up. He follows this with "We're Editorial, we'll just give them the courtesy"—the meeting, I assume, is to give them background on the matter. He sends one of the assistants off to look for an old copy of PhilNews from the '70s, including an editorial detailing the search for Marcos's gold.

The newspaper arrives in my mailbox that Thursday. The headline reads: "Imelda Marcos Admits Owning Certificates for Gold Bullion." The entire editorial page, already previously laid out, was scuttled for a reprint of a 1978 article called "$100 Billion War Loot."

Although this meeting was not necessarily typical of the newspaper's daily operations, the anecdote does give a sense of how meetings are conducted, and how Esclamado—who was, after all, the publisher and editor-in-chief—had his way. It also underscored how important the anti-Marcos struggle was to a newspaper that made its name from it.

The Philippine news articles assumed that the paper's readers had more than a passing familiarity with the issues and people involved. Political events were one thing, but show business gossip, concerning actors in films most of the readers may never see, was another. One of its own columnists, the immigration lawyer Rodel Rodis, decried what he called "a downright shame. These newspapers have a responsibility to their readers to focus primarily on what is happening here in the United States and only secondarily with what is happening in the Philippines" (1996, A4). As Rodis points out, whenever "the President" is mentioned in an article, the term almost always automatically refers to the then-president Fidel Ramos and not to Bill Clinton.[10] Still, when

---

[10] Rodis's article was prompted by the 1996 conference of the Federation of Filipino American Media Associations, where the main speaker was the former Philippine secretary of tourism Mina Gabor. The former Philippine News columnist (and current editor of *Filipinas* magazine) Greg Macabenta points to the headlines of Filipino American newspapers—"all about Philippine politics," he argues—and reminds the reader, "Simply put, America is our country too" (2006, 7).

In comparison to other Bay Area Filipino newspapers, however, *Philippine News* was the most rooted in its community in the United States. (Coming second would be the *Manila Mail*, which was embroiled in a bitter mudslinging feud with *Philippine News* in 1996.) Other newspapers like *The Eye* and *Manila Bulletin* (not related to the Brigadier-General Hans Menzi's former Philippine-based newspaper) are poorly laid out mishmashes of reprinted articles from Manila newspapers—with some articles literally cut and pasted from Manila tabloids. The rare local article, if not about Filipino veterans, is almost always a press release.

one takes into account the composition of the Filipino population, the constant focus on matters "back home" becomes more understandable. Many members of the population are recent newcomers; the relative lack of Filipino American "celebrities," whether in entertainment, sports, or business, also explains the reliance on articles from the Philippines.

One could argue that this focus on the Philippines was a clear reflection of the readership: recent, middle-class immigrants very much attuned to events back in the "homeland." In that sense, Rodis's criticisms of Filipino American newspapers as a "downright shame" were misplaced—the newspapers, after all, were only heeding their audience. But the newspaper did not merely reflect discourse on the Philippines and Filipinos in the United States; most important, it also *produced* that same discourse. Either way, the newspaper's staffers were quite aware of its responsibility in publishing good news or bad news: *Philippine News* was reflecting, and constituting, public discourse on Filipinos.

As Michael Billig notes, the nation-state is said to constantly reproduce itself, defining its identity and affirming its boundaries on a daily, passive basis. But these daily reminders, he writes, are "mindless, occurring as other activities are being consciously engaged in" (1995, 41).[11] In this sense, a newspaper, which "[maintains] a principle of news apartheid, keeping 'home' news and foreign news . . . separate" (1995, 118) functions as a venue for disseminating national identity.

In *Philippine News*, "Hometown Reports" dealt chiefly with news items from the provinces; it has since been retitled "Philippines," then changed back to "Hometown Datelines," more clearly cementing the Philippines as "home." A boxed section called "Worldscope" was subtitled "Read about Filipinos in Other Parts of the World" and featured short Associated Press items (almost always bad news) about Pinoys in Hong Kong and Saudi Arabia. Manila items were generally placed in the main part of the paper, however, betraying the editors' Tagalog bias; a special section entitled "Around Metro Manila" was later created, which also consisted of nothing but bad news: a drunken rampage, a murdered child, a mugged priest, for example.

But what kind of audience was the newspaper addressing? Would its vision of its readers have a direct relationship on the image of the nation-state being reproduced by *Philippine News*? Rodis's point about the newspaper's

---

[11] Eating Filipino food at home could be seen as an extension of the Filipino ordinary—that is, an act that reminds the consumer of "home" without it announcing itself as such. The presence of numerous Filipino restaurants in Daly City did not make eating Filipino food a constant, voiced reminder of things back home. That is, eating Filipino food did not have to be a special occasion that announced itself as something coming from the Philippines; the Philippines was already in Daly City.

responsibility is directly tied to its role as the definer and voice of cultural and political issues in the Filipino American community. Is it irresponsible for a minority newspaper to be "still" constantly oriented towards—or, perhaps, mired in—events in the "homeland"? This orientation calls to mind Alice Bulos's assertion in the previous chapter that Filipino American political empowerment has been hindered by people's "loyalty to the homeland." Rodis's unwritten assumption—that "real" transnationality is neither possible, nor desirable—is not unrelated to the commonly perceived ideal role of the immigrant: one whose new life should ideally be focused on one's new community as well. To do otherwise was seen as culturally and, most crucially, politically regressive. How was one to become a productive, contributing citizen when one was more conversant with the political intrigues back home? To dwell on events in the Philippines was, in effect, to dwell on the past.

The "B" Section

In many ways the anchor of *Philippine News*'s national coverage, and perhaps its deepest involvement with the community, is its Metro, or "B" section.[12] This assertion is something of a paradox, as almost half its contents—in 2002, the People, Showbiz, Arts, and Motoring sections—were directly rewritten or reprinted from Philippine newspapers and official press releases. What distinguished it from other newspapers was the depth and detail of its coverage of community events—organizational dinners in Kentucky, debutante balls in New Jersey, family reunions in Seattle, fund drives in the suburbs of Chicago.[13] Despite its ambitions to a kind of transnationalism, *Philippine News* also functions not unlike a small community newspaper, albeit one distributed nationwide. Nowhere else has the social life of the middle-class first-generation Filipino immigrant been so prominently on display.

A ubiquitous feature of *Philippine News* ever since its inception has been the publication of photographs, sent in by readers, of social events: medical

---

[12] The Metro section's format has changed since *Philippine News* changed hands: the business page moved to the National section, and the Showbiz section now reprints articles directly from the *Inquirer*. The paper's ties to the *Inquirer* have also allowed it to expand the sports section. In the mid-2000s this changed again to a sexier "Life &."

[13] A typical Calendar of Events, for instance, announced a University of Santo Tomas Club camp in San Dimas, California; a fund-raising variety show sponsored by the Catholic Filipino parishioners of Saint Boniface Church in San Francisco; a Life in the Spirit Seminar in New York; a Caribbean Craze Night sponsored by the West Visayan Circle of Houston in Sugar Land, Texas; and the annual reunion and dinner dance of the University of the Philippines Nursing Alumni Association of Northern California in Berkeley ("Calendar of Events," July 8–14, 1998: B2).

conferences, picnics, birthdays, weddings, baptisms, ophthalmologists dancing the macarena, and so on, sometimes occupying an entire page. Often the
community pages turned into a Filipino version of a mainstream newspaper's society pages, consisting mostly of pages of photographs of grand balls,
with doctors and their wives, lined up in a row, dressed in their tuxedos and
sequined finery.

The gathering of materials is facilitated because *Philippine News*—or
more specifically, the CommLink manager—actively solicited announcements and articles from its readers. Every week, dozens of informal "press
releases," accompanied by snapshots, arrived in the mail; it is the task of the
CommLink manager, along with one of the editorial staffers or interns, to
proofread the articles and match captions with the photographs. "These
aren't written by, you know, professionals, so they have to be edited a lot," the
CommLink manager told me. Editorial staffers every now and then would
swap examples of bad style—"the beauteous and dashing bride," one press
release read. "Naku, nagtingin pa raw nang thesaurus" (Oh my, someone
who "consulted" a thesaurus), the managing editor commented.[14] In this way
Philippine News is assured of a constant flow of articles and photographs
from all across the country. Unlike other newspapers, in which the "letters to
the editor" section (and sometimes, the Op-Ed page) is the only source of
feedback—in effect, the only channel of two-way communication—*Philippine
News* receives not only commentary, but actual articles from the readers
themselves.

The press releases rarely varied. The first paragraph would start with the
date, time, and place of the event, then a brief background of the occasion,
followed by a list of the organization's officers, from president down to public
relations officer. Photographs invariably would be what the editorial staff
called "shotgun photographs": people standing in a row in front of an imaginary firing squad; these were generally considered unfit for publication unless
no other photos were available. Shorter press releases would be condensed to
one paragraph and printed in the Metro Calendar instead.

Aside from attending local community events (mostly limited to the San
Francisco Bay Area), the CommLink manager, Ken Torres, told me that his
primary role was to follow through on CommLink's "commitment to unify
the different Filipino organizations." The Metro Calendar, he said, "lets or-

---

[14] Sometimes articles come unsolicited as well. In 1997 I was asked to write a profile on a cheerleader
for the San Francisco Giants baseball team; the "lead" was sent in by her grandmother, who had
supplied *Philippine News* with a short biography, a photograph, and a contact phone number.
Follow-up phone calls revealed that the cheerleader had not wanted to be interviewed at all, and in
fact she had scolded her grandmother for sending the materials. The newspaper paid no heed and
ran the article (very slightly rewritten by me), photo and all, on the front page.

ganizations know what other organizations are doing." He also cited examples of people finding "long-lost friends" or fellow hometowners through CommLink.[15]

The CommLink section provided moneymaking opportunities for the newspaper as well. Torres kept a massive database (originally put together by the information systems manager, Carlos Esclamado, the publisher's eldest son), containing the names and addresses of hundreds of Filipino American organizations throughout the country. The "blue binder" (as the database was referred to) was used to its full potential in May 1996, when for the first time in 34 years, *Philippine News* began a telemarketing campaign in search of new subscribers—indeed, a campaign that partially depended on the large number of Filipino organizations.

The CommLink manager started by mailing out trial issues of the newspaper to addresses that were already in the database. But Torres took the CommLink concept further by calling up organization heads, inviting them to send press releases for publication in the Metro section, and then asking for their membership rosters, complete with addresses. Trial issues were sent to every person on the list. For the telemarketers, Torres contacted various schools in the San Francisco area, looking for young Tagalog-speaking students, some of whom had been previously profiled in CommLink's Gallery of Graduates section. The telemarketers would then call those who had already received a month's worth of free issues and convince them to buy a subscription. The following passages, detailing the telemarketing process, are taken from my notes:

> The telemarketing project started in May. Torres recalled that Esclamado was dissatisfied with the subscription rate.
>
> The sales campaign started with five telemarketers that month, who only worked twice a week on "bad days," Friday and Saturday. (These were the nights when people they called were more likely out of the house.) Despite this limitation, they got thirty-nine people to subscribe.

---

[15] Ethnic newspapers in the late 1800s functioned similarly, attesting to historical continuities then and now:

> Often only his own press could give the immigrant the explanations his troubled experience demanded. The happenings of the old village and its environs were still of concern to him; yet that concern would not be satisfied in the general American papers. . . .
>
> The immigrants were interested in knowing about themselves. . . . Accounts of diverse noteworthy local occurrences found a place in these pages and nowhere else. To the extent that these people had begun to constitute communities, they wished to be contact with each other. Their own newspapers supplied the means of establishing that contact (Handlin 2002, 160–161).

By the end of June, with ten new telemarketers, the number of new subscribers had jumped dramatically.

A month later, the results were even more spectacular, more than doubling the previous month's record. By the middle of August, the telemarketers had already surpassed the total that they thought would be attained only by the end of the year.

The record for the number of new subscribers per week was broken every week. In short, the project exceeded all of Torres's expectations. Now he also expects to have a pool of 20 telemarketers by September.

"We have a special offer right now: it's 25 percent off the regular newsstand price, which means it's only as little as 11 cents a day, or 75 cents a week," says one telemarketer at the next desk.

Another telemarketer, a student at Mercy High School in San Francisco, is trying to convince the potential subscriber on the phone. "It's like loose change underneath your couch," she says.

A third telemarketer tries a different tack. "Do you drink coffee? Well, it's like buying a cup of coffee once a week."

Teresa Santos has just discovered that the person on the other end of the line is married to the president of a regional association. "*Philippine News* has a Hometown section where you can get news about your hometown," she tells her listener, zeroing in, quickly fashioning her spiel to fit her listener. "You can't get that from other papers, can you?"

At another desk at the other side of the room, Edgar Hofilena is speaking to someone in polite, but halting, Tagalog. "*Maganda pong offer ito. Mura lang po. Makakatipid po kayo* [This is a great offer. It's affordable. You can save on this]" he adds. He waits patiently for the reply. Hofilena, along with Santos, had helped develop the Tagalog version of the telemarketing script—the "fallback version" to use if the potential customer sounds like they don't speak English very well.

The "script" sitting next to their phones still reminds them "Always say, 'Marami pong salamat [Thank you very much],'" but they already know it by heart.

The reliance on youths for the telemarketing campaign is somewhat in contrast to the newspaper's image. The Lifestyle section, for instance, is very much geared to an older generation, with articles on home decorating and parenting. But twenty years previously, the Youngtalk section, which debuted in March 1978, was one of the paper's most popular sections, judging from its future expansion into YES!, or Youth Entertainment Section, a year later.

Questions on hot-button issues like "Is 'living together' an immoral practice?" or "Should Filipino youths be bilingual?" were posed; teenagers—again,
mostly in the San Francisco Bay Area—wrote in their answers and included
a photograph. Their answers to the question "Are you Filipino-American,
Filipino, or American?" display an interesting one-sidedness, one still uncomplicated by ethnic studies courses: "I consider myself a Filipino," said a
college student from Pittsburg, California. "Even though I've been in this
country eight years, I still have the Filipino in me. . . . Maybe when I'm an
American citizen I'll think different." A high schooler from San Francisco
answered: "I am a Filipino. So long as you are born to Filipino parents—you
are still a genuine Filipino. Only the mestizos whose parents are half-Filipino
and half-American are called Filipino-Americans," echoing the sentiments
of some recently arrived Filipino immigrants. (These answers appeared in
the Youngtalk section of the April 22–28, 1978, issue of *Philippine News.*)

A year later, Youngtalk was expanded into YES!—two pages of sections
including Dear Dolores (an advice column), Campus Capers (a schedule of
college activities), Spotlight (a profile of an exceptional youth), Metronomes
(capsule music reviews), Point of View (an opinion column), and Astroguide
(a horoscope for teens). Its most popular section, Short 'n' Sweet, consisted of
personal "love notes."[16] The new section marked, even until the late 1990's,
the most involvement or interaction the *Philippine News* has had with young
people in its entire history, especially after YES! was phased out in the early
1980s; even an Outstanding Youth Contest announced in 1979 was discon-
tinued as a result of poor response, and replaced with the Quest for Magandang [Beautiful] Filipina–USA contest instead.

One might argue that the currently popular Gallery of Graduates constitutes youth involvement, but it fails to draw young readers. The Gallery features Filipino American students who have graduated, from any educational
institution (elementary school, high school, or college), during a particular
year. As with the Metro section, photographs and a short biographical note
are solicited from readers. Students graduating with honors are featured on
the front page; the rest are published in the Metro section. But proud parents,
not teenagers, almost always send in the articles; it is doubtful that their targeted readership is composed of teenagers.

I stress this aspect of youth because it shines a light on *Philippine News*'s
audience and reputation—or rather, on what it is not. The newspaper's coverage has always been focused on the immigrant older generation (their social

---

[16] For instance, a note from K. A. to F. R. ("You better call or babatukan kita [I'll hit you on the
head]."), or one from James to Honey ("You're once, twice, three times a lady and I love you! It
may seem corny but it's what I feel. Never change.").

events, their politics, etc.). Arguably, the younger generation has better things to do than read an ethnic newspaper to keep up with current events. But perhaps *Philippine News's* larger focus on affairs in the Philippines already precludes their interest in the newspaper.

Indeed, this distinction between older and younger generation may be a false one; perhaps the more compelling operating division is between first-generation Filipino immigrant and native-born Filipino American. I am not suggesting that the American-born are naturally unconcerned with events happening in the Philippines. But they are unlikely to be interested in gossip columns on actors they may not have heard of, starring in films and television shows broadcast in a language they may not speak, or in politicians whose activities have little to no impact on their lives. The *Philippine News* largely operates in a vocabulary (or a tradition, or a history, or a stock of symbols) from which the native-born second generation is excluded. Its community of readers has, and will always be, the foreign-born, immigrant generation.

Of course, the most likely explanation for the paper's emphasis may simply be that the Philippine-born are the majority of its natural audience. But in the previous chapter I suggested that the second generation represented a form of assimilation, a generation of people who actually "belonged" in the new homeland, and are, in that sense, envied. It is the success of the second generation that is most often celebrated. They are viewed with some ambivalence, however, because they also represent people who have "lost" their traditional Filipino values.

As late as 1973, for instance, the newspaper was confident enough of its readership—the recently arrived, first-generation immigrants—to be able to publish material potentially offensive to some of its unintended readers. As Vic Mapa wrote, in an article entitled "The Most Beautiful Country in the World," "The second-generation Filipino, born, bred and educated strictly Yankee-style, with the inability to relate to his ancestry or to cherish the richness of his blood, [is a] creature to be pitied" (1973, 1). This unease with the second generation is analogous to the uncertainties regarding the relationship between ethnicity and class. But it is interestingly illustrated within the pages of *Philippine News* itself.

Consumption and Resistance?

In his groundbreaking ethnography, *Locating Filipino Americans*, Rick Bonus writes that newspaper advertisements, "tailored to immigrant readers via their ethnic immigrant coding . . . bridge the gap between what one doesn't have (yet) and what one needs to have in the new place" (2000, 141).

All ads are, in a sense, fantasies. They are the conduits for commodities or services for which readers or viewers construct images of themselves as consumers: I imagine myself drinking a Coke, I imagine myself watching TV on a plasma screen hanging in my living room, I imagine myself behind the wheel of a large automobile. Bonus's perceptive observation—that the advertisements display "what one *needs* to have in the new place" (emphasis mine)—theorizes a set of requirements, an assemblage of needs, for immigrant success. Indeed, according to Bonus, these "requirements" are coercive: "readers are very much aware of this pressure to 'act like an American' by 'buying like an American,' as one told me" (2000, 139). Here, consumerism is seen as an act of assimilation; as we shall see in Chapter Six, the equation of materialism and being American is widely circulated in discourse about Pinoy immigrants.

Bonus critiques Robert Park's classic 1922 study of "the immigrant press" arguing that "the implicit criterion Park uses in evaluating the 'success' of immigrant presses is their ability to be integrated into the commercial and cultural landscape of the United States—a landscape in which appeals to the 'universal' are desired, 'foreignness' is erased, and differences with the mainstream society . . . are suppressed" (2000, 146). But Bonus lets the Filipino American newspapers off the hook, as it were: "In view of mainstream media exclusion, these newspapers serve as alternative sites for meaningful and empowering constructions of Filipino American communities" (Bonus 2000, 163). They may indeed be alternative sites, claiming a separate cultural space, but *Philippine News* also claims a material Americanness and exemplifies, in its balls and organizations, a desire for respectability. The newspaper needs to be read—in precisely the same terms as Bonus's interviewees conceive the ethnic media—as an appeal to the universal, and as an erasure of foreignness.

It is in this respect that I differ from Yen Le Espiritu's conceptualization of Filipino immigrant practices. Building upon Bonus's pioneering work on Filipinos in San Diego, Espiritu's *Home Bound* (2003) is an intimate examination of transnational activities as a form of "home building" and, in particular, of the moral tenor of such practices and the resulting constraints on the daughters of the immigrant generation. Like Bonus, she argues that these border-crossing practices are fundamentally grounded in resistance:

> By living their lives across borders, Filipino immigrants, in effect, are challenging the nation-state's attempt to localize them; that is, to mold them into acceptable and "normal" subjects. . . . Filipino transnational activities must be understood in part as an act of resistance: an articulation of their deep dissatisfaction with and anger at the

contradictions between official state ideals of equal citizenship and state-sanctioned forms of subordination. . . . It is also an act of resistance against the violence of globalized capitalism . . . (212)

These immigrants, complaining about the drudgery of their nine-to-five jobs—"the 'costs' of migration and capitalism," as Espiritu puts it—are "in effect . . . exposing and challenging the unequal power between nations within a global system of racialized capitalist relations" (89).

Indeed, in her work, Espiritu is extremely attentive to globalized systems of power and their concomitant disruptions that created the Filipino diaspora in the first place. But such an interpretation—that the shoring up of status back in the homeland is somehow an act of defiance against the displacements of capitalist oppression—seems needlessly generous. Pinoy immigrants do, after all, purchase the products advertised in *Philippine News*, and this is surely done not just out of a dull, barely articulated anger at their alienation from the promise of liberal egalitarianism. Consumption in this case is a paradoxical mix of both assimilation and an assertion of ethnic identity.

Let me turn to an example. One of the fairly recent additions to the "B" section are the Motoring pages (later called "Awto," a Tagalog "rendition" of the word *auto*), with Associated Press articles on automobile safety, thinly disguised press releases on new car models, or, very rarely, pieces on traffic in Manila. The section does not fit the general tone of the paper at all; it features reprints of articles on wearing seat belts, for instance, and there is hardly any reference in the articles to ethnic identity—something that is paramount on every single page of the paper. Clearly the Motoring section is a marketing tool, as half of the pages are always filled by advertisements for automobile dealerships (usually highlighting their Filipino salesmen). By 2002 the section had transformed into a separate motoring supplement altogether, with the following blurb:

Place your display ad in the Automobile Section of Philippine News!
    Tap the rich market of Filipino Americans who are noted for their prolific spending on new cars and in accessorizing them. Direct your message to this ethnic group which has a per capita income above the national average and whose purchasing habits are geared towards buying automobiles. (Motoring Supplement advertisement 2002, C3)

The most interesting part of the Motoring section is a regular column called "FilAm On Board," where readers send in snapshots of themselves and their cars, describing what makes their cars distinctly Filipino. Beneath each photograph and its caption identifying the owner is the question "Is there anything in or about your car that gives away your Filipino-ness?" The paper subsequently invites readers to submit a photograph and a caption. "FilAm On Board"—the logo done in the style of the "Baby on Board" car signs—has proven to be quite popular, running every week for a few years now.

The facile interpretation here—and one I am loath to make—is that Motoring's reader submissions are proof of Filipino materialism. And indeed those suspicions would be easily confirmed by weekly photographs of people standing by their brand-new sport utility vehicles. (One memorable photo showed a *Philippine News* vice president pointing to the small sticker of a Philippine flag stuck to the bumper of his BMW convertible.) Look, the people in the photograph seem to say, we've made it. And here's the proof that we're Pinoy, the people say, pointing to a crucifix hanging from the rearview mirror. Sometimes the captions do all the work, describing how the car's owner listens to Filipino music on his CD player as he drives down the highway.

Philippine News—perhaps to alleviate the editors' unease about a section so nakedly commercial—gave the Motoring pages a Filipino "angle." (The name change from "Motoring News" to the clumsy "Awto" served this same purpose.) It provided a convenient venue for establishing immigrant success with a universal symbol: the car.[17] But further proof was needed to show that the car "gave away" the owner's ethnicity; this identity—the Pinoy "angle"— was then simply crystallized in the form of a bumper sticker or piece of car décor. In a sense, the car itself was a symbol of assimilation, one unrecognizable as Filipino unless the connection was pointed out. What the photographs displayed was, perhaps, the *absence* of discomfort; the owners could show that they, too, could spend like Americans and, therefore, already belonged.

The transnational activities Espiritu describes necessarily involve consumption of a conspicuous sort, but such spending, one can argue, would have two different audiences: one in the United States, for the reasons discussed above, and one in the Philippines. It is for the latter, Espiritu argues, that economic capital is converted into social capital, "as a disruptive strategy enacted by the migrants to challenge their differential inclusion in the United States as subordinate subjects" (2003, 212). Other scholars of Filipino migration have asserted this before, most notably Stephen Griffiths (1988) and Rhacel Parreñas (2005). In perhaps the single most important essay written on

---

[17] Mahler (1995, 87) relates that Salvadoran immigrants to the United States would pose in front of parked cars that were not their own, pretend the cars were theirs, and send the photographs to their relatives back home.

Filipino migration, Filomeno Aguilar (2002, 415) argues that labor migration can be seen as a "secular pilgrimage," a rite of passage that takes the migrant through a journey of dislocation and sacrifice, to be rewarded, upon return, by financial achievement, prestige, and a kind of social transcendence. But Aguilar's argument is chiefly predicated, like those of the three other scholars, on permanent return—something which neither Espiritu's interviewees, nor mine, are necessarily willing to do.[18] But such a "return" could at least be symbolically accomplished within the pages of a newspaper.

As a newspaper, *Philippine News* could be seen as a clear manifestation of a desire to be transnational, to transcend national boundaries—and therefore, in that sense, simply characteristic of immigrant identity. But another direction was evident, one in keeping with that same immigrant identity, and one that could be seen in the balls and parties and cars: that of belonging, and the need to prove one belongs—in the new land.

[18] Except for Griffiths, whose fieldwork on "Hawaiianos" returning to their home village in Ilocos Norte was conducted in the early '70s (and therefore predates the larger populations who would migrate later), the three other scholars significantly draw their data from migrants returning from countries other than the United States.

5

LOOKING BACK

~

Indifference, Responsibility, and the Anti-Marcos
Movement in the United States

The tension between the desire to demonstrate immigrant achievement and the need for political awareness may be directed "forward"
to the United States or, more importantly, "back" to the Philippines.
I argue that the call to remembrance, to a kind of nationalism outside of the
country's borders, is integral to understanding the Filipino community. The
call for more active, concerned participation in the affairs of the homeland,
demanding sacrifice, was most acute during the Marcos regime, and it still
is potent today. But Philippine nationalism was not only at cross-purposes
with a new life in America, it was also contradictory to the demands of immigrant success and, at least initially, to an upwardly mobile immigrant
middle class. At the same time, what was portrayed as the exemplar of
nationalism—the anti-Marcos movement—was itself riven with conflicts
revolving precisely around differences in class ideology. These ideological
disparities could be mapped onto generational and native-born/foreign-
born differences as well.

The play between these contradictions was perhaps most clearly manifested in the pages of *Philippine News*. The differences showed up in public
discourse—in this case, a feud between two newspapers. Both were against
the Marcos regime but took different approaches, for extremely different reasons. The *Philippine News*, with a more conservative political outlook and
from an earlier generation, allied itself squarely with the so-called oligarchy in
exile. *Ang Katipunan*, the official organ of the Kilusang Demokratikong
Pilipino (Filipino Democratic Movement), or KDP, in the United States, was

the resolutely radical newspaper, calling for an overthrow of the Marcos dictatorship.[1]

The newspapers had in common, however, a fervent and, I might add, courageous opposition to the Marcos regime. Both newspapers (the *Philippine News* in particular) appealed to their readers for support in protesting against the martial law regime, strategically using a discourse of guilt. That is, in looking back toward the homeland, immigrants also risked being looked at as well, subject to the (supposedly) accusing gaze of their fellow Filipinos. As one editorial put it, how were Pinoys in the United States supposed to face "[their] relatives . . . friends . . . countrymen, with the knowledge and realization that in their hour of need [they] kept silent?" (*Philippine News*, 1975a: 4).

In consequence, Filipino immigrants, especially those in the United States, seem to feel they must adopt a defensive position. An undercurrent of guilt and remembrance pervades discourse by first-generation Filipino immigrants.[2] This sentiment of guilt—whether manifest in feeling guilty or making other people feel guilty—shows the ambiguity of status of Filipinos in the United States. The reason for guilt does not necessarily have anything to do with colonialism, but it can be attributed to a combination of class status, increased purchasing power, and the need for *pakikisama*, or what Agoncillo and Guerrero define as "the intensive signification of camaraderie or

---

[1] President Ferdinand Marcos' reelection to office in 1968 presented a grand opportunity to consolidate his power over the institutions of the ostensibly democratic Philippine state. By the mid-1970s the Philippines would be enjoying economic success in terms of gross national product—but a success limited to Marcos's family and friends, and at the expense of state coffers and Filipinos perpetually living in poverty. Marcos, in this decade and the next, relied chiefly on military force to prop up his dictatorship: the mass rounding up of political prisoners, constant extrajudicial killings, and a protracted war against both Communists and Muslim separatists (13,000 of the latter dying in the '70s alone). As a consequence of disastrous economic policies (abetted by the Marcoses' profligate spending habits), high unemployment rates, and an increasing official dependence on the export of labor and on dollar remittances—one that shows no sign of abating—middle-class professionals left for the United States and Saudi Arabia, among other places; women, typically from the lower middle class, would leave by the thousands a decade later to work as domestic helpers and entertainers. See Abinales and Amoroso (2005) for a comprehensive historical and political analysis of the Philippines.

I must add that, the few applicants for political asylum notwithstanding, the vast majority of the 300,000 Filipinos who immigrated to the United States during the Marcos era (1965–1986) did not necessarily do so for explicitly political reasons. By this, I mean that these mostly middle-class professionals (and their relatives petitioned for via chain migration) were not necessarily the victims of political persecution. The depressed economic conditions, of course, were a direct result of Marcos's acts of plunder, but the migration of these professionals to the United States should be seen within the context of a larger worldwide dispersal of Filipinos beginning in the late '60s. The relatively small handful of political exiles I profile in this chapter were motivated to come to the United States for very different reasons entirely.

[2] I posit this guilt in contrast to a seeming *absence* of guilt as well, which I have discussed in previous chapters.

spirit of comradeship, the main elements of which are unselfishness and good faith" (1987, 13).

Indeed, characteristic of much Pinoy immigrant discourse is a silence concerning the colonial; that is, guilt and postcoloniality never seem to be discussed together. One may argue then that there is no connection between the two—but perhaps the silence has everything to do with it, that absence effectively marking off that very presence. A facile argument can be made here that colonial mentality has permeated Filipino discourse so effectively that it is invisible. But as we saw in Chapter Three, anxious thoughts about immigrating to the metropole and ending up in the belly of the beast have not bedeviled most Filipino immigrants in Daly City as they did the political exiles and journalists we will meet in this chapter.

Exiles

The politics of the *Philippine News* was emblematic of the conservatism of a certain immigrant generation. In its contents, and particularly its editorials, *Philippine News* spoke for members of the Second Wave generation, and later, those who embraced a particular kind of conservatism. An excerpt from an interview with Wally Curameng may serve as an illustration:

> You know, when I talk to some Filipinos who are—those who have been here long. Let's say . . . my uncle. When they see the news about Philippines, they would even laugh at them. Like during the Pinatubo [volcano eruption], they're making fun of them. Hey, it's snowing in the Philippines, they look really delighted, you know. I think those who came here earlier when they were like 26 to 30 years old, who came here in the '60s, and lower—from the '40s to '60s—their feeling about the Philippines is gone, you know, like—their nationalistic feeling, being a Filipino, they already ignore it.

Wally felt that his parents' generation, in their '60s, had "abandoned the Philippines." But he could relate to some of those feelings, "because during that time, there was really nothing. Not necessarily still nothing, but the Philippines was still a little backward when they left."

> They're more pro-American, because World War II had just ended, their feeling towards Americans are, they saved us, like that, they always think, General MacArthur, they're always—their hero is General MacArthur instead of Jose Rizal [*laughs*]. And during the Spanish time, their hero is—what? I don't know.

Arriving in the United States in the mid- to late '40s, the Second Wave came as intact families, a stark contrast to the thousands of single men who had arrived as labor migrants a generation earlier. Through the 1945 Brides Act alone, 118,000 spouses and children of U.S. Armed Forces soldiers were able to immigrate to the United States. The immigrants also came in the midst of a relative economic boom. McCarthy's anti-communist purges, as well as anti-Hukbalahap campaigns back in the Philippines, drove the Left underground and helped foster a long suspicion of groups allied with the Left. But perhaps the most crucial defining characteristic was forged in the Second World War. Enmity against the Japanese helped to produce a deeply rooted sense of gratitude and loyalty toward the United States. This generation, unlike the subsequent Third Wave immigrants, missed the fervent nationalism of late-'60s student activism in the Philippines; many of them were also perhaps a little old for the radical movements in the United States. Esclamado, who had arrived near the tail end of the Second Wave and the beginning of the post-1965 Third Wave generation, typified his generation in many ways.

Such conservative political leanings are not necessarily linked to the period of arrival in the United States, but to a generation *in the Philippines* born just before or during World War II. As Curameng said, it was his parents' generation—*Philippine News*'s target audience—and their seeming lack of national feeling that riled him. What differentiated him from his uncle was his sense of nationalism[3] –Curameng could not have "abandoned" the Philippines as his uncle, and the rest of his immigration cohort, did.

Included in this wave of immigration, amidst the doctors, lawyers, and medical technicians, was a group of self-proclaimed political exiles—there can perhaps be no other kind—from both ends of the conservative-liberal political spectrum. One group, however, spoke louder and had better press coverage. Formed in 1973, the mostly East Coast–based Movement for a Free Philippines, or MFP, led by Raul Manglapus, became the most prominent anti-Marcos organization in the U.S. On the other end of the spectrum was the progressive political organization KDP, headquartered in Oakland, California. Its official newspaper, *Ang Katipunan*, was *Philippine News*'s ideologi-

---

[3] What is called nationalism in the Philippines today is rather different from its conception at the turn of the twentieth century. Being a *nasyonalista* (or being called one) now still connotes the image of the student activist, Molotov cocktail in hand, protesting the Marcos regime before the declaration of Martial Law in 1972. This "radical" element of nationalism was somewhat diluted by Marcos's co-optation of it—all states create official nationalisms, in any case—via his Bagong Lipunan (New Society) program. State-sponsored (indeed, state-mandated) Filipino pride later gave way to the Marcos "oppositionist" of the early '80s (and therefore regaining something of its radical veneer), especially after the assassination of the ex-Senator Benigno "Ninoy" Aquino in 1983. The Second Wave generation missed these ideological upheavals, as Curameng notes.

cal opposite and, at least politically, biggest rival. It was also very much a product of the third generation of immigrants, written mostly by young Filipino American professionals and full-time activists who were already politically active in the turbulent late '60s. In many ways, the divide I mentioned earlier—of class, of generation, and of immigration time—can be seen in the difference between the two newspapers.

Yossi Shain and Mark Thompson write: "Operating from outside their country, and sometimes under the sanctuary of sympathetic governments, political exiles are in a unique position to discredit the regime's legitimacy and to expose its oppressive nature abroad" (1990, 85). But the exiles were, at the same time, the most vulnerable to accusations of selling out, particularly with respect to the specific configuration of neocolonialism and political persecution in which they found themselves.

Both camps were in the uncomfortable position of having nationalism—albeit a Marcos-constructed version—employed against them.[4] On one hand, Manglapus was dogged by persistent rumors, which continued long after he returned to the Philippines in 1986, that he was in cahoots with the CIA. On the other was the self-contradiction of the KDP, rightly railing against the American government's complicity with the Marcos regime, but at the same time located in, and seeking protection from, the United States. Casting doubt on their integrity was, in hindsight, easy for Marcos to accomplish; by simple virtue of their being physically outside the Philippines, the Filipino expatriates' credibility was already in question.[5] Teodoro Valencia, a newspaper columnist and Marcos mouthpiece, coined the phrase *steak commandos* specifically for the members of the MFP. What is interestingly appropriate about his phrase is that it not only casts derision on their class background, but on their being based in the United States as well.

The counterpropaganda was aided by more proactive efforts: in May 1973, Marcos published a blacklist of 150 newspaper writers and editors, mostly based in the United States. Most of them were already either U.S. citizens or permanent residents; Marcos took care of the rest by canceling their Philippine passports, hoping that the U.S. Immigration and Naturalization Service would deport them. *Philippine News* staffers were then forced to

---

[4] Throughout his regime Marcos showed himself to be a consummate political player: proud Filipino nationalist one day, *tuta ng kano* (American lapdog) the next. Marcos's 1976 visit to Kenya, where he suggested the formation of an anti-U.S. bloc, took American officials by surprise; his outburst was understood rightly by *Philippine News* as partly an attempt to smear political exiles in the United States by playing on anti-American sentiment (Psinakis 1976, 4).

[5] This portrayal of the exiles was not in contradiction with the *official* treatment of Filipinos based in the United States, as the regime could easily dictate which kinds of behavior were considered nationally loyal or disloyal. For Marcos, Manglapus and company were the only real "disloyalists."

apply for political asylum. By this maneuver Marcos essentially forced a rupture between his opponents and the protective ambit of the Philippine government. But because citizenship denotes, among many other things, which state is responsible for a citizen's welfare—and, more important, which state a citizen is responsible to—the question of national loyalty is almost rendered moot.

Traditionally, conceptions of legal citizenship and "patriotic" citizenship (i.e., citizenship as entailing certain "nationalistic" responsibilities) are conflated. Perhaps at least in the mind of the general public, being a citizen meant being a *good* citizen, an idea reinforced in the Philippines by Marcos's political rhetoric. (Obviously, a "proper" definition would take pains to separate the legal aspects of citizenship from the moral/sentimental aspects, as Kymlicka and Norman [1995] argue.) Any sins of commission (and omission as well, depending upon the circumstances) against the state—for example, sedition or dodging the draft—are quickly branded anti-Filipino, or anti-American (or un-American), as the case may be.

In the case of exiles, however, there is less ground to stand on, particularly for the essentially stateless. Immigrants, in turn, are perceived to have voted with their feet. This is perhaps the main reason why a change in citizenship is equated, at least by some of my interviewees, with a similar change in sentiment and identity. As should be clear from my discussion so far, however, physical and emotional uprooting is never complete.

Ideologies

Though the anti-Marcos movement in the United States may have seemed monolithic in the eyes of the Marcos regime, and to the gaze of those left behind, it was fragmented along lines of class and political beliefs. One major difference between the two anti-Marcos factions was the place of the United States within their ideology. The KDP and the similarly influential, affiliated East Coast–based organization, Friends of the Filipino People (FFP), as was to be expected, accused the U.S. government of collusion with the Marcos regime. The accusation, however, placed the Left in an untenable position, given that some of them had fled to the United States for protection. This fact was never quite explained in any of *Ang Katipunan*'s editorials, and it provided Marcos more ammunition against the left-wing exiles.

For the conservatives of the *Philippine News*, the struggle could only be accomplished with outside help. *Philippine News* explained the situation in one of the paper's most surprisingly neocolonial editorials, entitled "The US Can Redeem Its Honor in RP":

The American "defeat" in South Vietnam and Cambodia has raised the question of American honor. The US has been accused of not honoring its commitments to "allies" in Asia.

In our view America can very well, and very effectively, redeem its honor by demonstrating to the world that it can stand by commitments, especially ones that date back to the turn of the century.

For the Philippines has been an American child over the last 75 years. It was America who ushered the Philippines into the twentieth century. The Americans taught the Filipinos the basic concept of a democratic government. The Americans infused into the Filipino psyche the wisdom and value of such institutions as a free press and free and honest elections; the Americans . . . instructed the Filipinos on the intricacies of due process and the value of human and civil rights. Certainly the Filipino people have been thankful to the Americans for this. And now all those democratic freedoms have been deprived the Filipinos by President Marcos.

Whether or not the US consented, encouraged or connived with Marcos . . . is no longer the issue.

The issue now is whether or not Americans will realize and recognize that it will be completely and totally un-American to continue supporting . . . Marcos. . . .

America can still redeem its tarnished honor—in the Philippines! (*Philippine News* 1975c, 2)

Driving the editorial writer's plea was his fear that the Philippines would "turn communist"—despite the fact that Marcos had declared martial law because of the perceived Communist threat in the first place. Interestingly, the writer (very likely Esclamado) worried not about the underground left, but about Marcos's new relations with Beijing. The breaking of ties with Taiwan and the opening of Chinese consulates in the Philippines prompted this query:

Why then has President Marcos thrown a deeply God-believing, pronouncedly pro-American and fiercely anti-communist people, the first in Asia to successfully defeat a communist uprising, into the jaws of the Chinese giant . . . ?

Since the profligate and extravagant Marcos family . . . will never have the inclination to live the agnostic and Spartan life of the Chinese mainlander, why the haste throwing the doors of anti-communist Philippines wide open to communist superpower China? (*Philippine News* 1975b, 2)

The writer then conjectured that China could potentially use Mindanao as a launching pad for retaliatory measures against Indonesia[6]—not that the Philippines was safe from Indonesia, either. As *Philippine News* put it, "Who could next annex the Philippines? Will it be Indonesia . . . ? Indonesia, after all, has always considered the Philippines her geographic and ethnic kin, and rightly so. There are already enough people telling stories that the map of Indonesia hanging in the presidential palace in Jakarta already includes the Philippines" (*Philippine News* 1975b, 4).

Esclamado's paranoia, particularly about Marcos, was not by any means unfounded, however. It was evident that Marcos did indeed find the *Philippine News* a real source of anxiety—so much so that in August 1975, Marcos ordered the Secretary of Tourism, then Jose Aspiras, to put pressure on Filipino travel agencies to withdraw their advertisements from the newspaper. *Philippine News* managed to survive, however, despite the loss of about $50,000 a year in advertising revenues during the "Advertisers' August Massacre." Marcos agents continued to approach Esclamado and repeatedly offered to buy the newspaper (he considered the offers bribery), for amounts that peaked at $12 million in 1981. Various collection cases were filed against the newspaper as a result of mounting unpaid bills, which culminated on the brink of a forced closure by the IRS in 1985 for failure to pay more than $200,000 in back taxes (*Philippine News* 1985, 1). In 1975 one of the paper's writers, Primitivo Mijares (Marcos's chief media censor, who had defected from the Marcos regime),was the subject of a bribe attempt before he was to testify against Marcos before the U.S. Congress; he mysteriously disappeared in 1977, at the behest, it is believed, of General Fabian Ver, Marcos's notorious right-hand man.

It was no surprise, then, that Esclamado saw enemies everywhere. His dislike for left-wing organizations was not just mere whim, for it was written up in black and white in *Philippine News*'s style guide, distributed to its staff writers. I was told, for instance, not to interview certain community leaders who were formerly active in the Left; if I were to get a sound bite from them at all, it would have to be printed at the end of the article. Along with pointers on grammar and spelling was the following passage:

> There are certain stories that, as a policy, should not see print in Philippine News. Why?
>
> These are stories or press releases from known communist-leaning organizations and purportedly cause-oriented movements, both

---

[6] A convoluted and oddly paranoid reference to the murderous purges of ethnic Chinese Indonesians and suspected Communists in the late '60s.

U.S.-based and Manila-based, that have relentlessly sought to use the newspaper as a medium for their communist and revolutionary propaganda.

These groups, mostly composed of radical students and militant labor elements, and sometimes members of religious groups, are active in the United States and Canada, and they seem to be well-funded.

The newspaper's more public differences with the Left began in 1973, when *Philippine News* began an intermittent series of "exposés" publicizing what the editor called "red-tainted" anti–martial law organizations in the United States. The campaign culminated in a bitter feud with the KDP in 1979. That year *Philippine News* ran a series of articles on financial irregularities and "secret" left caucuses within the Friends of the Filipino People (reprinting KDP internal memoranda), but the eventual slant was on the "red" character of the KDP and its "clandestine" alliance with "extremist groups." Shouting in 60-point type, "KDPS ARE COMMUNISTS!" Esclamado reported on the "secret identity" of the KDP and how it was planning to replace one dictatorship with another, "hiding behind nomenclatures as 'national democracy'" (1979, 1). The KDP, Rosario Pineda alleged, "[operates] in clandestine fashion, hiding behind church organizations and other liberal groupings" (1979, 4). "It is clear," Esclamado wrote, "that the KDPs and their allies intend to convert all capitalist free enterprise states to communism through revolution" (1979, 1). *Ang Katipunan* responded:

> We find it hard to believe that anyone in the Filipino community . . . would be at all surprised or shocked at the 'news' that the KDP actively supports the National Democratic revolution, the NPA [New People's Army] and the CPP [Communist Party of the Philippines]. Alex Esclamado for one has known this for years. Ironically it is Esclamado and not the KDP who has tried to keep our work and politics a 'secret' from the Filipino community. For quite some time, the *Philippine News* has intentionally distorted the news in order to deny or downplay the active and leading role of the KDP in many progressive activities and struggles in the Filipino community. (1979c, 2)

The newspaper alleged that *Philippine News* consistently refused to publish press announcements about, for instance, fundraisers for the New People's Army.

During the first round of its rebuttals, an *Ang Katipunan* editorial "bestowed" a "[William] Randolph Hearst Award of the Year" on Esclamado for "sensationalism, distortion, and irresponsible reporting:"

This . . . is the singular accomplishment of the *Philippine News*'s brand of journalism: the distinction between news facts and editorial comment is shamelessly discarded. Thus, its reader is never fore-warned if he is reading facts or . . . Esclamado's interpretation of facts.

. . . Any fool who has the money to buy a mouthpiece can shoot his mouth off. Thus, ideas or opinions that would ordinarily be dis-missed as asinine . . . acquire a false sense of importance—if the per-son happens to own a printing press. . . .

Prior to its big 'scoop' on FFP and KDP, the *Philippine News* found any means possible to avoid mentioning the two organizations' existence, much less crediting their work. However, since the organi-zations' work did make important news in the Filipino community, the *Philippine News* found an ingenious way of chopping up FFP and KDP's press releases and tagging to them long quotes and comments from Raul Manglapus. The effect was to create the impression that Manglapus was at the forefront of the anti–martial law movement. (*Ang Katipunan* 1979b, 2)[7]

Still, the KDP was clearly genuinely worried about Esclamado's attacks, pub-lishing full-page rebuttals in its newspaper. "The whole attack," announced *Ang Katipunan*, "has the unmistakable stamp of . . . Esclamado. Once more he displays that he is politically as crude and primitive as a caveman" (1979a, 2). In perhaps one of the most cogent explanations of the National Demo-cratic movement (after all, the statement was written for *Philippine News* readers), the KDP attacked Esclamado's "reactionary position stemming from narrow self-interest," and alleged that his and Manglapus's class inter-ests were inimical to the movement. "At times, such reactionaries may stand for some political changes such as replacing Marcos. But they live in mortal fear of any talk, and especially action, in the direction of more fundamental, revolutionary change" (*Ang Katipunan* 1979a, 3).

Indifference

Although the opposition to Marcos may have been ideologically split, the two main camps were, at certain junctures, in agreement. One point of ac-

---

[7] In "such reactionary 'leadership circles,'" *Ang Katipunan* declared in a later article, "everything is orchestrated to highlight the few 'prominent leaders' . . . And so Manglapus's telephone call to a senator's office is basis for banner headlines in the News or Esclamado's luncheon with an aide to the mayor is the occasion for numerous photographs" (1979c: 2).

cord, of course, was their belief that the Marcos government had trampled upon democratic rights. That was a given. The other was the belief that the Pinoy immigrants in the United States were blissfully, shockingly, indifferent to the worsening situation back "home" in the Philippines. In this sense, the anti-Marcos opposition was also united against an apathetic middle class. The *Philippine News* attempted to appeal to its readers to look back and exercise their obligations to the homeland.

There was never any question, from the very beginning, about which side *Philippine News* would take in the split among anti-Marcos activists between sympathizers of the militant Left and MFP conservatives. Esclamado's joining the MFP in November 1975 received much publicity in *Philippine News*. But despite being blacklisted, Esclamado was not openly critical of Marcos until Geny Lopez, Jr., the son of his former employer, was jailed in November 1974. Only in April 1975 did Esclamado finally come out as anti-Marcos; quite understandably, he explained, "like most Filipinos, we sincerely hoped that Marcos would be true to his word about honest and genuine reforms" (1975a, 1).

Later he would write: "Upon the declaration of martial law . . . and during the few months thereafter, *PN* did not take a stand on the martial law question because it gave the benefit of the doubt to President Marcos, who was then serving a legitimate term of office under the old Philippine Constitution" (1975b: 14). Indeed, the very headline on *Philippine News*'s front page of September 28 to October 6—the week martial law was declared in 1972—proclaimed that the Philippines was "Calm and Peaceful," with the subheadline "Civil Rights Unimpaired."

In April, the same month Esclamado finally announced his opposition to Marcos, the newspaper issued the following strongly worded editorial, entitled "Are We Prepared to Meet History's Judgement?":

A very large majority of the Filipinos in America have opted not to express a view on the martial law situation now prevailing in the Philippines.

The primary reason for this, we have been told countless times, is their fear that should they express an opinion against the Marcos government, the lives and well being of relatives and close friends back home might be placed in certain jeopardy. . . .

Yet the relatives and friends of our staff have not been touched.

The same story holds true for many of the anti-Marcos leaders in this country.

What does this indicate?

It is our view that the element of fear . . . was used effectively by Marcos to intimidate the Filipinos in America into silence. . . .

Is the *Philippine News* then encouraging the Filipinos in America to come out in the open and express their views against the Marcos government?

Yes. Because we are cognizant of the fact that, rather than harm our people, this would be the best and most expeditious way to alleviate the plight of our countrymen. . . .

The voicing of an opinion, even the taking of concrete steps necessary to help terminate the martial law situation . . . has, in our view, graduated from a mere matter of exercising an option to recognize a duty, an obligation to our countrymen suffering. . . .

The longer we in America who are free remain silent, the longer our people will suffer. . . .

And then there are the millions of Filipinos who are enduring their excruciating agony in silence, looking wistfully across the Pacific Ocean to America, hoping, praying that we who are free, we who can do something or say something to help end their plight would do what we can . . .

One day, soon martial law will end. One day soon some of us will have the opportunity to go back. . . . Are we prepared to come face to face with our relatives, our friends, our countrymen, with the knowledge and realization that in their hour of need we kept silent? (*Philippine News* 1975a, 4)

Esclamado insisted, in repeated articles and editorials, that Filipinos in America had an obligation, as members of the same Filipino nation, to liberate a country they had seemingly already left behind. *Philippine News* (or rather, Esclamado himself) was quite aware of being in a unique position to be heard. Indeed, his pronouncements would become almost self-fulfilling, as he would later point to these same editorials as proof of his struggles against the Marcos regime.

The image of heroism was used by other activists as well. The MFP attempted to recruit future activists by explicitly invoking the ever-present ghosts of national heroes past. A *Philippine News* advertisement for Manglapus's book *Philippines: The Silenced Democracy* announced:

Our people back home cannot wait any longer. They need our help. The time is not for the faint of heart, the indifferent, the fence-sitter. Let us be inspired by the courage and foresight of Jose Rizal, Marcelo H. del Pilar, and Graciano Lopez Jaena who used their freedom in exile to work for the freedom of their countrymen at home. Filipinos rest their hopes on what we, their *kababayan*s [countrywomen/men] outside the Philippines, will do to help in the struggle for a Free Philippines as Charles de Gaulle led the Free French in England and Sun Yat Sen rallied the support of the Chinese in America. (*Philippine News* 1976, 2)[8]

I do not mean to understate the importance of *Philippine News* or other political exiles in the anti-Marcos movement. Copies of the newspaper were smuggled into the Philippines at a time when possession of subversive materials guaranteed incarceration or worse at the infamous Camp Crame. Photocopies of its articles, particularly those critical of Marcos, supplemented the underground press in Manila at a time when freedom of the press was curtailed.[9] *Philippine News* also reprinted investigative articles from local newspapers that otherwise would not be read by a nationwide audience—and *Ang Katipunan*'s was certainly smaller. But Esclamado may have overstated his importance to Filipinos back home, seeing himself as one of a small group of valiant crusaders.

Still, the newspaper was influential, and perhaps even inspirational to its readers outside the country. One could not wholeheartedly say the same for its "real" audience. A consistent tone throughout *Philippine News*'s editorials was disappointment and animosity at what the writers perceived as complacency among their middle-class readers. Tony Garcia's column right after the 1976 elections (during which various Filipino Americans won in prominent positions, including Monty Manibog as mayor of Monterey Park, California) was characteristically furious:

---

[8] The advertisement came with the headline "History Repeats Itself" and featured the following blurb:

> Rizal, writing in exile in Spain gave Filipinos in 1896 . . . *Noli me Tangere*, the novel that ignited the first successful national revolution in Asia and established the First Republic in that part of the world.
>
> Raul Manglapus, writing in exile in America, now gives Filipinos suffering under the Marcos dictatorship the new *Noli* in the fight to regain their freedom and lost Republic (*Philippine News* 1976, 2).

[9] Except for the underground *Balita ng Malayang Pilipinas*, or News of a Free Philippines, Marcos cronies had a stranglehold on the media: the former ambassador to Japan Roberto Benedicto and Enrique Romualdez owned the *Daily Express* and the television station RPN-9; Hans Menzi owned the former *Bulletin Today* as well as the magazine *Liwayway*, and Benjamin Romualdez, the former governor of Leyte, owned the *Times Journal*. But in the United States, the anti-Marcos press flourished: there were *Silayan* and *Makibaka*, put out by the NCRCLP; *Bangon*, based in Ann Arbor; *Pahayag*, based in Honolulu; the *Philippine Information Bulletin*, based in Cambridge; and *Tambuli*, from the Chicago-based Union of Democratic Filipinos, among others (Last 1975, 9). An interviewee who was a student activist in the '70s attested to *Philippine News*'s status among the political underground, as tattered articles were passed from person to person.

If Filipinos are good enough to get elected by Americans to respected positions . . . are they not good enough to enjoy freedom, democracy, human rights and civil liberties in their own country?

Probably one reason why Filipinos are given very little importance in America is that they do very little for the country of their origin. . . . No Filipino public official on the mainland has raised a voice in protest. . . . [Garcia then cites the case of Greek Americans, Jewish Americans, and Irish Americans.] Filipinos may indeed be the only ethnic group in America who do not relate to their own kind in the Philippines.

The almost criminal indifference of some Filipinos in America to the destruction of Philippine freedom is such that Colonel [N. L.] Manzano [the coordinator of the Northern California chapter of the MFP] . . . once asked whether these Filipinos came to America on the Mayflower with the pilgrims because of the airs they put on acting so detached from and so disinterested in a country they probably left merely a few years or several months ago. Worse, of course, are Filipinos who carry on as if they belong to another race by claiming to stay 'neutral' in issues involving Filipinos. (Garcia 1976, 4)[10]

In his column, Garcia went through a remarkable series of arguments. In a twist of the conventional meaning of civic participation, Garcia attributed the marginalization of Pinoys—still dependent on recognition by the American mainstream, it seems—to their lack of participation in homeland politics. He cited the lack of ethnic solidarity—and linked it interestingly with connotations of a class-based/racial "selling out" (as if "these Filipinos came on the Mayflower"). Assimilation—that one has become more "white," as it were—is therefore associated with the absence of *pakikisama*. One also notes an apparent shift in tone, in contrast to the editorials of a few months before. Fear of reprisals from the Marcos regime is no longer entertained as the reason for silence; now the readers—indeed, the entire Pinoy community—are accused of plain indifference.

---

[10] Similar to this diatribe was an essay by Elly Velez Pamatong—a fellow newspaper publisher and an activist for Muslim independence in the San Francisco Bay Area—titled "Weep, My Broken Land." He writes: "This national tragedy has been compounded by the shocking apathy and indifference shown by Filipino expatriates in this land of milk and honey. Like sadists, they approvingly look on with folded arms at their own people cringing in the midst of a frightful and monstrous reality. For this, I accuse these expatriates, and for which I believe neither time nor history will forgive them, of indirectly conspiring with the Marcoses to tear off the last shred of our people's humanity" (1976, 5).

The relative exclusion of Filipinos from the American political main-stream can be more easily attributed to other factors, however. It has been said by some Filipino leaders that the reason that the political empowerment of the Filipino community has been so relatively slow is that they were all involved in the struggle against the Marcos government. As Rodel Rodis[11] told me in a 1994 interview:

I was involved in coalitions with other Chinese and Japanese. And back in '71, '72, halos pareho-pareho lang kaming lahat [we were all almost the same]. We were all equally unempowered. You know, you couldn't see any Chinese in public office, you couldn't see any Japanese in public office back in '71, '72, so we were all the same. By 1986, virtually every commission in the city had a Chinese member; there were at least four or five Chinese in various elected positions. But there was not a single Filipino in any elected office; there were only a scattering of Filipinos in commissions. So what had happened during the whole period? Well, what had happened was the Chinese and Japanese continued to move forward, but the Filipinos were caught fighting each other because of martial law, pro and con, so no one united to address the issues of the Filipinos here. So we lost numer-ous opportunities to advance—I mean, we almost had what would be the equivalent of Filipinotown or Manilatown, but because of fighting, that was lost here in San Francisco. You know, so, what

---

[11] An immigration lawyer in San Francisco, Rodis (one of the founders of the National Committee to Restore Civil Liberties in the Philippines in 1972) also writes an anthologized column in *Philip-pine News*, "Telltale Signs." Highly visible in the Bay Area Filipino community, Rodis has served on both the Public Utilities Commission and the Community College Board in San Francisco. This is how he told his story to me:

I was a student [at the University of the Philippines]; I was a, what you might call a stu-dent leader, kuno. And I was a spokesman for some of the organizations on TV, radio, like that; I'll be speaking on issues of the youth, what were being struggled for. And then there was a rally in January of 1971. And several people were killed by the people. That night I was on TV and I was—'cause I was describing the murdered students, the people there—I guess I was calling Marcos all kinds of names, I was blaming him for killing, for ordering the killing. And it turns out that one of the people who was with Marcos was a congressman who was a friend of my father, and he told my father that you better do something to get your son out of the country because Marcos was very upset with the things I said. And baka-masalvage, ganoon [I might be killed, like that]. So my father got me to consider cooling off first, staying a few months in the States, and till things got a little better, then I could come back.

Rodis uses the slang term *kuno* in reference to his being a student leader. It is an odd term, short for *kunwari*, meaning "pretend"; the word is generally used in conversation to cast doubt on the veracity of something just said. It may be that he is just distancing himself (through false modesty, perhaps?) from the label "student leader".

happened in '86, was like being Rip Van Winkle, you wake up and, nalampasan ka na [you have been passed by], and then how, you're on the same level as the Vietnamese and the Cambodians and the Koreans, whereas the Chinese and the Japanese are way ahead. So it was time to start focusing on local—what we're talking about is political empowerment here now, not in the Philippines. They can take care of themselves.

Here, Rodis does not mention apathy, but directly faults the political divisions within the Pinoy community, and the struggle against the Marcos dictatorship as a whole, as the fundamental causes for the "lost opportunities" for community empowerment. He contrasts this, somewhat erroneously, with the Chinese American and Japanese American communities; other Asian American groups have been in the United States longer and in greater numbers, and so have had better opportunities to establish themselves politically. Rodis also acknowledges the immigrant predicament—but for himself, he has made a clear choice as to where his service lies.

This echo of Alice Bulos's statement—that Filipino American empowerment is slow in coming because of loyalty to the homeland—is only partially true. It is apparent that homeland politics have indeed distracted immigrants from domestic issues. But it is also clear that organizers from both sides of the political spectrum were faced with much rejection in mobilizing the Filipino community against Marcos. A letter from a reader in 1978 echoed what Esclamado had long pronounced:

> In general, the majority of us are apathetic to the plight of our fellow countrymen.
>
> We don't care if Marcos kills Filipinos like flies, as long as we are safe in the US. We don't care if he murders whole Muslim villages as long as he does not go after the Christian families.[12]
>
> We don't care about our fellow Filipinos, rotting away in the Marcos concentration camps, as long as we can hold our grand balls, play golf, have expensive cars and jewelry. We don't care if Marcos tortures our poor and unfortunate countrymen, as long as we make money and are fortunate to be in the US. . . .
>
> We respond to his Balikbayan call to visit the Philippines, and we go home to enjoy ourselves. . . .

---

[12] A very rare sentiment, for *Philippine News* has published some appallingly anti-Muslim statements.

For how many Filipinos have joined the Balikbayan Program and complained to Marcos . . . ? What they usually complained about is the mix up and loss of luggage at the airport. (Climaco 1978, 5)

Ang Katipunan also made a similar criticism in an editorial entitled "Stand Up for the Homeland":

As the resistance in the Philippines has grown, the substantial Filipino community here in the U.S. has also developed as a base of overseas opposition to the Marcos regime. Since 1972, hundreds of forums, pickets, cultural events, dinners, speeches, and publications across the country have opposed martial law. . . .

Certainly the existence of such a sizeable Filipino population . . . has and can continue to play a critical role. . . . And yet, within our own community some respond: "that doesn't affect us here," or "don't we have enough problems here to worry about."

There is no question that Filipinos in the US have many problems and suffer much hardship, especially discrimination because of national origin and even skin color. But this cannot be an excuse for us to divorce ourselves from the problems and needs of our homeland. Such attitudes are only a reflection of unpatriotic and selfish ideas. Because we were able to temporarily escape the dire poverty and oppression we faced in the Philippines, we should not ignore the conditions of our brothers and sisters who remain back home. (*Ang Katipunan* 1975, 2)

This constant exhortation illustrates, interestingly, a facet of the "diaspora"— though as I have said, the Filipino American community does not exactly fall within its strict parameters. It involves a kind of moral prescription, an admonition not to forget. Whether or not this remembrance entails the desire to return—one of the principal criteria of the diasporan paradigm—is beside the point. The editorials' thrust is that there must be sacrifice by Filipinos in the United States—indeed, *especially* those in the United States. As Khachig Tololyan writes, "the dominant view was that just as being the citizen of a nation-state had a cost . . . so also membership in a diasporic branch of the transnation must have a cost, a demonstration of loyalty that undertook the responsibility of sacrifice" (1996, 15).

But what was the cost? What would have constituted a "demonstration of loyalty"? Such questions became especially acute when placed in the context of what America represented: modernity, luxury, and a freedom unavailable in the Philippines. Those in the United States—mga nagpapasarap sa Amerika (those living it up in America), as is commonly said—had the responsibility to assist those in need back home, or at least to show some sign of sacrifice.

Rodis told me in his interview that he was supposed to stay with an uncle upon his arrival in the United States. After a while, however, he moved to the International Hotel to live with the *manongs*[13] about to be evicted from their homes. "I decided when I came here to San Francisco and I found out about the struggle of the Filipinos here," he said. "I thought, you know—well, I guess it was a feeling that it was a way to assuage my own guilt that I had left the struggle, so I would have felt bad if I was living in luxury or living while my friends were out there, so . . ."

Certainly Rodis had no reason not to remain politically committed. But here he attributes his continued political activism to guilt—that is, the idea that someone was looking at him, even from afar. His ambivalence about being in the United States was resolved by his choice to plunge into the plight of the Filipino elderly and, later on, to push for the restoration of democracy to the Philippines.

The editorial writer for *Ang Katipunan* understood the dilemma of belonging to two places at once: how was one supposed to live the reality of, let alone productively engage with, both racial discrimination in the United States and the "needs of [the] homeland" (*Ang Katipunan* 1975, 2) at the same time? The loyalty demanded of the Filipino readers in the United States was almost always placed in contrast to their living in relative luxury and comfort in America. In this way the exhortation was couched in an appeal to guilt. The excerpt from Garcia's column above posits, in fact, the opposite of transnationalism; Garcia decried what he perceived as abandonment. He saw not a repeated turning but a *turning away*.

The contradiction between luxury and sacrifice can be seen in the statement of a former core member of the MFP, Gaston Ortigas, who described the MFP as "the Filipino's neo-colonial political tradition transplanted in exile." He added: "The MFP was a distant reality . . . —a world of elite *kababayans* hobnobbing with American officials, with by-lines in the *New York Times*, well-chronicled arrests and escapes, anti-Marcos statements quoted in *Time*. . . . Besides well-heeled doctors who gave huge contributions and expensive restaurant receptions for exiled officials and oppositionists, the MFP was never a popular movement" (Ortigas and Mayuga 1994; 100, 118). Ortigas's stinging comments coincide with similar sentiments from the KDP.

In memoirs of prominent oppositionists to the Marcos regime, one can generally find tales of vacationing in Europe and childhood days in private

---

[13] A term of respect roughly meaning "older brother," and a shorthand reference to the first generation of Filipino migrant workers.

schools juxtaposed with passages relating deprivation and sacrifice (Fortich 1991, Ortigas 1994). For instance, Charito Planas, who would later become the mayor of Quezon City, reminisces about watching operas in Milan and living "in a big house with a swimming pool and sauna" (Fortich 1991, 99). This luxurious life is then contrasted with living in a basement (and having to disinfect a used mattress with gasoline):

> She prowled the flea markets and thrift shops and got a sofa for $4. Her plates, glasses and tableware were mismatched. When you can't afford much, you just have to settle for what the bourgeoisie would call eclecticism. . . .
>
> Charito soon became an expert bargain-hunter. She shopped at low-cost stores . . . and looked for items whose expiry dates were imminent. The prices of day-old bread, steaks, milk and other perishable goods were drastically slashed, and she outran, outpushed, and outpulled the black people who were her adept main rivals for these low-priced items.
>
> She got into the habit of picking up discarded newspapers, where she would look for discount coupons. . . . Then she also became a 'salad-bar filcher.' She would filch a tomato here, a carrot there. . . . In a month, she found that she could save $50 or more by using coupons alone. (Fortich 1991, 150)

One does not doubt the sincerity of such stories, but the details also have a less innocuous, legitimizing function, as if the teller's relative penury bolstered her commitment. The anecdotes are signs of sacrifice that belie the exiles' "steak commando" identity—"we too," the stories communicate to the reader in the Philippines, "suffered in the United States." But the spectacle of exiled members of the Philippine oligarchy buying secondhand furniture and bagging supermarket groceries does little to dispel the image of *walang pakisama*, or having no sense of camaraderie or solidarity. Because they were in the United States, after all, the political exiles were considered suspect, despite their contributions to the anti-Marcos struggle.

Luxury and Sacrifice

The contrasts between luxury and sacrifice were displayed most prominently in the Filipino American newspaper of record. For instance, for *Philippine News*'s 35th anniversary, important articles and the front pages of old issues were reproduced mostly in their entirety. Out of about 52 pages, only six articles were specifically about United States topics (the International Hotel,

Filipino medical graduates, World War II veterans, campaigning for the then gubernatorial candidate Jerry Brown, the National Filipino American Unity Conference, and a history of *Philippine News*). The rest were about the Marcos government and the so-called EDSA Revolution of 1986 that overthrew Marcos. In this way the newspaper chose to remember and immortalize itself as the publication that resisted Marcos, to fashion itself as heroic.

This positioning also, however, unwittingly underscored the paper's relative lack of attention to local community issues. The anniversary issues were spread across several weeks and broken down into historical periods; one installment focused on the '60s and '70s, the next on the years from 1980 to 1985, and a third on the years from 1986 to 1990. And as *Philippine News* put it, "The decade of the '70s was characterized by our initial struggle against the mighty forces of the Conjugal Dictatorship of Ferdinand and Imelda Marcos" (*Philippine News* 1996b, S1). The "tumultuous" '80s were similarly remembered as "the historic period of political movements both in the Philippines and in the United States centering on the issue of the Conjugal Dictatorship of Ferdinand and Imelda Marcos" (*Philippine News* 1996a, S1).

The last anniversary edition—"Entering the 21st Century—The Decade of the '90s and Beyond: The Struggle for Political and Economic Empowerment"—finally focused specifically on the Filipino American community. But the chronology of the issues gives the reader the impression that "the struggle for empowerment" had begun only in recent years. Furthermore, the anniversary edition's centerpiece article was a five-page list of Filipino American politicians (called "Bearers of the Torch on the Road to the 21st Century"), with their photographs, career biographies, and brief messages to *Philippine News* congratulating the paper on its anniversary.

The newspaper's heroic image as crusader for justice was in jarring contrast to another image it presented to its readers, as we saw in the previous chapter: the glitz and glamour of CommLink. For instance, in the same 35th anniversary section, an article on the Association of Philippine Physicians in America, which was selected by *Philippine News* as the "Best National Organization of the Decade," was composed of nothing but short biographies of past presidents. Capping the article was a full page of blurry photographs of the past presidents and auxiliary presidents (coincidentally, almost always male and female) dressed in tuxedos and long gowns (unwittingly calling to mind the "conjugal dictatorship"). In an editorial meeting, Esclamado explained why he wanted to choose a national organization of the decade—to show that Filipino American organizations were "not all about balls and parties." His ensuing front-page editorial was entitled "Beyond the Glitz." An accompanying article pressed the point further, with the title "FilAm Groups More Than Meet the Eye":

It is through membership in Filipino organizations that the presence of the Filipino is felt. The organization is the Filipino's unit of action as well as his/her forum for social and community life. In effect, the Filipino's membership in an organization serves as his/her formal declaration that he/she has arrived in America and is ready to perform his/her role as a member of the Filipino community. (Ong 2000, 1)

Membership in associations has long been considered one of the first steps to Americanization—but, as the historian Sucheng Chan somewhat erroneously argues, "Belonging to clubs was definitely not a habit [Filipinos] brought from the homeland, where kinship formed the basis of virtually all aspects of social life, but they readily became joiners in the New World out of necessity" (1991, 78). Whether created out of necessity or not (and certainly Filipinos even joined the same associations they had belonged to in the Philippines) Filipino organizations were venues for making employment connections, organizing community activities, and raising funds for political candidates, disaster relief, and the like—all, in their way, part of the immigrant's "role as a member of the Filipino community," as Esclamado put it. But there is no denying the fact that membership in such clubs is not necessarily a political statement, and even less a "formal declaration that [one] has arrived in America." As Handlin writes, "The magnetic element at the core of all . . . was always the opportunity for sociability. . . . The balls and picnics had the additional virtue of raising money; but their true end was sociability" (2002, 158).

Indeed it could be argued that *Philippine News*, as the Filipino American newspaper of record, was instrumental in the creation of this "balls and parties" stereotype. This aspect has been the object of derision among some people—whether readers, or Bay Area Pinoys I have interviewed, who have reacted with embarrassment and have questioned, for instance, the newsworthiness or professionalism of the society pages. Even up to the present, the *Philippine News* has been notorious for the same kind of ostentatious display that the newspaper itself condemns. As Teddy Encinas put it,

The *Philippine News*, it was created to show off about Marcos, bad news about Marcos, that was what it was like then. I bet that's how they got started, I think. I don't know, I haven't been reading it lately but now they say it's like there is too much social news than actual news. . . . Who got married there, whose anniversary, whose party, fiestas of whoever, it's more like that, there's more of that, rather than actual news.

He qualified his opinion, however, by saying that it was "good for the community too"—but "sometimes you have to think that the purpose why you have to make a newspaper, either you produce a news back home or a news here or social events." The Filipino Channel, however, had fresher news items than *Philippine News* did, so for him television almost always won out.

The clash between a nationalistic, service-oriented agenda and "balls and parties" was brought to the fore in 1979, when the newspaper's call for an Outstanding Youth Contest was cancelled for lack of response. "In place of it," they wrote, "we are announcing the start of a new contest which according to our survey is the kind of contest you want us to run."

Open to any permanent resident of "Filipino or Filipino-American descent, irrespective of blood ratio)"—an interesting throwback to the days when *Filipino American* exclusively referred to people of mixed racial heritage—the Quest for Magandang Filipina–USA was launched. Regional finals in eleven different cities culminated, after much front-page hype, in the crowning of Yvonne Flores from Suisun City, California, after her "stirring vocal rendition of George Benson's 'The Greatest Love of All.' "[14] What *Philippine News* de-emphasized, however, was that contestants had to buy 35 subscriptions each to enter the pageant—earning $56,000 for the newspaper altogether. *Ang Katipunan* went straight to the politics of the contest, describing it as "a strange blend of fashion show, talent contest, an anti-KDP lecture, and slideshow all rolled into one." The rival newspaper pointed out that such pageants promote sexism, calling the swimsuit contest "downright disgusting." But part of its ire was reserved for how *Philippine News* portrayed its role in the community, as Willy Briones wrote in a scathing article:

> To give clout and justification to the pageant, Esclamado started the program with a 20-minute 'historical perspective' on the Filipino-American experience. With the assistance of 'historical consultant' Rodel Rodis, he turned the truth upside down and re-wrote history!. . . .
> Worse yet, slides of the various struggles of the community, like the International Hotel, Narciso-Perez[15] . . . were shown followed by

---

[14] Sponsored by the Fil-Am Veterans and Federal Retired Association of Fairfield, California, Flores defeated, among others, the first runner-up Lisa Manibog from Monterey Park, who performed a "very symbolic American-Indian ritualistic dance"; Theresa Abueg, who "played 'The Entertainer' on her flute"; Jacqueline Guerrero, who danced "a jazz-ballet interpretation of Gary Wright's 'Dream Weaver' "; and Rose Tibayan, who performed "a Malayan dance interpretation on disco roller skates" (Aljovin 1979: 1, 12).

[15] In fact, the newspaper's coverage of the protests about the demolition of the International Hotel in San Francisco, one of the catalyzing moments in Filipino American history, began quite late,

Philippine News's front page coverages of the same issues. Displaying the worst sort of opportunism yet, Esclamado was able to create the impression that HE and HIS NEWSPAPER were leading these struggles. (Briones 1979, 1)

Briones added that KDP members distributing leaflets during the pageant were "roughed up" by Esclamado's associates.

Not surprisingly, *Ang Katipunan* followed up the article by lashing out at the contest in an editorial:

The pageant's sponsor, *Philippine News* . . . [claims] that the contest was meant to promote Philippine heritage and unity. Anyone . . . however would surely agree that there was neither a performance nor presentation . . . which vaguely resembled Philippine culture or heritage. . . . .

No, the Magandang Filipina pageant was not an innocent competition, a meeting of the community's "best and beautiful." Rather it was a masked business venture which exploited the contestants and sections of the community. . . .

Like grand *terno* balls [ternos are formal Philippine gowns], cocktail parties and other expensive forms of social activities, the beauty contest diverts our attention from more pressing concerns. . . . If we expended the same amount of money, energy and time on a fund raiser for some community cause or for the political refugee problem . . . we could justifiably claim that our efforts were progressive, positive and productive. A beauty contest can hardly claim the same. (1979d, 3)

Paradoxically, *Philippine News* would probably also agree with the statement just quoted; as it was, the newspaper constantly trod a fine line between the two images of heroism and profligacy. But the tension was in keeping with the contradictory impulses of the newspaper: to demonstrate immigrant success, and to strive for political awareness by highlighting the community's marginality.

---

well after the eviction process was under way. One suspects that the delay was probably because mainly young Asian American student activists spearheaded the protests concerning the eviction of *manongs* from the I-Hotel. "Radicals" of a more leftist persuasion, they were the kind of people Esclamado would have avoided.

Filipinas Narciso and Leonora Perez were Chicago nurses accused of murdering two patients in 1976, a case which spurred many Filipino activists both in the Philippines and in the United States to rally to their defense. The case was finally thrown out of court in early 1978.

The rivalry between the newspapers exposes the contradictions that underlie a particular paradigm of exile/immigration. The slash in *exile/ immigration* seems appropriate, for it highlights crucial differences within the Filipino population: some spurred on by the exigencies of political persecution, and many others motivated by growing economic dissatisfaction. The Marcos regime may have been an aberrant period—though arguably there was no major impact on immigration patterns to the United States either during or after it—but it also illustrates what happens at the extremes, at the edges, and illuminates, in turn, what occurs in the center.

Though the political exiles were in the minority, their discourse, as seen in their newspapers, dictated the parameters of heroism—specifically, a particular heroism located outside the boundaries of the nation, or even of national belonging. Middle-class Pinoys in the United States were enjoined to exercise a national loyalty to two nations, one seemingly incompatible with their new lives in America. For them to be able to belong to the category of the "good Filipino," sacrifice had to be involved. This sacrifice was not merely symbolic; being Filipino in the United States, at that point, demanded a demonstration of responsibility for fellow Filipinos in the Philippines. But in this act of sacrifice the political exiles were thwarted, or at least regarded with much suspicion, simply because of their presence in the United States. Furthermore, the rift in the Marcos opposition demonstrated the difficulty of ideologies based specifically on provoking guilt about one's class position, particularly in a milieu where immigrant success was expected.

The *Philippine News* presented a characteristically "transnational" perspective for an audience that was ostensibly the same. This was a mostly middle-class readership of people whose lifestyles allowed them to consume ethnic media, to remain conversant about happenings in the Philippines. For many of them, families and friends were back home as well. Why else would a newspaper in America focus on events in the Philippines? Aside from anticipating the demands of its audience, the newspaper has made no grand statements on political or economic connections: we find no discussions of postcolonialism, or of the struggles of "people of color" the world over. The politicization of the relationship between the two countries was, in a sense, unnecessary; what already "naturally" bound them together were sinews of memory and kinship.

It is the elision of boundaries, even during the editorial process, which makes *Philippine News* noteworthy. To be sure, modifiers of place such as "dito sa Amerika" (here in America) or "doon sa Pilipinas" (there in the Philippines) were always employed. But discourse about the Philippines and the United States tends to naturalize a way of thinking about the two. Such public discussion and circulation of information meant that the Philippines was constantly watched, thought of, and talked about, in the lives of Filipinos in the United States.

Readers of both newspapers were constantly asked to imagine, to place themselves in the stead of those they had left behind, to display *pakikisama*, to conceive of a nationalism and national identity that stretched across borders. But in a sense, all that imagining had already been accomplished, in a more comfortable fashion. Could it not be said that all the pageants, the beauty contests, and the festivals constituted a kind of cultural nationalism, one that created and re-created a Filipino identity nostalgically removed from the everyday horrors of the Marcos regime—or, indeed, the "horrors" of everyday life in the Philippines? Middle-class Pinoys in Daly City, it seemed, were already practicing a nationalism without guilt, for they already saw themselves in their newspapers, ate the same Filipino food, and danced in the same grand ballrooms—just as they had back home.

6

BETRAYAL AND BELONGING

~

MICHAEL SANTOS (MS): How about you, if you were given the chance—you've already worked here, you're already earning a big salary, and then you're offered [a job] there . . . maybe, I don't know, if there's anything that loyalty or being nationalistic can do. Anyway, all of us, we're all thinking of—materialism is what we—we're materialistic.

BV: Is that what you think, that's how we are, the Filipinos who are here?

MS: Maybe. However much you love your country, you don't want to leave it, but you see that your life is not improving, then what are you going to do there, right?

Many scholars have used the push-pull model of migration, but it has been criticized for its neo-functionalism and assumption of discrete, autonomous receiving and sending states (Rouse 1992). Rouse adds that "the emphasis on a bipolar framework has obscured the ways in which many settlers . . . have managed to maintain active involvements with the people and places they have left behind and . . . have often helped create new kinds of communities that span the international border" (1992, 25).[1] His reconcep-

---

[1] Indeed, the bipolar framework (and the easy separability of "here" and "there") has its echoes as well in the semi-racist conceptualizations of immigrant or ethnic identity as either/or, e.g., *either* Asian *or* American, and not both.

tualization is a valuable reminder that places like Daly City (and the people who reside in them) perhaps inevitably derive their identities from at least two different places. The conceptualization of a more unified framework has its effects on anthropological fieldwork and writing as well: George Marcus, in an attempt to represent the larger systemic context of his subjects, has suggested a focus on multiple locales in ethnographic writing rather than on an artificially bounded community (1986, 1992).

In the two preceding chapters, I looked at the contradictory obligations of Pinoy immigrants. In simplified terms, these responsibilities can be seen as looking back to their homeland and looking forward to their adopted country simultaneously. In this chapter, I will explore how Filipinos in the United States are perceived outside, in the Philippines, as manifest in popular discourse. Class intersects with Filipino national belonging in a variety of ways—in this specific case, materialism is used as proof of immigrant betrayal. These notions of Filipino identity and belonging are evoked to regulate the class and national inclusion or exclusion of middle-class individuals outside the country. I will highlight the points of comparison and contrast between discourses from different locales, partly to emphasize the "global" quality of discourse by and about Pinoys in general.

One chapter cannot exhaust the particularities of an unstable, heterogeneous mass here conveniently called "middle-class Filipinos." I will examine only the homogeneities it presents for inspection. It seems difficult to discuss identity—particularly when national identity is concerned—as being relational when on the ground it is perceived by many as essentialized and timeless, despite efforts to uncover the ideological trickery engendering it. But, in this case, distinctive identity formations are produced in the intersections of conceptions of class and nation.

I will look at Daly City—or rather, a fictive "Daly City"—from the outside. By *fictive* I do not mean a Daly City that exists in literature, but a place that is created in discourse and fashioned by sentiment. Certainly the reality of living in the United States also exists, if to a lesser degree, in the social imagination of Filipinos in the Philippines. The *image* of Filipino immigrant life in America, as held by Filipinos in the Philippines, is a relevant social fact, as it both informs, and is informed by, the actual conditions in the United States. This constant act of looking back, of turning and re-turning, is, I believe, integral to any analysis that involves a transnational framework. And so to begin, I leave Daly City for a moment to take a detour and focus on its origins back home.

Departure as Betrayal of the Nation

In 1993, a book edited by Isagani Cruz and Lydia Echauz appeared in Manila bookstores. Titled *1001 Reasons to Stay in the Philippines*, the monograph, presented in a format admittedly cribbed from U.S. self-help guides like *Life's Little Instruction Book* and *The Portable Life 101*, manifests a particular class's fantasies, as well as its perspectives, concerning notions of Filipino identity. (Noticeably, the interviewees' credentials—schools, occupations—are easily interpretable by Filipino readers as shorthand for "middle class" and "upper middle class.") According to the editors, the book, was meant to be a collection of "positive thoughts about the Philippines" in order to "make life more enjoyable for the millions of Filipinos who prefer to live in their home country rather than face isolation, alienation, and prejudice outside" (Cruz and Echauz 1993, preface). It was also clearly a reaction, if a rather lighthearted one, to Filipinos' dissatisfaction with life in the Philippines—a dissatisfaction that, as I discussed in Chapter One, was by no means abated by the time of the Pulse Asia survey in 2002, which indicated that one out of five Filipinos would choose to live or work overseas.

Consisting of two or three pithy, somewhat decontextualized quotes on each page, the 1,001 reasons are by turns droll or touching, and are often surprisingly revealing. Most of the reasons given revolve around platitudes concerning the beauty of the country—"the implacable enchantment of its 7,100 islands," says the poet Anthony Tan (Cruz and Echauz 1993, 132) and having one's family and friends nearby—"I want to be able to bump into old friends and people I grew up with when I walk the streets," claims Glicerio Sicat, the president of Interpacific Capital Philippines (Cruz and Echauz 1993, 9). But a significant number evoke some form of nationalistic service to the country, as may be seen from these sample quotations given by Cruz and Echauz (1993):

> Times call for every Filipino to think of self last and country first. This is not the time to desert our country for convenience of selves. Happiness, dignity and recognition come first before material possessions.
>
> —Isidro Cariño, President, Asia Research
> and Management Corporation (25)

> Each Filipino has the obligation to help improve and uplift the country economically, politically, and spiritually. I would like to fulfill my obligation in whatever way I might be able to, no matter how small and seemingly insignificant.
>
> —James E. Festejo (183)

There is a need to develop a critical mass of Filipinos who are willing to sacrifice personal interests for national good.
—Roberto S. Sebastian, Secretary of Agriculture (45)

I'm trying to live up to my name—nagpapakabayani [letting myself be a hero]!
—Bayani V. Evangelista, Publisher/Editor-in-Chief, *Mediawatch* (136)[2]

As these comments suggest—another interviewee of Cruz and Echauz says that those responsible for Philippine development are "silent heroes" (1993, 158)—leaving the Philippines is tantamount to a betrayal of sorts, a non-fulfillment of an obligation to contribute to the nation. Departure is a betrayal of the nation to pursue what are seen as purely personal interests.

The comments above imply a binary opposition between money and nation.[3] It should be clear, of course, that the material and cultural conditions are much more complicated. But it is a cognitive model that, despite its pervasiveness, has not existed for long in the Philippines—perhaps only since the '60s and '70s—and one repeated throughout Filipino representations of the balikbayan. Those who leave, ostensibly in pursuit of money, are seen as unwilling to sacrifice for the nation, as thinking only of themselves. In this twist in the definition of "heroism"—for merely staying in one place!—nationalism is also tied up with the naturalization of the link between ethnicity and place: the idea that people of a certain ethnicity, and for that matter people of a certain nation, belong to one particular geographic place.

Remaining home, in turn, is linked with the invocation, preservation, and consequent reification of "traditional" Filipino character traits depicted as nothing but positive in these quotations given by Cruz and Echauz (1993):

Neighbors still care enough for each other to drive a sick child to the hospital.
—Gloria S. Chavez, College of Business and Economics, De La Salle University (18)

---

[2] In a previous version of this chapter I carelessly translated *nagpapakabayani* as simply "being a hero." The idea of giving oneself over to heroism is more interesting and reinforces the notion of a sacrifice made in the name of the nation by staying in it.

[3] The silence about the burden of the colonial and neocolonial relationship is quite interesting to note, and is somewhat beyond the scope of this book—or, indeed, may have everything to do with it, at the very least as it concerns fantasy as social practice. The trope of betrayal is hardly ever couched within the framework of a "return" to the former metropole.

Strong extended family ties. Good formative years for children. Opportunity to help less privileged ones.

—Roman F. S. Reyes, senior partner,
Sycip Gorrez Velayo & Company (143)

I am a first class citizen in my country. It is the only country where the people understand utang na loob [debt of gratitude], pakikisama, and bayanihan [cooperation].

—Roberto Benares, Insular Investment
and Trust Corporation (34)

Those who don't have reasons for staying should leave, so we can have this beautiful country all to ourselves.

—Barry Ponce de Leon, civil engineer,
Department of Public Works and Highways (189)

A plant warehouse head working for the San Miguel Corporation puts it aptly when he likens "the Filipino tradition of togetherness and support" (Cruz and Echauz 1993, 29) to being in a mother's womb, stressing the primal, essential character of tradition and, interestingly, its connection to place.

The implication is that when one leaves the Philippines, one also leaves its protective environment, and one's sense of service, behind. This concept is similar to Daly City residents' experience of the absence of solidarity, as discussed in Chapter Three. Of course, there is a certain idealization on the part of the Manileños themselves, but that is not the point here: the Filipinos who choose to stay deem the parameters of nationalism and national belonging to coincide squarely with the state's own borders.

The comments define what it is like outside the Philippines, but they also perform another duty, which is to solidify the boundaries of "Filipinoness." What is involved, however, is not the mere enumeration of "ethnic" stereotypes, but the structure of a prescriptive, almost moral order, which is reiterated and deeply woven in various discourses. Certainly this association of morality with an ethnic "authenticity" is nothing new, for each nation has its own list of stereotypes, but it illustrates how such associations are perpetuated and taken for granted in the everyday world. The middle-class rhetoric of betrayal—one not traceable merely to class resentment—suggests that emigration is more akin to the loss of *pakikisama*, rather than an act of flagrant unpatriotism. That is, the expatriates are not necessarily branded as traitors, but as former fellow countrymen and countrywomen who abandoned their country rather than share in the common, everyday sacrifice of living in the Philippines.

Most interesting of all is how the trope flies in the face of apparently successful attempts by the Aquino, Ramos, Estrada, and Macapagal-Arroyo administrations to crown overseas contract workers, or OCWs, as "bagong bayani," or new heroes. In February 1998, the theme of the celebrations for the EDSA uprising, "Every Filipino Can Be a Hero," was specifically meant to honor the more than four million overseas Filipino workers, or OFWs. In the first quarter of 2002 alone, OFWs[4] were responsible for contributing $1.9 billion to their families in the Philippines (Batino 2002), underscoring the government's parasitic dependence on the export of cheap labor to countries where workers' rights are fraught with uncertainty.[5] All together, OFWs are the largest source of foreign exchange for the Philippines, earning about $6 billion a year, or 8 percent of the country's gross national product (Prystay 2002). The average OFW, to illustrate the chain of dependency, supports five people; one out of five Filipinos "directly depends on migrant workers' earnings" (Constable 1997, 34).

The reference points of Cruz and Echauz's interviewees may really revolve around the difference between leaving and staying away. The title of their book—not to mention the very reality of its being written—already confirms a desperation of sorts to stem the hemorrhage of "deserters." But "staying" can only be the opposite of "leaving" as long as those who have "left" stay away for good. Rey Ventura reminds us, writing about Japan, "there is no Japanese Dream, and yet Japan, for the Filipino, has become a second America. There is no Statue of Liberty in Yokohama—and why should there be? A statue of the Yen would be more appropriate. We do not dream of becoming Japanese citizens. . . . We do not imagine that we will settle there for ever" (1992, 165). Though a statue of the Dollar would not be inappropriate—as should already be clear from my Daly City interviews— Ventura's point here is that the option of settling permanently is really open, in practical terms, only to Pinoys in America. But restrictive immigration policies, in Hong Kong and Italy, for instance, which keep Filipinos in a semi-permanent "guest worker" status, are only part of the reason for not settling. The United States occupies a central position in migration

---

[4] *OFW* became the more accepted term by the mid-1990s, and it included workers without contracts. Republic Act No. 8042 uses even more generic language, as it is commonly referred to as the Migrant Workers and Overseas Filipinos Act.

[5] As Rosario Ballescas writes, the government is "utilizing the young women of the Philippines in exchange for immediate but temporal and artificial financial alleviation; utilizing the . . . women to try to resolve poverty, a role which should rightly be borne primarily by the government" (1992, 114). In fact, $2.79 billion were sent as remittances by Filipinos in the United States in the first nine months of 1995—financial links that contribute to the maintenance of familial ties strained by the calls of global capitalism (*Philippine Daily Inquirer* 1996, 4).

studies because it is, after all, the preeminent "receiving country" in the world; it is also, among the industrialized countries, the state with the most relatively liberal immigration and naturalization laws. This reason alone is seen as enough incentive for permanent relocation.

What I am suggesting is that the interviewees in the book are defining themselves and their country specifically against the United States, and against Filipinos in the United States. The latter are the Other—though not exactly Other, but really Otherwise. For Filipinos in Abu Dhabi, Jeddah, Singapore, Yokohama, Kuala Lumpur, Melbourne, Madrid, Cologne, London, and Hong Kong, staying away permanently is not an idea that is as viable—or a possibility that lodges itself as deeply in the national imagination—as the notion of eventually settling in Chicago, Hialeah, Houston, Baton Rouge, Kodiak, Fresno, Seattle, or West Covina. I am not discounting those Filipinos in the United States who do not intend to stay permanently, but the lines outside the U.S. embassy on Roxas Boulevard in Manila are an obvious manifestation of how deeply woven into the national fabric the possibility of relocating to America is. And within this horizon of expectations lies Daly City.

Betrayal versus "Home Service at Its Best"

The distinction between leaving and staying away can itself be subsumed under a broader opposition between Filipinos in the United States and in the Philippines: it is that of money and of the nation. As we see from the interviews above, the self is posed against the nation: the self, with its dreams of material success, is to be renounced in the service of the nation. E. San Juan, Jr., in his inimitable overripe way, has described Filipinos in the United States as having "dutifully internalized the ethos of bureaucratic individualism, the ABC of vulgar utilitarianism, inculcated by the media and other ideological apparatuses in the Philippines and reproduced here in the doxa" (San Juan 1994, 7). But though he follows his pronouncement with a discussion of his frustrations concerning the apolitical Filipino community in the United States—"fragmented and inutile" are his words—his rhetoric similarly falls within the binary construction of money versus nation.

For the interviewees of Cruz and Echauz (1993), the "pull" of money goes against the strictures of nationhood and an untainted Filipinoness. One of my interviewees from Daly City, Michael Santos, makes the same distinction between Filipinos in the Philippines and in the United States through his reference to a conflict between "matiryalismo" and "nasyonalismo." Though it was possible to be a Filipino nationalist in the United States, he said, how can you be nationalistic here if the culture that, you know, is westernized . . . ? You're in a different country, unless you're in the Philippines, where you can really devote your being, you know, there. Here, there's nothing [you can do], even if you're nationalistic, you're doing something for a cause, but you don't know what's happening there because you're not there. In a way, it's possible, you can send support, if there is fund-raising for a cause in the Philippines, that's a possible way to help, just to show that you still, you know, your country.

In the course of our conversation, Santos told me that Pinoys in the United States. can certainly be "nationalistic" too, if they contribute to relief programs in the Philippines and the like. After a pause, he added, "I guess that's not much." The paradox here is that it is precisely money, thought to be antithetical to loyalty to the nation, that itself provides the catalyst for heroism undertaken for the nation's sake. The quest for money, amidst the privations of other lands, can make heroes of OFWs. The acquisition of money, then, does not taint equally. Its corrupting power lies in the seemingly singular capacity of the United States to evoke feelings of betrayal among the "nationalistic" middle classes who have been left behind.

This difference partially explains the odd erasure of the figure of the overseas contract worker from the nostalgic sweep of the interviewees' answers reported by Cruz and Echauz. Again, the contrast between leaving and staying is employed rhetorically. In the case of OCWs, the circulation of money is controlled, kept mostly within the confines of the nation's borders, in a comparatively straight path from worker to family. It is the money earned and circulated outside by green-carded immigrants in the luxury of the United States that is detestable. Nowhere do Filipinos in the book admit that some people seek their fortunes overseas because they must, in order to support their siblings and children.

The irony is further compounded by other reasons given in Cruz and Echauz (1993) for staying:

> I detest housework. I need someone to keep house for me, cook meals, wash and iron clothes, so I can pour my energies into development work, helping the poor and making this country a better place.
> —Victoria Garchitorena, Executive Director,
> Ayala Foundation (19)

> The orchids I have grown. Efficient maids to prepare meals while I rest from the day's work.
> —Edna Formilleza, former Undersecretary
> of Education (31)

Maids, *yayas* [nannies], and drivers—home service at its best! Bora-cay, Dakak, and Palawan [expensive beach resort areas]—heaven next door!

—Isabel Yotoko, writer (83)

I don't have to do house chores. I have four maids and a driver doing everything for me. I'm a queen at home.

—Mariela Corpus Torres, housewife (113)

I don't need a weather report to help me decide on my wardrobe for the day. My housemaids give me freedom and leisure time for a job and entertainment outside the home. At present, in terms of the inflated-peso value of my old house, I can call myself a millionaire.

—Sylvia Ventura (133)

I can wake up in the morning and not bother making my bed, know-ing somebody else will do it.

—Antonio Concepcion, Senior Vice-President and
Chief Marketing Officer, La Tondeña Distillers (191)

"Home service at its best," indeed: the irony of this class blindness is not lost on most readers, who will remember the hundreds of lower-class Filipino women working as maids and babysitters overseas. The convenience of hav-ing maids not only affirms one's class standing, but gives one a reason—or indeed, *the* reason, as some interviewees admitted—to stay in the Philip-pines. The people quoted see maids as better off working for Filipinos and earning paltry wages than working abroad and being able to stretch the riyal or Hong Kong dollar further.

My position contrasts with Rey Ventura's rather simplistic and often-echoed assertion, "The richer you are in the Philippines, the more likely you are to go abroad and to settle there for good" (1992: 164). This is true perhaps only to the extent that the Philippine income of those who have left for good has been able to support partially—but not fully—the re-quirements of their class position. Hence their departure in pursuit of the "fundamental" accoutrements of middle-class status (the wide screen tele-vision, the car, the house in the suburbs—all products advertised in *Philip-pine News*) already attained by those who can "afford to stay" in the Philippines.

The interviewees of Cruz and Echauz (1993) also suggest a link between class and nation: that one's class perquisites allow one to grow more fully as a Filipino. Their maids not only purchase more time for their jobs, but more opportunities to pursue and gain cultural capital.[6] Ironically, it is the emigrants, then, who tentatively put themselves in a better position to consume these more legitimized products to shore up their class standing. But from the perspective of Manila, to live in the United States inhibits the possibility of leisure that the middle class requires; "Here we are real people, not shadows holding two to three jobs to survive," says a deputy manager of the Lufthansa office in the Philippines (Cruz and Echauz 1993, 191). As Pierre Bourdieu writes, ease "represents the most visible assertion of freedom from the constraints which dominate ordinary people, the most indisputable affirmation of capital" (1979, 255). As we have seen, the efficiency of maids—which includes removing the burden of making one's bed—makes the middle-class Filipinos "real people" and frees them up for "more efficient service" to the nation, to make it "a better place."

To be maidless in America (and losing that particular class marker) seems reason enough to keep the upper middle class in its place.[7] Its members can therefore be "silent heroes," in contrast to those who have left the homeland in an act of betrayal. Perceptions of this betrayal are parlayed into interesting stereotypes—not really perpetrated through social power, but through their numbing repetition—which at many times, however, seem completely contradictory to each other. Filipinos in the United States can both be praised (and reviled, at least by San Juan) for their financial successes and condemned for their abandonment of the sinking ship that is the Philippine state. Only those deemed to have been extraordinarily successful (and therefore worthy of a certain worldwide acclaim)—in the nineties, the actress Lea Salonga and the businesswomen Loida Nicolas-Lewis and Lilia Clemente, for instance—escape the clutches of cash and its ability to taint, and are embraced by national belonging once more. The contradictions in these stereotypes are even more clearly seen through the relatively uncomplicated prism of Philippine film.

---

[6] The paradox, of course, is that most of the cultural capital to be acquired in Manila comes in forms engendered by American media, particularly films and television (with cuisine and, to a lesser degree, fashion as exceptions). I hasten to add, however, that the products and experiences in which cultural capital inheres are not necessarily of American provenance. The advent of globalization has, in interesting ways, standardized what it means to be "middle class" or "upper class."

[7] A few may remain undaunted by the "problem" of maidlessness, such as wealthier Filipino immigrant families with their own *yayas* in tow, allegedly paid well below minimum wage. But for most, the need for a maid is usually met by petitioning for one's parents who, if already retired, end up staying at home to take care of the grandchildren.

Material Success and Filipino Authority

A movie starring the Filipino comedian Dolphy produced in 1994, called *Home Sic Home*, paints the same sort of portrait of life in America. A widowed repairman leaves his family behind in the Philippines after being petitioned for by one of his other sons, who resides in the United States. (Both visa and plane tickets arrive in the same envelope.) The son has "changed" and become irrevocably yuppie: he and his Filipina American wife drive an expensive car and live in a comfortable home in the suburbs of Los Angeles. After the obligatory travel to San Francisco, Hollywood, and Las Vegas, the widower soon realizes that life in America is not what he expected. His son leaves him at home on weekdays, and he is afraid of using the phone to call long distance without his son's knowledge. Things get worse, for he is essentially left at home to take care of his grandson, who is bratty, thinks his grandfather is odd and, worse (at least in the context of the film), does not understand or speak Tagalog.

Efren Jarlego's film follows the widower's misadventures in looking for a job with his friend, played by the late comedian Panchito: they find employment as hospital attendants very easily. The bad guys come in the form of two INS agents who investigate the widower's green-card marriage to another Filipina, played by the much younger Dina Bonnevie (they eventually fall in love with each other). Dolphy's character gets into a car accident and, at his hospital bed, the grandson, blinking away tears, promises to learn Tagalog. The widower recovers and decides to return to his less well-off son in the Philippines.

The 1995 film *Sana Maulit Muli* (Would That It Happen Again), directed by Olivia Lamasan, illustrates the same conflicts, but the pressure of money in this example is most strongly contrasted to romantic ties. Aga Muhlach plays Jerry, an advertising executive in Manila who refuses to give up his career to be with his fiancée Agnes, played by the Tony award–winning actress Lea Salonga. Agnes's mother, who had abandoned her at a young age, has just petitioned for her to come to the United States. But Agnes grows more despondent each day: she is shown getting terribly lost in San Francisco, she ends up cleaning bedpans, her mother treats her as a servant, and her new, bratty siblings dislike her. "I don't belong here," she says, and thinks of returning, but realizes, "Ang daming halos magpakamatay na makarating dito" (There are so many who would almost give their lives trying to get here). Despite her pleas to join her, Jerry decides to wait instead for his promotion, telling Agnes that he is not ready to marry.

Deserted by Jerry, Agnes finds a job doing difficult, menial work in a seniors' home. Then the film fast-forwards a year and a half: Agnes has now become a successful real estate agent and has already bought a beautiful A-frame house in Half Moon Bay. Jerry suddenly reappears, to face a completely different Agnes: harried, consumed by work—but also self-confident, aggressive, her voice without a trace of her old Tagalog accent. Jerry finds a series of odd jobs as an illegal alien, chopping up logs at a lumberyard, cleaning cars on a lot, and washing dishes at a Filipino restaurant. But their occupations are not the only tables that have turned. Agnes is now unwilling to commit to their relationship: "inagaw ka nang ambisyon sa akin" (ambition grabbed you away from me), she tells Jerry. After quitting his job (where he is cheated out of his wages by the Filipino manager), he asks Agnes to marry him now or go back to Manila with him. Agnes refuses him twice. "It's not true that everyone wants to live here," Jerry says before he leaves for the Philippines. The film ends improbably with the woman (of course) abandoning her career, the couple reunited on the streets of Manila.

These films reflect and distill the image of the Pinoy in the United States according to beliefs held by people I have spoken to in the United States, and by Filipinos in the Philippines as well. The films work with tropes easily recognizable to their audiences in Manila, alluding to a familiarity of sorts with images and situations of the Filipino immigrant life. The films' success in Manila depended not on novelty, but on how they reinforced expectations of what immigrant life in the United States was like. The long, back-breaking hours of work, victimization by fellow Filipinos, the personal transformation of immigrants upon their arrival (however "accurate" these perceptions may be) and, most important, the "inevitable" return to the Philippines, are images the two films produce and affirm. Dolphy's son has earned his money at the expense of his soul and is redeemed later only by his belated profession of allegiance to family. Evoked in these films are transnationally shared standards of class—the house, the car—signs recognizable in a transnational grammar of wealth. Similarly, the naturalized, mythic trajectory of upper-middle-class wealth is reaffirmed, although the films upset it by (of course) making romantic or familial love triumph over a lucrative career, or the possibility of one.[8]

Another stereotype affirmed in these films is the widely held notion that Filipino children raised in the United States are spoiled and rude to their elders. Their bad behavior is attributed to their upbringing in a different environment. But more integral to *Home Sic Home*'s theme, which is echoed in *Sana Maulit Muli*, is its obsession with language. Language becomes a more

---

[8] Indeed, as can be seen from newspaper columns, films, and television talk shows, the biggest toll exacted by the circulation of migrant labor worldwide has been on the family, regardless of what form it may have.

potent national symbol in a foreign context, and it is used to patrol the perimeter of national belonging. As we saw in Chapter Three, one often hears such comments from first-generation immigrants as "But she's not Filipino, she doesn't speak Tagalog" when referring to Filipino Americans (especially young people) who were raised in the United States.[9] Filipino Americans in a symposium I attended at Skyline College (with predominantly Filipino American students) in San Bruno, California, complained that recent immigrants, on finding out that they do not speak any Philippine languages, would say, "Sayang [Too bad]. You should learn"—thereby, in their words, questioning their identities as Filipinos.

Another complaint that I often hear is that some Filipinos in the United States pretend they do not speak Tagalog. For instance, Mike Santos told me, he "[got] really annoyed at Filipinos here who, what do you call it, I don't know if they do it on purpose, those who you think do not know how to speak Tagalog, but know how to speak Tagalog, and don't want to speak Tagalog, and keep using English." He continued: "It's most annoying of all, lalo na kung halata mong marunong magsalita [Especially if you can tell that they know how to speak]," he added.

Certainly, distinctions are tricky; by no means does every immigrant understand Tagalog. But the regular irritation displayed by those who cling to Filipinoness reflects the seeming artificiality of English when spoken by a Filipino, who, regardless of location, *must* speak a Philippine language. English and an American accent are also connected, as in the Philippines, to status. "Anong klaseng pataasan nang ihi iyan?" an informant colorfully commented, comparing American accents among Philippine-born Filipinos to a pissing contest. The borders of the nation are constantly defended in the minutiae of everyday life.

The movie protagonists' easy ascent into the reaches of the upper middle class, and the price of that ascent, ties in with other stereotypes as well. In 1974, in the early days of Marcos's balikbayan program, Letty Jimenez-Magsanoc wrote a rather catty essay in *Philippine Panorama* derisively describing the people referred to by the newly coined term:[10]

---

[9] In the mid-'90s film *Ang Syota Kong Balikbayan* (My Balikbayan Girlfriend), Anjanette Abayari plays a beautiful Filipino American who visits the Philippines and keeps getting into fish-out-of-water situations, and whose heavily English-accented Tagalog is milked for laughs. But a great deal of the movie's humor comes from the action star Fernando Poe, Jr., whose clumsy attempts to speak English provoke much of the audience's laughter.

[10] The balikbayan program was, in essence, a massive public relations campaign for Marcos to drum up positive publicity to conceal the terrors of martial law, and to show expatriates in the United States that his *Bagong Lipunan* (New Society)—a phrase that did not outlive his regime—was for the good of the country. Balikbayan season officially began on 1 September 1973, reaching out to

She gushed forth with all the Americanese adjectives she'd picked up . . . that indicate beyond a doubt to her friends . . . that their *Balikbayan* really knows her English. She even pronounced Tondo with a long O.

This particular *Balikbayan*'s name used to be Patsy but since she migrated to the Land of the Free and the Land of the Brave, she's become Pat.

When interviewed, a *Balikbayan* [with no green card, the writer stresses] blurted out: "I'm so glad to be back in your country . . . er . . . I mean, our country."

When the *Balikbayan* goes shopping (bless his darling dollars), he strains his arithmetic, multiplying and dividing dollars by *"paysus"* whenever applicable. If the figures add up right, he goes on a buying spree.

Throughout the essay, Jimenez-Magsanoc's pointed remarks revolve around either the balikbayan's increased capacity to spend or the horror of how expensive imported goods are: "The prices of goods imported from the States dismay the *Balikbayan* . . . shaking his head feeling sorry for his brother Filipinos who will go to their grave without ever having sunk their teeth into the luscious softness of Three Musketeers or *Playboy*'s Playmate of the Month" (Jimenez-Magsanoc 1974). Again, she refers to the immigrant's relationship with money, coinciding with the loss of qualities of Filipinoness.[11]

---

about 700,000 Filipino "residents and their descendants" in the United States. Marcos rolled out every come-on he could think of: a temporary tax holiday from the Department of Foreign Affairs; the creation of a special military tribunal focusing on crimes committed against tourists, to try and decide cases within 24 hours; a National Hospitality Committee, headed by his wife, Imelda, to ensure that "government officials will see to it . . . that guests at all times will enjoy courtesy, honesty, convenience, safety and security; that the generosity of the guests is not abused, even by their own relatives, through a public education program"; discounts on airline fares and hotel and food rates, and in shops selling "native handicrafts"; and free medical and legal services, in case "some of these Filipinos may have legal problems about property or inheritance cases" (Alvarez-Bihis 1973, 15). The program also paved the way toward the institutionalization of the OCWs' monetary role, beginning with the early temporary migration to Saudi Arabia in the mid-1970s.

[11] The quaintness of the "Three Musketeers" aspect of Jimenez-Magsanoc's observation is due to the fact that extremely liberalized import laws in the mid-'80s—part of the International Monetary Fund and World Bank structural adjustment programs—have allowed the huge influx of imported candy bars and such into local *sari-sari* (variety) stores. Even now, fewer and fewer locally made products are on supermarket shelves in the Philippines, and many of the commodities—from

Interestingly, her irritation also registers on a linguistic level, as she mocks pronunciation, vocabulary, the changing of names, and slips of the tongue. The implication is that the betrayal of the nation is perceived and played out not only on an everyday level, but on a practically unconscious plane—or it may even be, as Jimenez-Magsanoc seems to imply, a deliberate linguistic affectation.[12] (This is in interesting contrast to the so-called glamour of English—indeed, its very currency—as seen, amusingly, in the phrase *spokening dollar*, a reference to speaking English, but with a sly, knowing distortion of grammar.) This general loathsomeness attributed to the upper-middle-class Filipino immigrant, whether in the United States or back in the Philippines—she calls them "Balikyabang" (*yabang* means "to boast")—plays out on both class and national levels.

Filipino Class Divisions in Daly City

The very obvious class differences within the Filipino immigrant population of the last thirty years complicate the usually homogenized image of Pinoys in America as successful and upper middle class. The image of Daly City as suburb triumphant, coupled with the "model minority" myth that some Filipinos seem to celebrate gleefully, obscures a significant number of declassed laborers. As noted earlier, the years following 1965 saw the migration of mostly middle-class medical and scientific professionals. Today, as a result of the aforementioned demographic shift to family-reunification preference immigrants (and economic decline), many Filipinos have ended up employed well beneath their educational attainments:[13] as babysitters, parking attendants, security guards, clerks, Navy cooks, waiters, janitors—all members of the so-called service industries. Stories abound of nurses and physical therapists being underpaid and forced to work only on night shifts.

These occupational woes, in turn, allow for the formation of distinctly class-based epithets like "mga patapon sa atin" (trash back home) and "halatang biglang yaman" (noticeably nouveau riche), descriptions uttered by

---

milk and paper napkins to potato chips and cookies—are imported, usually from Australia, Malaysia, Hong Kong, and the United States.

[12] The epithet *Amerikanong hilaw*, loosely translated as "unripe" or "uncooked" American, is usually used (derogatorily) to describe biracial Filipinos, but is also employed against Filipinos who speak Filipino languages heavily accented with American English.

[13] As I mentioned in Chapter Three, only three Philippine universities—the University of the Philippines, Ateneo de Manila University, and De La Salle University—are recognized for "accreditation" purposes in the United States. But diploma mills are, unfortunately, a dime a dozen in the Philippines, and so this "underemployment" is not as prejudicial as it may seem.

some of my informants. Certain Filipino restaurants in the Bay Area, for instance, are said to be frequented by the "sosyal" (higher-class), and others are said to be "bakya" (lower-class)[14]—despite the fact that the main differences in the restaurants' clientele more often have to do with age than with perceived economic standing.[15]

Daly City reflects these class differences behind a screen of upper-middle-class homogeneity. The late activist-scholar Helen Toribio—interviewed for this book in her capacity as a former counselor with the Pilipino Bayanihan Resource Center based in Daly City—describes the city as having a "kind of this superficial image like it's very upper middle class," citing its "projection overseas in the Philippines." She stresses how Daly City is seen abroad: "They don't show this side of Daly City," she says referring to the Top of the Hill district, bordering the Ingleside section of San Francisco. "These are poor neighborhoods of Daly City," Toribio explains to me; about 2,000 Filipinos, constituting almost 31 percent of the population in that census tract, inhabit this older, somewhat rundown neighborhood. It is mostly in the Philippines, and in crafted images like films, that Filipino immigrant life takes on the glow of the successful bourgeoisie. This image coexists uneasily with often-recited stories of immigrant sacrifice, of being "shadows holding two to three jobs just to survive," stories that are ultimately blurred into the soft glaze of upper-middle-class prosperity. It is, in effect, a similar kind of class blindness that glosses over the countless nannies and gas station attendants.

For instance, a statistic often cited by Filipinos ranging from community leaders to magazine publishers is that the annual median household income of a Filipino family is about $14,000 higher than the United States average, according to the 1992 Census Bureau Current Population Report (U.S. Bureau of the Census 1992). (In fact, average Filipino household income, at $43,780, is even greater than the comparable white household income, calculated at $38,909.) But these numbers are misleading: Filipinos have a higher number of persons per household, which certainly inflates total household income. Among Asian families, Filipinos have the highest proportion of families with three or more income earners. Such households constitute 30

---

[14] A reference to the wooden clogs worn by "the masses," *bakya* also has the connotation of being gauche. The *bakya* is not worn much anymore, but the expression lives on.

[15] To return to maids: Raul Pertierra astutely observes that "much of the media outrage about Filipinos working overseas is directed as much to the fact that they are working as maids than that they are potentially exploitable. The growing image overseas of the Filipino as maid is what is objected to. This low view . . . undoubtedly reflects the views of the Philippine elite who resent that the country's image is shaped by their social and cultural inferiors" (Pertierra 1992, xv). A class-based blurring again occurs when one considers that many domestic workers are college graduates or former professional employees.

percent of all Filipino households; for the whole United States, the comparable figure is only 13 percent.[16]

Being in the United States does seem to make it easier for declassed workers to acquire certain markers of the middle-class life even as they lose others. An interviewee marvels, for instance, at how easily one can put a down payment on a new car in America. All this is in contrast, the interviewee says, to the conditions in the Philippines: he pays his taxes, "and nothing ever happens; look at our roads," he adds. In the United States, a car and a house in the suburbs are, for many Pinoys, not far out of reach, thanks to the magic of credit and thirty-year mortgage rates. Ultimately, money in America gains a kind of elasticity not seen in the Philippines. Money goes further and allows the consumer to choose from a wider variety of products.

I want to pose what newspaper columnist Hermie Rotea called, as early as 1972, "the six-times mentality in relation to the dollar-peso exchange rate" (4) as a contrast to the reasons given earlier—typified by an atmosphere of so-called traditional Filipino values—for staying in the Philippines. My informants often cite corruption and inefficiency of the government as reasons for leaving the Philippines. But it is clear that frustrations concerning money and the dimming purchasing power of the peso are what primarily spur the immigrant to leave. Nevertheless, standards of living in the United States are deceptive, San Juan claims; he writes about the "mutable exchange rate of dollars to pesos" and how, "ignoring cost-of-living disparities," this becomes the true "opium [*sic*] of the masses" (1994, 4). Actively computing the exchange rate, particularly before purchases, is described as something only tourists and very recently arrived immigrants do. This mathematical slippage, an operation revealing a primary orientation towards the homeland, conceals the class disparity behind the monthly paychecks.[17] The differences in cost of living are glossed over; it is the sum that counts—and the car and the house that go with it.

A related paradoxical "state," in opposition to this affluent veneer, is "second-class citizenship," an often-cited condition of Filipino immigrants

---

[16] John Silva, the former associate publisher of the San Francisco–based magazine *Filipinas*, bemoans the lack of recognition of "consumer strength" in the Filipino community in the United States. "We buy cars, we have 20 billion dollars' spending power," he said in a talk at the University of California at Berkeley on the future of ethnic publications in April 1995. Citing a study showing that *Filipinas*'s subscribers' second car is a Mercedes-Benz, Silva went on to say, "I get so upset that up to now, there is no recognition of Filipinos as consumers." *Philippine News* (1995; 2,4) similarly cites "a reliable 1991 marketing study" that estimates Filipino buying power at $52 billion annually.

[17] Mahler describes the same phenomenon among Salvadoran immigrants: "It may be difficult to believe that people can make these calculations without figuring in the cost of living in the United States, but this is precisely what happens" (1995, 56).

in the United States, which suggests, as one of the interviewees above puts it, a "first-class" citizenship in the country of one's birth and, by extension, belonging. ("Second-class citizen? Serbisyong-bayan muna [Service to the nation first]," Aga Muhlach says in the movie *Sana Maulit Muli*, once again evoking the binary opposition.)

The concept of second-class citizenship implies a certain political awareness: of a denial of rights to minorities, for instance, or the experience of racism. But in this case, second-class citizenship has nothing to do with the traditional associations of rights or responsibilities. Perhaps it really revolves around "class" rather than "citizenship." Living first class in the Philippines, "as a Filipino should," and according to the dictates of one's class, primarily entails a capacity for consumption; it also means not having to work two or three jobs, or not working at a job incommensurate to one's education. (Indeed, the phrase *second-class citizenship* is hardly used in the Philippines itself, even to refer to the poor or ethnic minorities.) Once again, this concept highlights the importance of money, the lack of which brings one a step closer to tainted money from overseas. Those without the wherewithal to live as they "should," or "could," leave, and stay away, and are in turn branded as outside the ambit of Filipinoness.

This second-class citizenship in the United States has its peculiar "advantages," however, which are illustrated by this conversation with Wally Curameng and Debbie Patron:

DP: [Wally] didn't like the social system, financial—the class system back home.

WC: Here there is less—

DP: Less discrimination.

WC: Yeah. Separate the rich from the haves and the have-nots. The haves and the have-nots can mingle . . . as opposed to the Philippines. [There] the haves look down on the have-nots.

BV: And the wealthy Filipinos here, they don't look down on Filipinos who—?

WC: Not as bad. Not as bad.

DP: They're not as bold about announcing—they're not as bold at expressing the fact [that they are wealthy] than they are back home.

WC: They're too conscious—

DP: —their power is lessened.

BV: Because it's not—

DP: Because it's not their birthright to be able to act that way when they're here. Versus in the Philippines, it is your birthright when . . . you are wealthy. A birthright to look [down on] the masses—and when they go here, that's hard.

This semblance of an equality among Filipinos was not part of Curameng's many preconceptions prior to coming to the United States. Neither was it cited by my interviewees as a reason for leaving the Philippines, though one assumes that the so-called injuries of class partly impel a search for better opportunities abroad. But the loosening of this caste-like rigidity in class status after migration to the United States is not seen as the triumphant result of American liberal democracy. Rather, the wealthy Filipinos' "power is lessened"—a recognition of their common lot as first-generation, second-class citizens finding their footing and relearning marketable skills in a new homeland. In contrast to the "discrimination" in the Philippines, this was an unexpected improvement for Curameng, but as he and many of my interviewees learned, that perception of being in the same boat together was not the basis upon which solidarities could be built.

Filipino immigrants in the United States are caught between parallel discourses of heroism and sacrifice—one issuing from the country they left behind, the other from political exiles and Filipino American activists—and they are seen to fail to be accountable to both. Their perceived cultural transformations as immigrants in a harsh (but ultimately generous) country, and their seeming inability to sacrifice and serve the nation have turned them into something less than Filipino. But the fact that the films discussed here end with a return to the Philippines is not lost on the Filipino audience—the prime targets of the films—as it affirms the rightness of their beliefs: that Filipinos are corrupted by wealth and American culture, and that they should just stay where they really belong. The message is that there is hope for a kind of redemption, but one that cannot be achieved without a physical participation in the common sufferings (and everyday heroisms) of the Filipino nation.

In interesting ways, however, little of this filmic discourse mattered much to the Filipinos in Daly City. The films I have mentioned, for instance, are all readily available for rent or purchase, and are locally distributed in Daly City. But the consumption of these images in Daly City is largely unremarked. A good number of my interviewees had actually seen *Sana Maulit Muli*, but had surprisingly (and disappointingly) little opinion regarding the movie, saying "Ganyan talaga dito" (that's the way it is here) or commenting on how good the acting was. If anything, the film provided some amusement in Daly City precisely because it was filmed in the San Francisco Bay Area; this was also why posters of the film were displayed prominently in Daly City video stores at the time of its release. As in the *Philippine News*, the audience members could see themselves on the big screen; the Daly City viewers saw themselves in the old immigrant narratives—of the importance of hard work in a harsh and lonely place—already fashioned for them.

This form of recognition is crucial, particularly because the films— far from being "just" fantasies—reflect particular empirical realities as well. For starters, the films reinforced commonly held beliefs regarding second-generation Filipino Americans. Similarly, some immigrants proved "lucky" in their gamble (or worked backbreaking jobs) and struck it rich; others ended up working below minimum wage. This the audiences knew. For both audiences in the Philippines and in the United States, the films provided a form of validation of their beliefs. But Pinoy viewers in Daly City see themselves as both Filipino immigrants *and* from the outside as critical Filipinos from the Philippines. This doubleness is perhaps what enables them, as spectators and as participants, to navigate the palpable cultural differences without having to acknowledge feelings of guilt overtly or to internalize accusations of betrayal. But the problem with this doubleness—this immigrant predicament turned transnational fantasy—is that it cannot be sustained emotionally for very long, and certainly not physically.

This sense of recognition (or, to be more precise, misrecognition) could be channeled into legitimate, and not just symbolic, resistance, and I turn to a more recent example to illustrate this. In late September 2007, the ABC television network broadcast an episode of its hit show *Desperate Housewives* which unwittingly resulted in a mini-firestorm of controversy. Horrified at hearing from her doctor that she may be going through menopause, the ditzy housewife (played by Teri Hatcher) blurts out to her physician, "OK, before we go any further, can I check those diplomas? Because I would just like to make sure they are not from some med school in the Philippines."

The response was swift and angry. An online petition demanding an apology from ABC—a lukewarm one was later delivered—was promptly circulated and as of early 2008 had received over 128,000 signatures (obviously not all from the medical profession); a few weeks later, the writer of the petition, Kevin Nadal, was profiled on the front page of *Philippine News*. This newspaper, as did practically every Filipino media outlet both in the United States and in the Philippines, featured the ongoing controversy prominently, with updates on the case running every week.

The petition said, in part:

As members and allies of the Filipino American community, we are writing to inform you that this type of derogatory remark was discriminatory and hurtful, and such a comment was not necessary to

maintain any humor in the show. Additionally, a statement that de-
values Filipinos in healthcare is extremely unfounded, considering
the overwhelming presence of Filipinos and Filipino Americans in
the medical field. Filipinos are the second largest immigrant population in the United States, with many entering the U.S. (and successfully passing their U.S. licensing boards!) as doctors, nurses, and
medical technicians. In fact, the Philippines produces more U.S.
nurses than any other country in the world. So, to belittle the education, experience, or value of Filipino Americans in health care is
extremely disrespectful and plain and simply ignorant (Filipino
Americans Demand for Apology from ABC and Desperate Housewives
2007).

A month later, the Northern California chapter of the National Federation of Filipino American Associations (NaFFAA) was reported to be filing a
$500 million class-action suit for defamation (which was later abandoned)
on behalf of the Filipino medical community in the United States. NaFFAA
would later demand that ABC hire Filipinos both on and off screen, and that
ABC incorporate plot lines or characters in its TV shows that portrayed Filipino doctors and nurses in a positive light. Similarly, the newly-formed Filipino American Leadership Council, a coalition of prominent Filipinos and
doctors quickly assembled at a conference in Las Vegas, insisted on the airing
of an historical documentary on Filipino physicians in the United States, and
on the deletion of the scene from future broadcasts or DVD versions of the
TV series. Calls for boycotts of ABC and its affiliate stations were circulated,
and photographs of Filipinos picketing in front of the ABC studio offices
(and in front of branches of Disney Stores, ABC's parent company) were published in Filipino American newspapers.

The reaction from Filipinos was not unanimous, however. Some readers
of the *Philippine News* argued, in letters to the editor, that the show's writers
surely got the idea from a recent scandal regarding the leaking of answers
during a nurse's licensure examination in the Philippines in 2006. (This resulted in the blanket denial of U.S. certification to Filipino nurses who took
the test that year, but it is doubtful that the writers were aware of this.) Nonetheless, it was rightly perceived as an insult—except, most crucially, by writers from the Philippines.

In a *Philippine News* column entitled "The Disconnect" from October
2007, the characteristically intelligent Rodel Rodis soberly analyzed the reaction to the controversy from Philippine-based columnists like the *Philippine
Daily Inquirer*'s Conrado de Quiros (who, by his own admission, "laugh[ed]
out loud [at] Hatcher's remark"). Rodis concluded that, with "their 'get over

it' attitude", there was a "disconnect": that "Philippine commentators get to watch Filipinos on TV every night, in various roles both positive and nega- tive," in contrast to the absence of Filipinos on American television. More- over, "Philippine television is generally not subject to the same 'fairness' standards that American TV networks are subject to" (A7). But De Quiros was not alone in suggesting that Filipinos in the United States were too thin-skinned, or lacked a sense of humor, or had misplaced priorities.[18] An- other Philippine-based newspaper columnist, William Esposo, similarly wrote in the *Philippine Star*:

> ... In typical Filipino fashion, we've over-reacted once again over what can be considered as nothing more than one issue in [a] long line of misinformed racial slurs that are commonplace on US televi- sion. I say over-reaction because why should we be so enraged and incensed over a one-line put-down in a TV fiction-drama when we can be so quiet about the high crimes that are being committed on our people by our own elite and political leaders? (Esposo 2007)

Such campaigns against the U.S. media are, in fact, not new. Some of the controversies of the last two decades that have prompted the most outcries have been about misrepresentations of Filipinos in the mass media. Invoking hurt national pride, people have protested the equation of the word *Filipina* with "housemaid" in one edition of the Oxford Dictionary (a false rumor), the disc jockey Howard Stern's on-air insults ("I think they eat their young over there," he said, referring to the Philippines), and the characterization of Filipina mail-order brides on the NBC TV sitcom *Frasier*, among other recent mini-scandals. But as Rodis argues, "'expatriate' Filipinos have united on this 'Desperate' issue more than any other issue in recent memory." Why, then, the curious dismissal from writers in the Philippines, who seemed to downplay the importance of the incident?

The answer may also lie in the dynamics of recognition and misrecogni- tion. Indeed, this occurs on two different levels: that at the lone moment that Filipino doctors are recognized on mainstream American television, they are

---

[18] There is no question that the writers of *Desperate Housewives* were indeed ignorant, and that such a line was predicated on the enforced invisibility of Filipinos in the American workforce. Such a sentiment, particularly if circulated through a medium like television, can indeed be damaging to the reputation of Filipino doctors everywhere. But to have this be the primary issue to galvanize the Pinoy community in the United States is indicative of an anger tied to a particular class-based privilege. At most Filipino-based protests I have witnessed in the Bay Area—whether for affirma- tive action, or outside the Philippine Consulate in San Francisco over extrajudicial killings, or against deportation—the protesters are overwhelmingly native-born and in their '20s.

in fact "misrecognized." The angriest people of all were those Filipinos in the United States who recognized themselves being slighted on TV. This did not seem to matter to those Filipinos in the Philippines, who, as those people who stayed put back home, simply did not see themselves on the screen.

It is ironic that this "exercise in empowering a community" (Rodis 2007, A7)—indeed, a genuine effort at resistance—should be viewed as "conforming to the predatory Filipino character" (Esposo 2007). But such are the associations with arrogant balikbayan from the United States, suddenly insecure about their own statuses; medicine, in particular, is considered by Filipinos to be one of the most prestigious occupations, with its practitioners therefore the recipients of the most wealth in the United States. When the Philippines regularly deals with other diasporan emergencies—domestic helpers in peril, or truck drivers held hostage in Iraq—perhaps a campaign against a three-second line on American television seemed petty in comparison.

Questioning the Postcolonial

The past colonial link still haunts the present and renders the relationship of Filipinos to the United States problematic and therefore quite different from the experience of Filipinos elsewhere. But the case of the Philippines in relation to the rest of the world is, of course, by no means unique; one can see Filipino migration as merely part of the long history of migration from peripheries to cores (or colonies to metropoles) and vice versa. Still, postcolonial (or, as some might argue, neocolonial) relations set Filipino migration apart in this regard from other traditional reasons for migration like economic or political pressures alone. Although financial reasons may ultimately be the primary impetus, Filipino migration is necessarily complicated by history and America's lingering place in the Pinoy consciousness. The Philippines' historical position as a former colony of the United States, and the inculcation of "American values" through the educational and political system, are factors that must be considered in any contemporary analysis of the two countries.

Seen through the prism of postcolonialism, the Filipino immigrant experience seems to take on a different cast from the circumstances of many other immigrants to the United States. But does this automatically complicate ideas of home and belonging? How does it affect the attitudes of Filipino immigrants and, in turn, the attitudes of Filipinos in the Philippines toward those immigrants in the United States? Does the past colonial link between the United States and the Philippines render the Filipino immigrant experience substantially different from that of other immigrants to the United

States? Such questions seem to lose some of their power when seen in the less rarefied light of ordinary life. Current Filipino immigration to the United States can be understood as less a postcolonial effect than as simply part of a worldwide movement. Filipinos may idealize and fantasize about the United States no more or less than do other immigrants.

"Americanization" is certainly an observable phenomenon: America's hold on Filipino fantasies can be vividly seen in my interviews, for instance, which are testimony to the social power of imagination and the cultural and economic power of the United States.[19] But Americanization is by no means unique to the Philippines. For instance, it could easily be argued that globalization, or at least worldwide popular culture, is largely American in flavor and provenance. Much of the technology, capital, ideas, commodities and popular culture that spreads unevenly across the globe is centered in the United States (Hall 1991, 27), and therefore the Philippines, in that sense, is hardly exceptional. The late-capitalist "Americanization" occurring in the Philippines is perhaps merely part of the same process overwhelming the rest of the world and not necessarily continuous with the Americanization of the colonial period.

Much has been written about the idea of colonial mentality—that Filipinos hold their former colonial masters (in this case, in reference only to the United States, and not, in an interesting example of historical blindness, Spain) in absurdly high regard as a result of their colonial subjugation. Much historiography and contemporary Filipino American scholarship has directly proceeded from this assumption.[20] In this respect, Filipino immigrants to the United States would be held most guilty. The notion of colonial

---

[19] One can constructively compare what has long been called the Philippines' "love/hate relationship" with the United States to the latter's place in the South Korean imagination, as Nancy Abelmann and John Lie (1995, 62) describe it:

> Through military and civilian contacts, the United States became at once an object of material longing and materialistic scorn, a heroic savior and a reactionary intruder. Material desire and moral approbation, longing and disdain, have been twin responses to many of the trappings of American culture. . . . These are not fixed positions with adherents who espouse one or the other, but rather reside together both in the South Korean collective imagination and in private memories. It does injustice to the full-bodied nature of the South Korean engagement with the United States to assume that images of the United States are fixed or one-dimensional.

Similar vacillation—by Filipinos in the Philippines and in the United States—can be seen clearly in my interviews.

[20] It is worth noting as well that many discussions of Filipino colonial *mentality*—and, therefore, colonialism and postcolonialism in general—necessarily foreground the subjective as influenced by the material; in slight contrast, discussions of economic imbalance, core-periphery relations, etc., take place under the rubric of the *neocolonial*.

mentality, in the last three decades, has been naturalized as part of Filipino identity. It is the ideological burden that confronts nationalism in the Philippines and at the same time haunts immigration to the United States. "The reality of U.S. colonial subjugation and its profound . . . effects," the writer E. San Juan, Jr., has asserted repeatedly, "distinguish the Filipino nationality" (1994, 2).

Like many scholars and activists, Renato Constantino has argued that this colonial history has produced "a pervasive cultural Americanization of the population, exhorting Filipinos to regard the American culture, political system, and way of life as superior" (1987, 2). Americanization, San Juan writes, overdetermines immigration even at a somatic level: "So long before the Filipino immigrant, tourist or visitor sets foot on the U.S. continent, she—her body and sensibility—has been prepared by the thoroughly Americanized culture of the homeland. . . . Filipinos find themselves 'at home' in a world they've lived in before—not just in Hollywood fantasies but in the material culture of everyday life" (1991, 117).[21] I find interesting San Juan's provocative claim that Filipinos find themselves "'at home'" in the United States—that is, that there is a *lack* of disjunction between the two places at the moment of arrival—but I find it grossly insufficient as well, for it glosses over the many cultural adjustments immigrants have to make. "Infused with images of U.S. abundance," Yen Le Espiritu writes, "Filipinos quickly took advantage of the 1965 changes in the immigration law" (1995, 19).[22] Colonial mentality and the configurations of colonialism/postcolonialism are therefore seen to impel immigration itself and, ideally, assimilation into the metropole.

But the entrenchment of "the colonial" in discussing Filipinos in the United States is so strong that even non-Filipino scholars have followed suit. Lisa Lowe writes, for instance, that "the American citizen of Filipino descent [is] simultaneously immigrant and colonized national" (1996, 8). Such ahistorical pronouncements, smoothing over the complexities of the immigrant experience, do not advance the field. This same "crippling" history of "colo-

---

[21] Oscar Campomanes also writes that "Filipino Americanization can . . . be understood as a function of U.S. colonialism and its aftermath in the Philippines (the term 'Filipino American' can be thus recharged, instead of the conventional problematic of immigrant hyphenation). . . . Americanization for Filipinos does not so much as commence at the point of arrival on American soil as it does from the point of departure itself" (1995, 147).

Alejandro Portes (1990) makes a parallel argument concerning Mexican migration, as he points out that the United States had already created and shaped the flow of labor out of Mexico long before the government declared crossing the border illegal.

[22] I hasten to add that immigrants from numerous countries, even those with strong states, were similarly beguiled by American prosperity.

nial subjugation" has, in many ways, permeated much of Filipino American studies in general.

To take one example: in her introduction to a compendium of contemporary Filipino American scholarship, Maria Root writes, "Colonization ravaged the souls and psyche of the indigenous people of the archipelago. . . . The traumas associated with colonization that lasted almost 400 years scarred us all, regardless of our nativity, language, class, or gender" (1997, xi).[23] There is not much room for resistance here. Similarly, in an essay (in the same volume) entitled "Coming Full Circle: Narratives of Decolonization among Post-1965 Filipino Americans," Leny Mendoza Strobel relates her apparently successful "decolonization" sessions with U.S.-born Filipino youths, in which "[naming] internalized oppression, shame, inferiority, confusion, anger" is "a necessary phase in the development of a healthy Filipino American cultural identity in the United States" (1997; 63, 66).

The impact of colonialism is seen as reaching across borders and generations, and deep into the recesses of the unconscious: "Acknowledging themselves as victims and understanding how they were victimized are today the most urgent challenges for Filipinos everywhere" (Rimonte 1997, 59), writes another scholar in the same collection. But it is unclear how colonial "trauma" is inflicted upon the current generation of Filipino immigrants and even Filipino Americans, as Root and Strobel claim. Starting at a point of "internalized oppression" and victimhood makes unsupportable assumptions about an entire ethnic group's psyche and glosses over more subjective determinants of migration.

One may, for instance, compare the numbers of Filipinos worldwide and place the United States in a more properly global context. In 2007 alone, 1,012,954 migrant laborers—only about 200,000 less than the year before—were processed by the Philippine Department of Labor and Employment for departure overseas (Department of Labor and Employment 2007, Philippine Overseas Employment Administration 2006). Primarily working as domestic helpers and factory workers (together the two occupations accounted for almost 50 percent of the total new overseas hires in 2006), overseas Filipino workers were responsible for a record-breaking $11.9 billion (from January to October) in remittances (Department of Labor and Employment 2007).

Here I juxtapose these numbers with the almost two million Filipinos in the United States, about a million of whom emigrated between 1981 and 2006. This comprises the largest population, as could be expected, but the numbers need to be considered in comparison to the yearly migrant exodus

---

[23] See also Vergara (1999) for a review.

alone. As of December 2006, for instance, there were eight million Filipinos outside of the country (Department of Labor and Employment 2007). Whether they are maids in Hong Kong or in Rome, or engineers on an oil field in Saudi Arabia, or construction workers in Baghdad, or merchant seamen aboard an oil tanker, or musicians in a Beijing hotel lounge, this empirically clear scattering of Filipinos around the world belies the teleology of a mere postcolonially motivated migration to the United States. It is but one country, though a particularly large one, among many, with the main difference, in terms of immigration and labor policy, being a crucial one: the possibility of citizenship.

There are numerous variations on the reasons for immigration. Assertions regarding colonial mentality, though they inform discourse on Filipino immigrants, are not necessarily characteristic of Filipino immigrant lives. Pinoy migrants are neither simply pulled by the call of the postcolonial nor willingly plunged headlong into the embrace of American society. Filipinos come to the United States to live "better" lives as Filipinos, even though better lives may require the loss of what they wish to preserve their Filipinoness. To focus on postcolonialism alone is to miss how Filipino migrants see and experience the world. Reliance on the postcolonial as a general explanation for Filipino immigration to the United States obscures more complex circumstances for individuals and deprives migrants of agency.

I do not argue that colonialism and immigration are unconnected. There is no question that the excesses of colonial governments (and, now, an increasingly globalized world economy) created, or exacerbated, the gross economic inequalities that push people out. And colonialism surely does operate on a "semi-conscious" level: it can be argued that its absence in my interviewees' statements places it, at least, in the realm of the inarticulable, whether through repression or poverty of vocabulary. But the colonialism is neither a necessary nor a sufficient condition for immigration. Even accusations of betrayal, while clearly referring to immigration to the United States, are not associated with any kind of anti-American ideology, but are simply linked to the corrupting power of American currency. Pinoy immigration to the United States needs to be understood as a more complex, economically pragmatic process, and not just as a "progression" simply reducible or attributable to the colonial. These complexities can be seen, as we will view in the next chapter, in the tenor of immigrant anxieties, as expressed in nostalgia and homesickness, or, indeed, their absence.

7

CITIZENSHIP AND NOSTALGIA

~

If the immigrant predicament requires the careful balancing of obligations to homeland and new home—as manifested in the acts of turning
and turning back—then it is made all the more difficult by perceptions of
betrayal. Citizenship, or the act of naturalization, is one of the more defini-
tive acts that can foreclose the possibility of "turning back." To become an
American citizen is to accept that state's protective guidance and, most important, to uphold that country's practices and beliefs and ostensibly re-
nounce another's. This characterization is, of course, not entirely accurate, as
such a scenario is not encouraged in today's self-avowed multiculturalist society. Nor is it likely to happen in real life. Culture is not a zero-sum game,
but citizenship is still seen as casting one's lot in another place, deciding to
belong somewhere else, and forgoing the possibility of return—and therefore
seen as a lack of *pakikisama*.

Filipinos are said to covet American citizenship highly; anecdotes abound
of pregnant women in their third trimesters attempting to enter the United
States and deliver a child there to "guarantee" an immigration petition in the
future. Filipinos from the Philippines who enter the U.S. Navy, for instance,
are generally understood to be doing so to gain a foothold in applying for a
green card and later citizenship.

My interviewees from Daly City reveal a wide range of attitudes toward
naturalization, from ambivalence and rejection to a strategic practicality.
They are able, however, to "return" another way, through nostalgia, homesickness, and the simple assertion of ethnic identity. Such a turning back is in

itself socially generative, but not in any conventional manner; it is, perhaps, what characterizes Daly City and the Pinoy immigrant community. Although both processes figure in the emotional lives of my interviewees, they occupy a larger role in the public sphere in the form of commercialization and consumption.

Citizenship and homesickness/nostalgia can be seen as turns in opposite directions, as different manifestations of a longing to belong: one, to the place of origin, and the other, to the place of arrival. But what looks like nostalgia on the surface may be its opposite. What appears to be an eagerness to gain U.S. citizenship is not always what it seems, either. Is it still possible, or even desirable, to go back?

Going Back

"Are you going back?" is not the most politic of questions.[1] The notion that one could be merely a temporary American has been offensive to many (politicized) Asian Americans. Though the significance of sojourning has long been established in Asian American history, particularly among Chinese American laborers in the late nineteenth century, contemporary scholars and activists have taken great pains to stress the transition from sojourners to settlers. The idea that Asian Americans, some of whose families have been in the United States for generations, are somehow less rooted (or committed)—or, to stretch the implication further, less American—is misleading and sometimes fatally wrongheaded, as the internment of Japanese Americans during World War II demonstrates.

But insistence on the permanence of Americanness obscures a kind of flexibility seen among immigrants in a more globalized age—a fluidity, if not in identity, then at the very least, in life options. People do go back and forth; some people, like Teddy Encinas's father (who is retired and a U.S. citizen), want to spend their retirement in the Philippines. Some people can afford to spend half the year in the United States and half the year in the Philippines. Aihwa Ong's work (1999) on Hong Kong businessmen[2]—who travel back and forth between the United States and Asia, leaving their wives and children in

---

[1] A corollary is "Where are you from?" Asian American Studies classes (like political speeches by Asian Americans, I might add) I have attended or audited, particularly at the undergraduate level, invariably begin with prodding the Asian American audience to recognize how they are seen by the mainstream as "not belonging." As a discursive strategy, it is employed largely successfully because it keenly resonates with its listeners. But the Filipino respondent—or rather, the immigrant Filipino respondent—will not necessarily take offense.

[2] Or "astronauts," so called because they are said to spend more time in the air than on the ground.

the United States—focuses on people under heightened transnational circumstances.

But it is also in the traveling that the difference between Ong's subjects and my Daly City interviewees lies: most Pinoy families in the United States cannot afford to travel often, much less shuttle back and forth between the two countries. For all the talk about transnational migrants constantly shifting between boundaries, there are many others who are, in a sense, physically immobile. The world of the transnational—of airplanes, faxes, e-mail, and satellites—is, as always, limited by money. And for most, it is not a matter of returning, but simply of visiting. Teddy Encinas and his family, for instance, have always wanted to visit the Philippines—he has not been back since he arrived in the United States in the '70s—but the cost of travel, he says, has prevented him. One deterrent is that he does not have anyone to stay with, and his family's properties (which were uninsured) burned down some time ago. His father's relatives in the Philippines have also been squabbling about their property. "It's like I want to, it's like I don't want to. . . . That's what's hard about the Philippines, the government is a mess and stuff—in the event things suddenly become chaotic, I don't want to get stuck."

He started to tell me that there would be "high emotions" all around if he returned, as he was the one (among all his siblings) who was closest to their cousins, because he grew up with them. But then he continued:

The others are struggling because you know, the trends in their lives are changing, it has become either you're rich or you're poor, and they're the ones that are like—they're not really poor, but they're making money just to survive. When I leave, they're going to go back to the same level where they're struggling, they're trying to survive. It's like I'm thinking of the emotional, they're happy when I'm there, when I leave they'll return to where they were before [masaya sila nando'n ako, pag-alis ko balik na naman sila sa kagawian na dati]—that's what I'm thinking.

Encinas's reasons for not going back, aside from the cost, are due to factors in the Philippines itself, like family quarrels and his fears about safety. Part of his hesitation also had to do with his mixed emotions concerning the relatives he left behind. He feels some guilt—guilt because his migration to the United States has made life better for him, unlike those he left behind.

Nancy Navarro seldom returned to the Philippines, primarily because there was "nobody to visit anymore." But as with other interviewees, unsettled assets created friction between family members. In her case, the lack of wills in the Philippines made it impossible to determine who inherited a deceased relative's property. Navarro's husband's family had the same problem—"we're finding out that some properties are ending up in somebody's name already even though you own them," she explained.

Navarro told the story of some friends who wanted to retire in the Philippines, but had to return to the United States because their renter of 13 years refused to leave and threatened them at gunpoint. "So a lot of Filipinos are realizing that going back home is not going back home." As in Encinas's case, home was, literally, not home anymore. Dislocation can be both physical and emotional; one cannot go home to a place that is not—literally and figuratively—home anymore.

My second-generation Filipino American students often speak about "going home," referring to the Philippines. But the Philippines is technically "home" only for their parents; members of the second generation cannot "return" to a place they have never been before. Such an imagined home may exert much influence on the thoughts of the younger generation, but they may find that their conceptions have little to do with the reality of life in the Philippines.

Navarro's children have also been to the Philippines, but it was not, in any sense of the phrase, "going back home."

> They've gone back there twice, to look at it. They said they liked the people, Filipinos are nice, they're very friendly, they're very caring, but it's not a place they'll live in. They said, they freaked out on nobody paints the houses. Because there, right, nothing is painted. They said the bathroom is always wet. And then, the flies, that really freaks them out when they step on food, and they don't know where it's been stepping all over the place, it could be stepping on poo or something, and that freaks them out.

Indeed, Navarro's children's comments sound much like the complaints that Jimenez-Magsanoc placed in the mouths of her "balikyabangs" in her 1972 essay—perhaps more reason, then, to feel ambivalent about homecomings.

A deacon at a predominantly Filipino church in Daly City told me, humorously, of older members of his congregation who would say farewell to him before their retirement in the Philippines. A few months later, he said, they would be sitting in his pews again. When asked why they came back to the United States, the returned parishioners would cite "in order: the traffic, the heat, the mosquitoes."

Alice Bulos's political commitment meant that going home is not an option for her; her sense of belonging is already deeply rooted in the United States. She has not been to the Philippines since 1986 (when she went to visit her remaining relative, a sister), and she has no desire to move back because she foresees problems of adjustment—primarily because her expectations have already changed. "Because here in America, straightforward, it's black, it's black, it's white, it's white, it's a yes, and it is a no," a reference to the difference in politics in the United States and in the Philippines.

Kiko Novero is very clear about not going back:

> I don't want to go back any more. Because the only reason I would want to go back is to see my friends. But you see, when you go back there you still think, oh your friends are still going to be there. But you have to realize that all of us have grown up. And in a way you might still think that they're still the same. But in reality, they too have moved on, they too have their own lives now, they take care of their own families, their own jobs. You still might think that they'll still be there for you the way it used to be. I'm sure it's not that way anymore.

He is faced with a dilemma, however. His parents are now saving up and working hard, said Novero, because they are planning to retire in the Philippines in two years. "By that time my mom's gonna be 62, 63, which means she's still not qualified to get a bigger retirement check, so she's saving as much money as she can for the retirement in the Philippines."

Novero has also thought of going back, although he thinks he should finish school first to get the credentials. But the problem of security in the Philippines prevents him from embracing the idea of returning wholeheartedly.

> KN: You could be rich and you could have all the material things, but then again, like the authority figures which are supposed to maintain law and order, you can't even trust them, I mean, what if I'm gonna raise my kids . . . ? So I'll just try to stay here, where at least you can trust the authorities.
>
> BV: So they're going to retire there. And leave you again here?
>
> KN: Um-hmm. That's why I'm working very hard too.
>
> BV: So are you thinking of going back?
>
> KN: If I go back, everything that my parents had sacrificed—my dad still looks back sometimes and "you know what, Kiko," he says to me sometimes, "I think Kiko, the things I'd sacrificed, all the things that I had in the Philippines"—'cause my dad originally didn't wanna come here, only my mom. My mom was thinking about us, my dad was thinking about himself, and his position . . . and his security would be nice, and sometimes he'd tell us, for

instance, "if I only stayed, I'd probably . . . be high up . . . already, and getting a good pension plan and everything, but because of you guys, because we wanted you guys to have a brighter future, we sacrificed," and they really did. In fact sometimes I feel sad because it's like, they don't really have a lot to show for it? It's because all the work is basically been given to us. It's a very selfless kind of thing.

Novero's story illuminates the paradox at the heart of his parents' migration: they migrated to give their children "a brighter future"—in a place where "at least [one] can trust the authorities"—which resulted in their children being left alone in the Philippines.[3] But now that Novero's parents want to retire, their son cannot be with them either, because leaving the United States seems to invalidate his parents' sacrifice. There is a very real emotional price to pay for the decision to migrate.[4]

What seems clear, however, is that the possibility of return no longer appealed to many of my interviewees. For some, return was not an option because they had already gotten used to a higher standard of living in the United States, whether in hygiene, or politics, or job opportunities. But for most of my interviewees, the passage of time (and not really the distance) had irrevocably altered what was "home": friends had moved away and lived different lives, houses had changed hands, and so on. Or, perhaps, it was the opposite, as with Encinas: *he* had changed, and time, tragically, had done nothing for his relatives. The distance from looking back to going back seemed, sadly, unbridgeable. One may as well stay.

On Citizenship

Perhaps homologous to the historical transition from sojourners to settlers is a similar transition from Filipino immigrants to Filipino Americans. There are, of course, problems with such a comparison: nineteenth-century Chinese immigrants were branded "sojourners" (and other things besides) as justification for denial of equal rights. But the homology works in the sense that both are changes toward something more permanent. One may argue that a kind of politicization, or political awareness, takes place (or should

---

[3] Rhacel Salazar Parreñas (2005) writes movingly of women who work as nannies overseas while leaving their own children (who grow up without their mothers) in the care of other domestic helpers. The recent Filipino feature film *Anak* (Child) by Rory Quintos gets most of its melodramatic mileage from such circumstances.

[4] Novero's parents have since returned to the Philippines and retired with the rest of the family in tow—except for Kiko, who is still at his same job of almost ten years.

take place) at that juncture; another may say that the passage into the category of Filipino American is conferred only through citizenship. Some activists claim that there should be no political difference between "FilIms" (short for "Filipino immigrants," as one interviewee put it) and "FilAms," for they are subject to the same social structure and system; others distinguish very clearly between Asian Americans and members of the Asian diaspora. For Alice Bulos, the political activist, being Filipino American is intrinsically tied to the responsibilities that come with residence in the United States.

Ultimately, conceptualizing a pattern for such a transition hews closer to earlier, more rigid models of assimilation and integration. This theorization is by no means intellectually spurious, even if I use a largely discredited model here. Robert Park's concept of assimilation (1950), as the final stage of a cycle of interactions between immigrants and mainstream American society, posited the inevitability of the dissolution of ethnic differences. Park's theories were intellectually allied with those of anthropologists who challenged biological conceptions of race, but disregarded the indelible inscription of racial difference that prevented any total integration. Ethnicity as an "insurgent" paradigm against race was largely based on the experiences of white European immigrants, and was therefore seen as inapplicable to people of color (Omi and Winant 1994, 14). But Park's formulation—as taken from migration studies to race relations—still exerts a fierce hold on popular, extra-academic discourse about ethnicity and race, as seen in my interviewees' views about assimilation in Chapter Three.[5]

Of course, external factors from bureaucratic classifications[6] to acts of injustice may animate or intensify a more self-conscious formulation of identity. Previously established categories (particularly regional identities), on arrival in the New World, change gradually into something new and more inclusive—moving from seeing oneself as Sicilian to seeing oneself as Italian American, for example. This is the generally accepted paradigm for immigrant identity. Espiritu (1992) similarly observes that Asian American "pan-ethnicity," or a pan-Asian consciousness, is only a recent phenomenon born from the civil rights movement of the '60s; even then, cleavages between ethnicities, the native-born versus the foreign-born, and even generational lines (as seen in the Daly City election) prevent pan-ethnicity from being a potent political force. But in most cases, definitions of belonging and identity—or

---

[5] My Asian American students, for instance, often speak contemptuously of "whitewashed" Asians, listing a catalog of their traits. Such characterizations are a direct offshoot of sentiments of ethno-racial pride.

[6] Censuses have historically slotted—or rather, forced—individuals into orderly state-formulated ethnic, racial, and ancestry categories. One Daly City interviewee, Simon Romero, told me that he was "Filipino American, of course. That's what I check on application forms, is why."

"Filipinoness," or "Americanness," or "Filipino Americanness," for that matter—are ultimately arrived at subjectively.

When I began my interviews, I overestimated the importance of belonging to particular categories. U.S. citizenship is popularly thought of as a long-sought grail for immigrants. But for my interviewees, great ambivalence still surrounds the decision to opt for American citizenship.

Wally Curameng had no plans to apply for U.S. citizenship; his experiences in the Air Force made him see "what Americans are." Indeed, the only change he foresaw with gaining citizenship was the chance "to travel all over the world without applying for it. That's the only reason." For him, practicality in traveling (an erroneous belief, at that) was its only benefit. His disillusionment had to do with his naïve expectations and his experiences with racism:

> BV: But was this feeling that America was discriminating—you were unwilling to become part of America because of what you experienced and what you saw?
>
> WC: I just ignore that, because the more I think about discrimination, the more I would hate the country. But what's the use of staying here if I regret coming here—it's as if I don't want to make things harder for myself [parang ayoko pang pahirapan ang sarili ko]. I'm already here in the States, if you cannot fit, just try your best to fit in.

Curameng actively repressed his recognition of racism—the more he thought about discrimination, the more he would regret his decision to immigrate. Things would be harder, he said, if he did not perform an act of repression within himself. This, perhaps, is another facet of the immigrant predicament, similar to the stereotypical "caught-between-two-worlds" image of the "marginal man": the best way to deal with cognitive dissonance was repression.

Michael Santos, who has been a permanent resident for two years, was not interested:

> I don't know if I'm even willing to give up my [Filipino] citizenship. If there was dual citizenship I'd like that better. As far as—I still don't know what the advantages are if you become a citizen, what benefits you'll be getting, so I still want to find out, if it's more, maybe. But I know some people who are not giving up their citizenship, although they can already [apply for citizenship], they still haven't done it.

He explained that most immigrants enjoyed the rights of a citizen anyway, except for voting. He cited the example of his mother, who was able to receive the same security benefits citizens received even though she had only permanent resident status. He added that he was not very interested in politics in the United States because he could not vote.

In retrospect, Santos's comments were surprising, coming from a social worker involved with recent immigrants—surely he was aware of the rights (or lack of them) that an immigrant, documented or undocumented, had. But his comments perhaps exemplify the strong orientation toward the homeland that he and other Filipinos in the United States have. Santos did not elaborate on his reasons for not opting for American citizenship, but understandably he was most interested in its possible benefits.

A form of "cultural" loyalty is reflected in Jun Bautista's conception of citizenship, different from Santos's more utilitarian considerations. Bautista's family had considered the possibility of American citizenship, but it was not a pressing issue. As the eldest daughter put it: "Maybe it's possible, but it's only in name anyway. But of course, your real self ['yong talagang sarili mo], of course, whatever happens, is still Filipino. You will never lose the culture you grew up with." For her, American citizenship (and culture, by extension) is an overlay over the "real" Filipino culture; it would be a change "in name" only. Again, for her, being Filipino was an essential category, and it was immutable regardless of change in citizenship status or location. The category of "U.S. citizen" does not diminish, an indignant immigrant might say, any sense of Philippine national belonging.

Bautista started enumerating the advantages of becoming an American citizen, particularly the right to vote—"that's when you will be able to speak [doon ka na makakapagsalita], about politics, that's when you can get involved in politics." But in contrast to his daughter's conception, the disadvantage was the removal (*pagtanggal*) of "something, 'yong code ng Pilipino [the code of being Filipino]." I asked him what this *pagtanggal* meant, and he cited as an example the way many immigrants would break into tears after taking their oath of citizenship. Bautista interpreted this phenomenon not as tears of joy for finally gaining U.S. citizenship, but as tears of sorrow for "renouncing" Filipino identity. His interpretation revealed how he personally felt about naturalization.

Bautista's family has still not decided whether or not they will stay in the United States permanently, primarily because they have just arrived. They still feel quite ambivalent about immigrating. "Hindi naman sa gusto, hindi rin sa hindi gusto, parang in-between" (It's not that we like it, it's not that we don't like it, it's kind of in-between), one daughter said. "Siyempre medyo high ka pa rin" (Of course we're still kind of high), Bautista said.

His enthusiasm was still there, and he was not losing hope, he added. "All I'm saying," he said to me, "we are still unable to answer that question."

And so I was left dangling, and so were they. But is this state of perpetual indecision characteristic of an immigrant community? That is, was it possible that, as Filipinos in the Philippines left their life options open, so did Filipinos in the United States? Or was this ambivalence simply a manifestation of a need to hold on to the possibility of return to prevent the obliteration of ethnic identity by assimilation? Bautista's ambivalence is reflected as well in the pages of *Philippine News*, in the way it expresses different longings and straddles national boundaries. His statements represent a contrast to the previous answers from people who were sure they were never going back; for Bautista, belonging or not belonging was a decision deferred. For some Pinoy immigrants, going back may not be an option—a possibility they may not have realized yet—but perhaps they performed their repeated turning in other ways.

Homesickness

At the very beginning of my study, I had specifically planned to investigate homesickness and nostalgia, to look at the conditions under which they emerged and at the objects of immigrants' longing. I thought that those emotions would be prevalent and would be part of the process of repeated turning. Crucial to the emotion of homesickness are the recognition of difference between the two places ("here" and "home") and the heightening of those differences. Intrinsic to the nostalgic impulse is an act of self-delusion, where the faraway (or the past) is reconfigured as closer to the ideal. The work of nostalgia involves a rewriting of the past that selectively discards experiences that may not be pleasurable. Recovery (or more properly an attempt at recovery) of the past in the nostalgic process is necessarily predicated on a distortion of reality in which events are cast in a warm, fuzzy glow.

Initially, nostalgia, which was once thought to be a disease, had the same meaning as homesickness; it is clear that nostalgia in the seventeenth century referred only to a spatial distance. By the twentieth century, particularly in America, nostalgia and homesickness had diverged in meaning. In the 1950s, nostalgia had come to signify any vague yearning for the past. By the 1970s, both nostalgia and homesickness increasingly revolved around images created by mass media—not the homeland, nor the small town, nor childhood, even—and functioned as a commercial enticement by which products and events could be pitched to consumers. By that point one reached the correspondences held popularly today: homesickness with space, nostalgia with time. Here I roughly conform to the space-time distinction between homesickness and nostalgia as presented above, although it should be apparent that they could be interchangeable, depending on their usage. "Home," for instance, may be a vague notion of a literal physical space or location that is also associated with the past; in that sense, a longing for home can be construed as both nostalgia and homesickness.

Although Philippine literature, for instance, is suffused with nostalgia, the American penchant for nostalgia for particular decades—the '20s, the '50s, the '60s, et cetera—and its resulting commercialization, has little relevance in the Philippines. The most prevalent nostalgic image in the Philippines is that of bucolic peasant and village life in the nineteenth century, as depicted in Fernando Amorsolo's paintings, for instance.

Homesickness in the Philippines is a different matter. More often than not, the English word *homesick* is used; for instance, "naho-homesick" (being homesick) is cited by the *Overseas Filipino Workers Handbook* (Philippine Overseas Employment Administration 1996) as one of the problems facing OFWs, a condition which writing home and engaging in hobbies (playing the guitar, playing chess) would alleviate. Tagalog, for example, has no specific terms for homesickness, though the word *nangungulila* (being or feeling orphaned) is sometimes used interchangeably with homesickness. It connotes a generalized longing for home, but *nangungulila*—the root word is *ulila*, which means "orphan"—also literally refers to bereavement. There is something wonderfully poetic about the term, as it refers to a kind of mourning for one's parents, which here are conflated with one's homeland.

Most of my interviewees missed their friends the most—not just their friends, but the time spent with them, and the ease with which that time could be set aside. The hectic pace of life in the United States indirectly triggered a longing for home. Santos said:

> Now, I get sad because, things are different in the Philippines, here, you can see, it's different. There, every Friday, even if it wasn't Friday, all of your officemates could go out together, wander around, [see] neighbors; here, you can't, things are different here. You aren't able to do that. I could do that before, because I had a friend in my office who was also a recent immigrant. But now of course s/he's busy with her/his own. . . . I'm still trying to get used to that here. Homesickness, same thing, I miss the old stuff there, your friends, your relatives who you left behind, and the—the lifestyle there is different, it's different here, here you really have to be persistent and assertive, that's necessary, because—ah, he's shy, when you come here you have to learn to get along with others, to get along with the whites, they say they're outspoken, here, we Filipinos don't speak our minds,

but now I'm learning how to cope. The adjustment, my transition period, I think I've [gotten used to it], not like when I first arrived, of course, whites would be speaking English, you won't be able to pick up everything, the slang, but little by little you get it. But adjustment in the beginning was difficult—we didn't find it so hard, our families were near, so adjustment as far as loneliness—some people are unable to bear it, right, because you're alone. For us, almost all of us are already here, so it isn't that difficult.

Santos's train of thought in this quotation moves in interesting ways: from homesickness, to differences in lifestyle between the United States and the Philippines, to passiveness, and to difficulties in language. But his comments are also indicative of how homesickness is triggered: the pressures of the here and now—the alienation, the workload, the loneliness—impel the creation of an image of home, one always rosier than the present or the real. What provoke nostalgia and homesickness are circumstances in the present, and not from the past.

Santos elaborated further:

Maybe the time, the time I spent with my friends, my peer group—here I can't spend it like that, time here is always busy . . . That's what I like here, they're punctual about time, when they say sharp, they're there. In the Philippines it isn't that way, we'd have no plans, we'd just go. What do I miss there? Your company, you can't get that here, even from your fellow Filipinos, they're not that—they're not that hospitable—back home it's different, of course, Filipinos . . . here it's like you feel that you're not too welcome, something like that. There are also Filipinos who have similar feelings like that, probably because they're also in a hurry, they have their own things to do, you know. Take, for example, you have a friend . . . who's always with you. When he arrived here . . . but sometimes we don't even get to see each other because he's working, and now he has a family already, and now it is as if his time, he can't really spend on hanging out, he's always at home. At work, he's already really tired, he wants to go out, his body can't take it because he's too tired from work. . . . You really work to death here, you're tired from work.

For Santos, there is an interesting twist in the semantic drift between nostalgia and homesickness: he is homesick for time. But much of his feeling is related to the apparent coldness between fellow Filipinos; the exigencies of work (again, partly attributable to the obligations of immigration) make time unavailable.

Similar in tone was the answer given by Bautista's daughters. I had asked the same question (what do you miss in the Philippines?), and Ellen answered: "Megamall." (Megamall is an enormous shopping mall in Manila.) But it was mostly her friends for which she longed:

> EB: Like that, for instance, afternoon, you're not doing anything, even if it's late at night you can still be out, chatting with your friends, like that, but here, of course, the weather, like that, you can't do that, and of course it's hard to just go anywhere . . .
> BV: What do you miss in—what do you like here that you can't get in the Philippines?
> EB: Um—food is expensive here. Not that we find food so expensive, but it's not, here, even if you're poor, even if you're a laborer, you can still afford food. . . . Then, there are lots of sales.
> Jun Bautista (JB): Lots of what?
> EB: Lots of sales.
> JB: Ah.

Ellen enumerated things she liked about America: the shopping, the way one can do whatever one wants. But one disadvantage was that people were "independent," and the "other side" of being independent was that people were unable to become "close" to each other. People kept working and working, she added. The latter comment is similar to other interviewees' comments about life in the United States in general—the lack of time to be with friends, the hectic pace. Although immigrants understandably have to juggle their obligations to families both in the United States and in the Philippines, life in Manila is hardly more relaxed. But nostalgia works to efface the pollution and the traffic. This would be a refrain familiar to scholars of other immigrants, of other periods: "As the passing years widened the distance, the land the immigrants had left acquired charm and beauty. Present problems blurred those they had left unsolved behind; and in the haze of memory it seemed . . . they had formerly been free of present dissatisfactions" (Handlin 2002, 232).

My interviewees' homesickness and nostalgia were manifested in very different ways. For Novero, his nostalgia was intertwined with music and memories of a girl with whom he was in love. Indeed, he bought only Filipino music CDs "because I wanted to be reminded of her."

> Sometimes once in a while I'd still get into those moods when I miss the Philippines. Or I miss the way that it used to be—of course when you're in the Philippines, and then sometimes, we kind of always

wanna stay with how it used to be, for example, especially when you're young, you're not working, all that mattered to you were your friends, and then your friends were always there for you, and then you compare your life now—gosh, time is always on the go, and then sometimes you get depressed, or you get sad, and you think about those times, and sometimes you wish that those days were back again.

He admits, however, that he does not listen to Filipino music too much, "because it's gonna be pretty sad."

This is quite similar to how homesickness is triggered: not as a positive act of recollection, of active longing, but as an uncontrollable remembering of an undetermined set of associations—in this case, brought on by music. But the source of nostalgia always seems to come unexpectedly, and most importantly, from outside one's self: from a song on the radio, from the smell of crayons. In this respect, nostalgia has a processual similarity with Freud's concept of the uncanny; it resembles the recurrence of the repressed. Novero's memories are literally uncalled for.

Food is generally associated with homesickness, but few of my interviewees mentioned it explicitly. Santos, for instance, did not miss Filipino food, because most of the time he ate out at Filipino restaurants. Daly City could relieve that kind of homesickness more easily than almost any other place in the United States. "Before, I was in the Philippines, of course I would always crave American—McDonald's, like that—but now because there's so much . . . you want Filipino food all the time." He did miss vegetables; he considered vegetables in the United States to be tasteless. He added that he grew tired of meat here, particularly since here it was just "ordinary." In the Philippines, he said, one wouldn't be able to afford to eat meat every day.[7]

Most of the time, however, there is nothing to miss. As we saw in Chapter Three, many of the interviewees had discovered that home was not home anymore. Curameng said that he does not feel homesick anymore. For him, "the Philippines is just a place for me to visit." This was confirmed for him four months before our interview when he had tried calling up a college classmate (the only phone number he had), only to find that the man was working in Thailand. Nancy Navarro told me that she did not feel homesick

---

[7] Vegetables are often conspicuously absent from menus in Filipino restaurants in the United States—and, for that matter, from Filipino restaurants in the Philippines as well—most probably because they are seen as ordinary "poor people's fare." Except for *laing*—taro root leaves simmered in coconut milk, with chopped shrimp, and therefore difficult to prepare—regular dishes, if they are served in Filipino restaurants in the United States at all, often come smothered by little chunks of meat.

anymore. She was 19 when she left the Philippines, and she is now almost 50. "So I've been here longer. When I went back there, as a matter of fact, I felt homesick for here. So it was already the reverse." The dust and the heat of the Philippines were also too much for her, she said. As for her two children, "they'd never thought that was their home. They believe this is their home." Jun Bautista misses his relatives back in the Philippines, though he does not think he misses the place any more—only the traveling throughout Luzon. "Tapos na 'yon, siyempre, another chapter sa buhay 'yon eh" (That has ended, of course, that's another chapter in life). He does not get to talk to his relatives, either, because calling by phone was too expensive; they communicate only through letters.

Establishing connections with the Philippines, if only temporarily and indirectly, was a way of curing homesickness. During Novero's last visit to the Philippines, he brought a videotape camera and taped "everything [he] pretty much did," which resulted in about six videotapes. He even taped Philippine TV. Souvenirs—which arise only "out of the necessarily insatiable demands of nostalgia" (Stewart 1993, 135)—are therefore crucial to forestalling the possibility of the nostalgic past's permanent loss. Novero said,

So now I've begun to realize that gosh, everything changes, and the things, the people you care about, they're not always gonna be there for you, and it's sad reality but I think the truth. So the implications of what happened, I became more like a moments person, every time I'd start a big gathering, I'd always videotape them, every time we're gonna go out or just hang out with friends, I'd always take pictures, I'd tape it, or when I get home from work, I used to have a microphone like that and do my audio journal. I was doing that. But after a while, I just had all these stacks of tapes and pictures, I had twenty different rolls I hadn't even developed yet, it's so expensive, and I've probably 700 pictures I have developed and spent money on, so much money too. So I got over that stage, and I've accepted the fact that, hey, I've captured so many loving moments and great moments in my life already, this is enough. [*laughs*]

Teddy Encinas said he was certainly "curious" about what was going on in the Philippines—he read the news on the Usenet newsgroup soc.culture. filipino and watched the news or Philippine basketball games on TFC, "just to see the scenery, mga buhay-buhay [everyday life]. Kasi wala nang uuwian sa Pilipinas, eh [Because there's nothing to go back home to in the Philippines]." TFC was "his pipe"—"I'm not really completely disconnected; that's my way of knowing what's happening back home," he explained. He doesn't feel homesick, he says, just sometimes envious of people who are able to go back. "If money were easy, we'll probably—I mean, if we win the lotto, we're probably gonna go there right away."

But in other cases, television triggered a different emotion, as Curameng related:

I always feel bad when there are disasters that happen. In fact, that Ozone [fire], when I found that out on TV, I even cried. I even cried when I found out that many died. So there's—really, I really cried. Then, [the] Pinatubo[8] [eruption], I was even—no, during that time, Pinatubo, that was still shallow [medyo mababaw pa], I could still kind of ignore it. Then, what struck me at Ozone—I felt sad. And they were high school students, they were just having a good time. And I thought, during that time, when I was that age, I was happy. And they, they end up trapped in the fire.

Curameng's reactions to bad news are interesting, because they illustrate an association of empathy and nostalgia. The Pinatubo eruption he could still shrug off; the Ozone fire affected him primarily because he could see himself in the disaster; he could see himself on TV, as it were. This in itself was tinged with nostalgia—"when I was that age, I was happy"—in contrast to his current state of indecision about citizenship and repression of feelings of discrimination. Such empathy, and the reaction elicited from him, is perhaps only natural. But the crucial difference, one that prevents him from truly identifying, was the fact of distance; he was, after all, sitting on his couch in his living room in Daly City.

The bridging of that spatial distance could be effected more concretely. *Philippine News*, within its pages, reflects the "global," immigrant nature of its reading audience, and the Filipino community in general. Now let us look briefly at other "sites" of immigrant identity: Filipino "fiestas" and a cable network, where nostalgia is displayed in contrasting ways.

Movable Feasts and the Consumption of Filipinoness

I had initially thought of studying how Daly City's residents displayed what I saw as the nostalgic impulse. And yet nostalgia or homesickness did not

---

[8] "Ozone" refers to a disastrous fire at a nightclub in Quezon City called Ozone, where 160 students, celebrating their graduation, were trapped and burned to death in 1996. "Pinatubo," of course, refers to the eruption of Mount Pinatubo in 1991.

seem, on the surface, to be a constant preoccupation for Daly City residents. What most of my interviewees missed—as they said when pressed—were the times they spent with friends and family. That is, their memories represented a time when there was less work to do, and fewer obligations to fulfill. Homesickness was mostly experienced as a feeling of generalized longing, and not one that necessarily resided in places and commodities. I have suggested that this was perhaps because the originals were already everywhere to be found; one could not mourn for lost objects if they were not missing in the first place. Like Michael Santos, someone in Daly City would not have to miss or long for Filipino food because it was readily available. The global flow of commodities, in effect, hinders feelings of homesickness.

At the same time, however, the purveyors of goods and services are clearly capitalizing on a particular niche. Nostalgia and homesickness are incorporated into marketing strategies. There is therefore a direct relationship between nostalgia and consumption (and profit), and this, in turn, encourages a political and cultural dynamic in the Pinoy immigrant community in Daly City. We return full circle to an elaboration of one of the social functions of imagination: how nostalgia permits the conceptualization of different worlds and realities.

Every year, many Pinoy communities all around the United States hold events—fairs, festivals, and fiestas—of various sizes and degrees of lavishness. Vallejo, for instance, has a yearly Filipino celebration; Daly City has been holding a low-key, annual Fil-Am Friendship Celebration in the Westlake shopping center since 1994. There are at least two major events in the San Francisco Bay Area: the Fiesta Filipina in June, mostly funded by the Philippine Consulate, and the month-long Filipino American Arts Exposition in August. The latter is set up by a loose coalition of mostly Filipino American members of the community; many are artists, and so the exposition—held in conjunction with the Center for the Arts at Yerba Buena Gardens in San Francisco, and therefore receiving the benefits of the city's humanities grants—has had a highbrow, more intellectual feel. Art exhibits, book signings, and short film screenings sometimes run concurrently to the exposition.

Fiesta Filipina is a slightly different event, but the similarities between the two productions are remarkable, and understandable. Corporate sponsors are lined up for each festival, and so are companies and community organizations that will be hosting booths on the festival grounds (for Fiesta Filipina, at Civic Center Plaza in front of San Francisco's City Hall). With few exceptions, however, the sponsors (for both events) have almost always been the same, year after year. So are the booths, as the major sponsors generally get one. And so are the performers, who consist mostly of local talent;

for Fiesta Filipina, the headline act has almost always been from the Philippines.

For instance, the sponsors for the 2001 Fiesta Filipina included MCI, AT&T, Pacific Bell (all long-distance telephone carriers), LBC Air Cargo, Philippine News, TFC, Wells Fargo Bank, *Filipinas*, Jollibee, Philippine Airlines, KTSF Channel 26, Western Union, and the Philippine Children's Fund—with little change, the same sponsors as for the 1996 Fiesta Filipina (and, not coincidentally, some of the biggest advertisers in *Philippine News* as well). Large corporations typically have sizable outlays for ethnic-targeted advertising and public relations, and fund-raising becomes a matter of tapping the same sponsors every year. But the hugely corporatist presentation of the entire cultural event—with a religious parade as its centerpiece—strikes one as nakedly commercial. Although there is nothing altogether surprising about this commercialization, it should be clear that the festivals' self-avowed mission of promoting Filipino culture and pride are secondary to their function of gathering and showcasing businesses—from ambitious mom-and-pop stores and restaurants to multimillion-dollar corporations—under one roof. The $10 entrance fee to Fiesta Filipina—much of it going to the security company in charge of cordoning off a public square—underscores the financial nature of this "celebration of Filipino culture" and its odd distance from the community itself.

I attended one Fiesta Filipina in 1996. It was held in Union Square, in the middle of San Francisco's toniest shopping district. I arrived at about 9:30; people were still setting up their booths, except for the food stalls. About five or six stalls were selling the same greasy food, at the same prices: barbecue for two bucks each, *pansit*, *menudo*, and other Filipino meat dishes. One booth specialized in mango nectar and other tropical fruit juices.

The Philippine Consulate had a booth, with a dollar raffle for beach vacations to the Philippines. In one corner of the booth were musical instruments—guitars and such, seemingly lifted from some exhibit at the consulate on Sutter Street and left forlorn to one side of the tent. Teresita Marzan, then the consul general, was greeting people; on the main table were forms and brochures about remittances and balikbayan programs. I found it ironic to read the inscription on the Dewey Monument in the middle of Union Square and discover that it commemorated the "victory of the American Navy under Commodore George Dewey at Manila Bay"—in short, the beginning of American colonial domination in the Philippines after Spain's defeat in Spanish-American War. Before the Santacruzan parade made its way from the Civic Center and up Geary, I wandered around and collected lots of free loot: a pin with both Philippine and U.S. flags from the Philippine National bank, a magazine called *Hoy!* from the Filipino American Arts

Expo (they were also selling a black T-shirt reading "From San Francisco to Daly City" and showing a jeep crossing the Golden Gate Bridge), free copies of the *Manila Bulletin* and the *Filipino Monitor*, and various brochures (TFC, LBC, *Filipinas*).

Subsequent fiestas have been much the same. To entice people to visit the booths, hourly raffles are held, or freebies are given out: refrigerator magnets, pencils, calendars, newspapers, rubber erasers, condoms (from the Asian AIDS Project booth), magazines, ballpoint pens, and so on. There is not much variation in the stores and organizations that set up booths every year and at every festival—the same two bookstores (Arkipelago and Reflections of Asia), Regal Films (selling videos and CDs), a chiropractor service, a travel agency, and at least half a dozen booths selling more or less the same food. The booths at these festivals are almost always largely oriented toward the Philippines; except for the Asian AIDS Project and the Pilipino Bayanihan Resource Center booths, most had nothing to do with Daly City or Filipino life in the United States per se. But the composition of the booths reflected many of the Filipino businesses in the Bay Area anyway, catering largely to an immigrant clientele with immigrant desires and obligations.

I stood at the corner of Powell and Geary and watched the parade. The usual grandly sequined matrons preceded a phalanx of cheerleaders from Vallejo, the *Santacruzan* itself, the theater troupe Teatro ng Tanan's big puppets in a pickup truck (Jose Rizal, Andres Bonifacio, Tandang Sora—all Philippine national heroes—and three others who represent ethnic minorities), a *kulintang* band, and girls in native dresses playing a reggae version of the Filipino children's song "Bahay Kubo."

The Santacruzan is a traditional Philippine Catholic ceremony reenacting the search and finding of the cross of Christ by Emperor Constantine and Queen Helena (or Reyna Elena). It is perhaps the most enduring of festival processions in the Philippines, and the lavish production involved has long since turned it halfway into a beauty pageant. The gowns alone, along with the arches of flowers the participants walk under, run up costs considerably. A retinue of equally well dressed men accompanies each *sagala*, or lady-in-waiting, as it were, to the Reyna Elena. (There are sixteen, representing different virtues—Reyna Fe, Reyna Esperanza, Reyna Caridad [Faith, Hope and Charity]—and characters such as Mary Magdalene.) But beauty is not the sole criterion for being selected as a *reyna*, as a combination of community and political influence (of the reyna's parents) is also factored in.

The anthropologist Martin Manalansan has written brilliantly about cross-dressing Santacruzans in New York and how Filipino gay men "[reconfigure] the whole structure of the ritual" (1996, 61) via explicitly political or parodic images. The San Francisco Santacruzan, however, was much like those back in the homeland in almost every detail, as its main organizer, Ferdie Villar, told the *Manila Bulletin*. The gowns and tiaras were imported from the Philippines. One minor difference was that the parade itself had wound only a few blocks, from the Philippine Consulate to Union Square, its participants dwarfed by gigantic Calvin Klein and Levi's advertisements on the tall buildings above.

What struck me, however, was the fact—or, at least, what I think I observed—that most, if not all, of the reynas were half-white. A mestizo reyna is by no means out of place in the Philippines; Western/Caucasian standards of beauty have long held sway there, and half-white Filipino Americans have managed to get acting and singing jobs in the Philippines fairly easily, despite a lack of talent. For every reyna in the Santacruzan to be of mixed race was somewhat odd, however. (At first the perverse thought came to mind that the girls were the embodiment of Filipino-American Friendship Day.) But as I noted in Chapter Three, the figure of the Filipino American (and, perhaps even more, the mixed-race Filipino American) symbolizes a form of literal assimilation. This particular Santacruzan was not just a perfect replica of the homeland version, but one that "improved" on the original.

In the 1996 version I witnessed, the program began about 45 minutes late. A woman sang the American national anthem with the words "O Say Can You Sing." Everyone stood. Befuddled tourists took photos the whole time. Marzan came out and anchored her talk to places: Mactan, Bagumbayan, Pugadlawin, Kawit, Bataan, Corregidor, EDSA. High school students from Fremont performed an excellent *pandanggo sa ilaw* (the Filipino dance in which women dance with candles in their hands, or sometimes balanced on top of their heads). The program slipped after that, when the emcees started "padding" the moments spent waiting for performers to get their act together. Five guys wearing Hawaiian shirts and sunglasses did an Apo Hiking Society medley in Tagalog, complete with choreographed arm gestures, and then sang the Carpenters' "Rainy Days and Mondays." When I left, most of the crowd was huddling in the shadow of the Dewey Monument, trying to avoid the noonday sun.

Many Filipino cultural events (and those I have attended) are notoriously late and disorganized, and this one was no exception. But more to the point was the succession of Filipino folk dances (the *tinikling*, the *singkil*, etc.) and musical performances (folk songs and ballads from the '70s). Many of the performers reappear in festivals elsewhere—evidence of a relatively small pool of popular Filipino talent. But when I was watching the Fiesta Filipina in 1996, the general trend of the performances at that point, even at other events, was toward the Philippines; it has only been recently that local hiphop or rhythm-and-blues singing groups have been included. The lone stand-up comedienne, Ai-Ai de las Alas, who constantly made the festival rounds, lived and worked in the Philippines and performed her entire routine in Tagalog. The festivals' headline acts, even up to the present day, are almost always flown in from the Philippines.

In contrast, Daly City's annual Fil-Am Friendship Celebration, because it has less money, takes its roster of performers almost exclusively from Daly City. This year, for instance, the acts included a local dance troupe called Fusion, a white singer who sang Visayan songs, an *arnis* group doing a demonstration of their Filipino fighting skills, "the Filipino Elvis," and so on. Even though the sponsors were mostly the same—AT&T, *Philippine News*, Reflections of Asia, *Filipinas*, and Western Union all had booths—the performances were decidedly more low-key. (The less lavish nature of the festivities had to do with the location as well, as the event is always held in the empty courtyard in the middle of Westlake Mall, next to an everything-for-a-dollar store, a Linen Barn, a Christian bookstore, and a boarded-up J.C. Penney's.) My impression was that the more money the organizers had, the more they could afford to hire major entertainers from the Philippines—in other words, "the real thing."

Sometimes nostalgia may operate in divergent forms, pointing to a culturally different but perhaps more fruitful direction for Filipino festivals in the Bay Area. On a balmy day in August 2005 I attended the annual *Pistahan*, or Fiesta, organized by the Filipino American Arts Exposition, held at the Yerba Buena Center Gardens in San Francisco as it had been for the previous 11 years. The gardens themselves are something of a green oasis in the heart of the South of Market area, incongruously sandwiched between the Moscone Convention Center, the San Francisco Museum of Modern Art, skyscraping hotels, and, depending on the time of day, the shadow of the Metreon, one of San Francisco's largest shopping and entertainment centers. That afternoon, a few hundred people were out and about, either sitting on the chairs set up in front of the stage, or strolling through the booths. The usual corporate sponsors were there, but so were various community organizations (though the non-profit cultural groups were conspicuously exiled to the second floor, and therefore away from foot traffic). The emcees, politicians' spokespersons, and parade of performers seemed very much like those from previous festivals, including the requisite mini-skirted nine-year-old singing as if she were eighteen. (This particular one, however, sang " 'A'—You're Adorable," a song her parents probably picked out for her.)

There was a big difference, however. The dance troupes in "native" costume, specializing in Philippine dances, were supplemented by what seemed like half a dozen hiphop dance crews—all young, mostly Pinoy, Bay Area–based, and dancing energetically, with elaborate choreography, to high-energy R & B and hiphop. All this preceded that afternoon's musical guest of honor, the legendary hiphop turntablist DJ Q-Bert.[9]

This was clearly a different direction for a Filipino festival. Hiphop acts had always performed before, but this was a case where these mostly second-generation performers were grouped together with—indeed, even dominated—the more traditional cultural acts. There was, in effect, a disjunction, as the afternoon's program juggled genres. Nonetheless, it was clear that much of the festival was slanted towards a younger, American-born audience—one that did not question the legitimacy of hiphop as a Filipino American cultural artifact.[10]

But a sense of nostalgia still lingered over the proceedings, though this was very likely lost on many of the attendees. Over half of the seated listeners were senior citizens and veterans bused in from Daly City and from the nearby residential hotels in SoMa and the Tenderloin who, one guesses, sat patiently and probably wondered when the din—the alien scratches, the chopped-up beats—would all end. DJ Q-Bert, arguably Daly City's most famous former resident, had been in fact flown in from Hawaii, where he had moved in 2000 after the Invisibl Skratch Piklz effectively disbanded that same year. That afternoon, DJ Q-Bert played a characteristically spellbinding set, his fingers skittering like loosed birds over the vinyl, but there was something belated about the stellar performance, for turntablism's (minimal) commercial popularity and critical success had peaked at least half a decade earlier. One audience member excitedly told me that it felt "like 1994," and she was right: hiphop may have represented a newer, more vital generation,

---

[9] DJ Q-Bert, along with fellow repeat winners of the nationwide Disco Master Championship, formed the mostly all-Filipino DJ crew the Invisibl Skratch Piklz, and has been universally acclaimed as one of the greatest live DJs in the world, if not in the history of the medium.

[10] Some have expressed misgivings about the embrace of hiphop by Filipino Americans, who, like many whites before them, are seen as apolitically appropriating a black art form, as intruding nonchalantly on other peoples' musical turf. (Efforts to connect hiphop's orality and the phenomenon of the poetry slam with the Philippine *balagtasan* (debates in poetic form, or literary jousts) are simply misguided attempts to quell racial anxiety.) This has prompted suggestions in some quarters that, of all the Asian American communities, Filipino Americans are the most "blackwashed."

Such comments are understandable, but somewhat misguided, as they posit the existence of an "essential" Filipino art form and therefore confirm the museum-ized quality of traditional Filipino festivals. And while hiphop has clear roots in black resistance, to insist on hiphop's marginality as an arena of (only) black protest is to deny its lucrativeness as a material commodity and its decades-long position in the mainstream. The relatively comfortable multiculturalism of the Bay Area surely contributes to a kind of unreflective daring on the part of Filipino American youths to pick up the microphone, but one cannot deny that the officials at the borders of the Hiphop Nation have already relaxed, if rather reluctantly, their racial requirements.

but it was exemplified at the festival by a moribund musical genre that looked to its glories firmly situated in the past.

This annual festival was particularly significant because of its location: beginning in the mid-'50s, the San Francisco Redevelopment Agency targeted various properties (including most of what was Japantown, and the International Hotel, the heart of what was then Manilatown) for demolition. What was once a thriving Filipino neighborhood that comprised almost 5,000 Filipinos in 1972 (and had been home to Filipinos since the Gran Oriente Filipino Hotel was established in 1921) was gutted by "urban renewal" as a convention center, tourist hotels, and public art centers, including the Yerba Buena Center itself, took over the area. The struggle against tenant eviction and for the creation of a Filipino Center in the SoMa area continues, heroically, today.

The community activist and scholar MC Canlas (2002) perceptively points out that the presence of a Filipino Center in the South of Market area would make it the symbolic opposite of "white" Union Square, with its Dewey Monument, north of Market Street. Across from St. Patrick's Church, with a predominantly Filipino congregation, the non-Filipino Yerba Buena Gardens—along with Arkipelago Books, the Bessie Carmichael School (also mostly Filipino), the West Bay Pilipino Multi-Service Center, the Bayanihan Community Center, and the Mint Mall are in a census tract where the majority of residents are Asian (and the majority of whom are Filipinos, about 1,500 in total), and the median household income is below $24,000—a particularly low figure, especially for San Francisco.

That sunny afternoon I experienced a sense of nostalgia doubling into itself—a nostalgia for a thriving Manilatown community still unravaged by "development," and for a neighborhood, looking into the future, that could provide the comforts of home—say, a place like Daly City, with its garbage-free streets and manicured lawns. SoMa, perhaps, is neglected by the middle class of "Daly City"—though I must emphasize here that it is *not* by Daly City itself, but by the same Pinoy professionals disconnected from the struggles of SoMa by class differences. An ironic victory, then, to have a patch of green in the commercial heart of San Francisco, reclaimed, if only for one Indian summer weekend, by brown folk.

Transnational Television

The Fiesta Filipina performances manifest an interestingly static view of Filipino culture. Except for a few acts, much of the festival steers away from the contemporary, preferring to focus on the usual clichéd folk dances. At first the festival reminded me of the same bland performances held in the Philippines for visiting tourists; that is, these were dances and songs already over-familiar to the Pinoy immigrant audience and were, in an odd way, almost aimed at the (white) tourists visiting San Francisco. But there was something comforting about the whole scenario—that at some point, the *itik-itik* would be danced, that the bamboo poles would be brought out for the *tinikling*, that the dancers would then invite brave souls from the audience to participate. There was something, then, reassuring in the whole business, as the immigrant audience's expectations of Filipino culture were fulfilled. This was an ossified version of Filipino culture, displayed and replayed, forever mired in an innocent, rural, prewar Philippines.

This vision is at first glance similar to the kind of reified culture on display at Pilipino Cultural Night events. The Pilipino Cultural Night, or PCN, is, for many Filipino American college student organizations, the culminating event of the school year. PCNs in universities mostly hew to the variety-show format, interspersing folk dances with songs, much as does Fiesta Filipina. Although PCNs can be seen as examples of "strategic essentialism," as the ethnic studies scholar Theo Gonzalves (1995, 130) argues, the successful carving out of a particular Filipino space is done at the expense of an engaged and critical cultural discourse. As one might expect, there is little or no mention of homeland politics—"bad news"—and politics is brought up, if at all, in the domesticated form of comedians' patter. The festivals show an operative nostalgia at work. The audience "remembers" a Philippines unsullied by crime or poverty. "Highlights" of Filipino culture are on display: a "perfect" Santacruzan, people dancing happily, and so on. In many ways, I thought, it was the opposite of something like TFC, where bad news could be readily viewed at the touch of the television remote. Nostalgia was not a phenomenon it (or *Philippine News*) directly addressed, for the messy reality of life in the Philippines was always present.

But I was later struck by a comment made by Jose Ramon Olives, the managing director of ABS-CBN International, who remarked to reporters that, through TFC, he was "in the business of selling emotions" (quoted in Gutierrez 1995, B1). (John Silva, formerly of *Filipinas*, would also say, in a 1995 meeting with journalists that I attended, "We sell nostalgia, we sell emotions.") Another article about the channel quotes a radio broadcaster from Vallejo, California, who says that TFC "brought back memories of when I was growing up in Quezon City" (Salido 1995, 27).

Their comments reveal the abject commercialization of nostalgia and its acknowledgment as a sales principle. TFC and *Filipinas*, of course, are following the lead of advertisements for airlines, travel agencies, and most especially long-distance telephone companies. But any doubts about the use of nostalgia as a socially productive force should be dispelled; it generates discourse and income for the businesses.

The businessmen's comments are also interesting precisely because nostalgia is not the operative social force in this case: nostalgia deals more "properly" with temporal, not spatial, distance (Phillips 1985, 65). Temporal distance hardly characterizes TFC's up-to-the-minute programming from the Philippines. Unlike other ethnic television stations, TFC broadcasts no locally produced Filipino TV shows[11]; in contrast, TFC is expanding rapidly, with 24-hour programming of *Ang TV, The Sharon Cuneta Show*, and a whole slew of Filipino movies, all of them originating from the Philippines. An article in *Filipinas* quotes the marketing manager Manuel Lopez, Jr., who attributes TFC's popularity to "the desire of Filipino Americans to maintain their cultural identity and heritage." The article adds that Lopez has received "hundreds of letters" from pleased viewers, particularly parents who "tell [him] it's the best thing that's ever happened to their kids" (Salido 1995, 26–27).[12]

Television may be creating this transnational link, but the viewers' seeking out of current showbiz gossip is by no means nostalgic. The popularity of a television station that broadcasts programs that would seem so far removed from the everyday lives of Filipino Americans is remarkable. With its almost complete lack of coverage of Filipino American issues, the world of The Filipino Channel is oddly myopic, regaling its 25,000 subscribers with the immediacy of life, without satellite feed delay, in the Philippines. "Except for the commercials," Lopez tells the reporter, "you'd think you were watching TV in Manila." As a complete replica of Manila's ABS-CBN 2, TFC fills the need to assuage a certain sort of homesickness, one based more on spatial distance than on time.

---

[11] KTSF Channel 26 in the Bay Area regularly features *The Filipino American Report*, though much of the content is taken from Philippine-based ABS-CBN's *TV Patrol*, syndicated separately from TFC.

[12] Debbie Patron thought that it was easier for Filipino children growing up in the United States now than it was a decade before, at least in terms of role models and asserting one's ethnicity—and that the Filipino Channel has much to do with it:

> [T]he whole time you're here and that you're growing up, your identity is not buo [whole], it's not [whole] when you grow up bicultural. And all of a sudden, you go home, and you're back in the Philippines, and you realize, my God, I do belong somewhere, I do have roots. And so, when I was . . . growing up, there was only like two other Filipinos in the entire . . . Mercy High School. . . . Now you know Mercy High School has 50 percent of the kids are Filipino. So that's very different, so the kids now have role models, they open up the TV, they get Filipino television from back home. You know what I mean, that's available, if you wanna rent a movie that's Filipino and see images of yourself, versus when I was growing up, we didn't have that, our role models were all white.

But this homesickness is related to a kind of service to the homeland as well. I find quite compelling the way this particular discourse on immigrant responsibilities keeps resurfacing. Olives, ABS-CBN International's managing director, added in the same interview that "TFC's primordial role is to help scuttle the Filipinos' crustacean mindset so they can feel, think, and move *up* as one, instead of pulling each other down"—a reference here to crab mentality. The depiction of a business as a community service—in this case, ostensibly to foster unity among its viewers (indeed, the entire Pinoy community)—is not new, as we have seen in the example of *Philippine News*. But an interview I conducted with Olives in his Burlingame office gave a more nuanced, if contradictory, sense of TFC's "mission."

Olives was discussing their strategy for expanding the cable audience—"wherever there's a Filipino, ABS must be there"—when he started expounding on the Filipino diaspora:

JRO: Any cruise ship that you ride around the world, I assure you there'll be a Filipino. In countries where overseas contract workers are required. So we have it tough. That's why sometimes I think being in North America is all wrong.

BV: Why do you say that?

JRO: You know what happens is that—you know, it is nice to be working in North America with this vision. . . . The problem is, the Filipinos in North America are snobbish. They kind of think that I've come to the land of milk and honey, I've earned my keep, and I've three jobs, two cars, and I'm somebody. . . . You know, my vision is, I would have done my job if I get every Filipino in America to go back to the Philippines. Because it is our duty as Filipinos to do what we can for our country. Our role, as ABS-CBN in North America, is not to pander to Filipino Americans.

BV: Filipino Americans meaning Filipino immigrants, or—

JRO: Filipinos living here. I'll just use Filipinos—it's not to pander to their desires or whatever, it's to make them realize that the country they've left behind is not as bad as how they think it is. And it's because of people like them that we need the Philippines to change. We can't be fence-sitters, eh, you can't be sitting here, you can't be sitting driving your brand-new BMW after you work *x* numbers of hours a day, watching television on a big screen that you loaned on your credit card, and say that you know how to solve the traffic problem. Or you know how to solve the environmental problem. That's one side of me. The other side is, shit, well, you're really doing well, I'm proud of you. But don't you think that if you stuck it out in the Philippines things would have changed?

Olives invokes the same immigrant obligations as other interviewees: Pinoys in the United States have a "duty . . . to do what [they] can for [their] country." Filipinos may be everywhere all over the world, but Filipinos in the United States are the exception, precisely because of their class status; they are already, as Olives put it, "somebody."

He later gave an example of the "snobbishness" of Filipinos in America, sounding uncannily like a *Philippine News* editorial:

Like yesterday, [someone called] telling us we're ulol [crazy] and no-good Filipinos. Things said, for example—well, you can never please everybody. Like there was a newsbreak, very big newsbreak about the Bangsa Moro [the Muslim separatist group] right smack in the middle of a movie. And they call up and they say, shit, we don't care about that. I said, but fucking people are getting killed, don't you wanna know? See, that's the attitude we have here, eh. It's so pedestrian. It's so parochial. They only care about themselves.

But Olives's personal vision—"to get every Filipino in America to go back to the Philippines"—also reaffirms what the Filipino films preach: that Pinoys ultimately do not belong elsewhere, that their true home is in the Philippines. This is why the resentful accusations of betrayal (and thinly veiled envy) are specifically directed toward those in the United States: because those particular Pinoys chose to leave for good.

Olives's vision also requires a precisely nostalgic process: "to make them realize that the country they've left behind is not as bad as how they think it is." This is, however, in contradiction to the images his channel shows:

The Department of Tourism hates me. Because they're saying that we're derailing their campaign about the beautiful Philippine Islands. . . . But I'm just saying, they hate us. Not hate us, they talk to me many times, please—even [the former Philippine Ambassador] Rabe has called me and said . . . ano ba 'yung nangyayari sa channel [what's with the channel]? Chief, paano ba nating magagawa, ganyan talaga ang balita [what could we do, that's what the news really is]. The news is already sanitized. As it is. But we have to show the people the truth. And let them be the judge.

For Olives, a distorted, purposely nostalgic presentation of the news was obviously not the answer; "the truth"—one that forestalled any possibility of being homesick—was what TFC presented. ("Making people realize, showing them about the truth, is not painful," Olives added later.) But here we see two sectors complaining about bad news: one because it made the Philippines look "bad," and the other because it intruded on the film in progress.

Bad news, in this sense, has two effects. One is that it does force people to act. Olives cited a relief drive for a typhoon in 1995 that netted $68,000 in 24 hours, much more than he or anyone expected. Although the lesson he drew from this event had more to do with how their subscribers viewed TFC's integrity (since they entrusted money to it), his words also shed light on his perspective on mobilizing people and getting them to "do their duty as Filipinos":

> JRO: They don't have to physically go home. I think they just have to make a certain effort—
> BV: In giving back.
> JRO: In giving back. It could be being proud, understanding the national heritage, teaching their children what a warm, rich culture the Philippines really is.

Such an understanding of "the national heritage" could be accomplished by regular viewing of The Filipino Channel. As an immigrant, one could keep turning toward the Philippines and be able to "give back"—already an act of heroism—simply by knowing, or communicating, "the truth" about the country: that it was not as bad as one thought.

But the other effect of bad news—particularly, the constant barrage of it in the media—is that it reassures the Daly City resident. Filipinos come to Daly City to become better Filipinos, as it were, or at least to live as Filipinos in a more orderly, peaceful version of the Philippines. But this desire has left some people, like Teddy Encinas, with feelings of guilt, as Filipinos come to Daly City to become Americans as well. One is left with nagging questions, raised by nostalgia, about why one left in the first place, and whether one made the right decision to leave, and with this unease comes guilt. But perhaps guilt is assuaged, paradoxically, when one turns on the TV or opens the newspaper and sees the bad news. Each bit of bad news makes the decision more right every time.

Looking at Daly City from this perspective suggests that the Filipino community may be involved in something more profound than merely maintaining ties to the homeland. The latter can of course be seen as an eager response to the call of savvy marketing, but also, as with many other things in

Daly City, a collective assertion of Filipinoness. One can see this in the San-tacruzans, with costumes rendered authentic to the last glittering detail; the newspapers that seamlessly combine scandals from hometowns both in the Philippines and abroad; the easily rentable videos that bring into living rooms the latest from Manila's film studios; the countless Filipino restaurants mostly indistinguishable from each other. One can perhaps read these mani-festations as efforts to keep the nation closer, as part of a concerted longing to demonstrate national belonging, as part of a collective "giving back" by com-municating pride in Filipino culture. They are, in effect, a claim to a heritage that would be denied them back home, a production and consumption of things Filipino, which potentially fends off accusations of betrayal, in order to live perhaps as much as possible as if they were in the Philippines. Perhaps branding The Filipino Channel as completely removed from immigrant life is wrong; perhaps the homeland has everything to do with their everyday life in America.

It is a paradoxical situation, one that seems to contradict the assertions that Filipino immigrants possess a remarkable ability to assimilate. In Jimenez-Magsanoc's view, "no immigrant or alien resident absorbs America's attributes faster than the Filipino. That all comes from the Filipino's tried and tested ability to adjust to most any situation. . . . The Filipino automati-cally recasts his image after that of his adopted land" (1974, 9). Abdul Jan-Mohamed similarly concludes, too easily, that immigrant status "implies a voluntary desire to become a full-fledged subject of the new society. Thus the immigrant is often eager to discard with deliberate speed the formative influ-ences of his or her own culture and to take on the values of the new culture" (1992, 101). The post-1965 Pinoy immigrants to the United States do not readily fit such a portrait. Are we, then, speaking here of a redefinition of the immigrant, in terms of the retention of ties to a "homeland"?

At this juncture it is important to compare The Filipino Channel with *Philippine News* again. Their similarities as Filipino media outlets are only on the surface, however, for they stem from different impulses. There is nothing nostalgic per se about TFC's television content, but one cannot say the same for *Philippine News*'s news coverage—what is imparted most often is not ex-actly a wish to return to one's origins, but a clear display of an ambivalent desire to belong to America and not to forget the homeland at the same time.

When a Filipino viewer watches The Filipino Channel, what she sees comes exclusively from somewhere else—perhaps, from "home." That is, the viewers in Daly City are not on television, not in the same way that they are in the newspaper. But TFC's exteriority, which otherwise signals its differ-ence from the viewer, is literally domesticated. One watches it at home, and so it becomes part of the fluid, "transnational" background of Daly City. One is able, like Wally Curameng's uncle, to watch the eruption of Mount Pinatubo and make a joke about snow falling in the Philippines.

When a Filipino reader opens the paper, what she sees is herself, or her friends and neighbors. Indeed, the *Philippine News* enables the reader to find herself in the society pages. The CommLink features make the *Philippine News* function much like a community newspaper. And despite the potential embarrassments—for instance, the political shenanigans back home reflecting poorly on Pinoys in America—what one sees, in a generally idealized fashion, are Pinoys being successful. Furthermore, they are not successful just because they are doctors and lawyers attending balls and parties, but because they are living the kinds of lives—*as Filipinos*—otherwise unattainable in the Philippines.

The reader's identification with the newspaper prevents it from being nostalgic; despite its orientation toward matters in the Philippines, the *Philippine News* still reflects a yearning to belong to the new country—to live, as Filipinos do, in the United States. This desire is not dissimilar, then, from the narrative of assimilation. Filipinos are seen as belonging to America, but—aided by the opportunities that a globalized age affords—still living in a distinctly, perhaps stubbornly, Filipino way. In that sense one could easily argue for a reverse hyphenization, one running in a different direction from the "ethnicizing" of America: what we see in the pages of the *Philippine News* is the gradual addition of the suffix "American" to "Filipino."

But one can posit not only a Filipino audience for the newspaper, but an American audience as well—reading over the Filipino reader's shoulder, as it were. In effect, the *Philippine News* is telling the hypothetical American reader that Filipinos belong too, that Filipinos are successful in the United States. Seen from this perspective, little differentiates Filipino Americans from previous immigrants; they, too, want to belong, and show that they can and do.

Nevertheless, class desires prevent the endowment of a complete authenticity on these trappings of Filipinoness and the occasions for their manifestations. In other words, the Filipinos of Daly City cannot be authentic Filipinos, for a true bridging of the distance embedded in these material reminders would entail a return to the homeland. Perhaps the desire remains only for the striving itself, and not for its referent. This kind of consumption feeds off the luxury of distance: the humidity, the rampant crime, and traffic jams can only be felt through, and warded off by, the printed page and the glow of the television screen.

And therefore Daly City acts as an imperfect mirror. It erases the reality of the lower middle class but simultaneously reflects its residents' class and national anxieties and longings. This image can be seen as a product of the cultivation of class dispositions—which include migration and *a* Daly City itself, as the act of leaving becomes a more and more concrete possibility in the breadth of Filipino middle-class imaginings. But it is, at the same time, an image both resented and envied back in the Philippines for how it goes precisely against the same class and national standards. One can say that Daly City is a Quezon City where the buses run on time, a Laoag City where every house has a two-car garage, a Davao City where its middle-class residents can acquire their wide-screen TVs and minivans, as transnationally shared symbols of middle-classness, in a manner impossible for them to achieve back home.

8

PINOY CAPITAL

~

On a summer day in 1931, the writer Carlos Bulosan stood on the deck of a ship after almost a month in steerage and saw America for the first time. He felt he had come home.

> We arrived in Seattle on a June day. My first sight of the approaching land was an exhilarating experience. Everything seemed native and promising to me. It was like coming home after a long voyage, although as yet I had no home in this city. Everything seemed familiar and kind. . . . With a sudden surge of joy, I knew that I must find a home in this new land (Bulosan 1973, 99).

His reaction to the view, as described in his semi-fictional memoir *America Is in the Heart*, comes as a surprise. It almost seems drawn from the stereotypical arrival scene in immigrant novels (and later, films), dictated by the demands of the narrative and the genre, and dramatically enhanced by hindsight. Indeed, there is little foreshadowing in his account that he would set off for America, much less embrace it with such excitement. We are told, for instance, about the kindly American librarian who teaches him about Abraham Lincoln, but this is the extent of his fascination; mostly, we read about the discouraging letters his brother sends him from California, and this is all we know of the United States. Yet he arrives in Seattle already recognizing the "familiar" and the "native."

That this was Bulosan's actual reaction upon first seeing America is unlikely. Writing for an American audience, Bulosan was very much aware of the form of the immigrant narrative, and his grand entrance fits squarely within this tradition. The memoir is, in any case, unreliable in its historical veracity. The "Carlos" of his semi-autobiography is actually a composite of other Pinoy migrant workers, including his brothers, and their experiences. The poverty that pushed Bulosan off the land and out of the Philippines is somewhat exaggerated; his parents were actually able to send him and his siblings to school, despite the loss of their lands. But the moment of recognition of home is important: how is his ecstatic reaction possible? How does one recognize home? How does one belong to a place one has never seen before?

On these matters Bulosan is silent. Paramount throughout the book is his unswerving determination to find a land of freedom in America—a country that, surely at the time of his many beatings and days of hunger, would make the Philippines look like paradise in comparison. By the end of the semi-fictional memoir, the narrator affirms his faith in the United States as a nation of equality and independence: "the American earth was like a huge heart unfolding warmly to receive me" (1946, 326).

Escaping relative poverty and finding freedom, however, were only a few of Bulosan's many reasons for migration. His friend and fellow writer P.C. Morantte writes, rather romantically, that Bulosan migrated simply to become a writer—and a famous one, at that—in America. But Morantte adds as well, "Carlos, like most of his contemporaries, was fascinated by the flood of all kinds of American commercial literature. . . . He said he liked to see the pictures of numerous goods being sold by mail which for him spelled the material abundance of America. He saw people rushing . . . orders for shoes, shirts, undershirts, handkerchiefs, and many other tempting items in the catalogs" (1984, 49).

Bulosan was hardly a typical figure—he was educated, ambitious, and highly talented, and affiliated with the American left, to boot—but he had similarities with his fellow Filipino immigrants. Like other immigrants, both then and now, Bulosan came to the United States with pictures of "material abundance" in his mind. Like other immigrants, he knew, even if misguidedly, what America represented, and he sought to uplift his economic condition. Like other immigrants, he also wanted to experience the freedom America was supposed to bestow. Like other immigrants, he came to reunite with his family (his brothers, who had left for the United States earlier) and make a new life for himself; like other immigrants, he left his home to find a new one.

Oscar Handlin's extreme image of dislocation in the "uprooted," alienated immigrant and Robert Park's paradigm of assimilation were the cornerstones of the study of American immigration for many decades, but they have long since been disavowed, perhaps too hastily, by scholars. Handlin, for instance, overemphasized the isolation and lack of preparation of migrants flung into a strange land, though it is now clear that migration networks have always existed to facilitate entry and employment. Most famously, he evoked the pathology of immigration in the opening words of his book *The Uprooted*: "I shall touch upon broken homes, interruptions of a familiar life, separation from known surroundings, the becoming a foreigner, and ceasing to belong. These are the aspects of alienation. . . . The history of immigration is a history of alienation and its consequences" (2002, 4).

The changing, apparently increasingly unstable notions of nation, place, culture, and identity have led scholars to attempt to reconceptualize migration and nationalism itself, paving the way for transnational theory. But the main assumption behind transnationalism merely reiterates what scholars of nationalism have long asserted: that the boundaries of nation and state have not always been the same, and that it is precisely the nature of state-programmed nationalism to try to ensure that those borders are the same. Forms of cultural dialogue linking different places have existed since precolonial eras, even before the birth of the idea of a nation. Migrants during the rise of wage labor–based capitalism itself could also be called transmigrants. The changes of the late twentieth century, I believe, are insufficient to declare the emergence of a new process. There is no question that global connections have intensified, but the phenomena that transnational theory and similar frameworks describe as completely new are not novel. Global movements and linkages seem ultimately to be merely more rapid, more numerous, more far-reaching, and not indicative of a paradigm shift as transnational theory purports these phenomena to be.[1]

Making sense of "the imponderabilia of actual life," as Bronislaw Malinowski put it, is one of the basic objectives of anthropological fieldwork. "There is a series of phenomena of great importance," Malinowski wrote, "which cannot possibly be recorded by questioning or computing documents, but have to be observed in their full actuality". By this he meant, in words

---

[1] It is telling that theorists of postmodernity—where "migrant rootlessness" is seen as its primary metaphor (Chambers 1994)—have latched on to "hyper" as their preferred prefix. As Doreen Massey wittily observes, "A special style of hype and hyperbole has been developed to write of these matters. . . . For amid the Ridley Scott images of world cities . . . the Baudrillard visions of hyperspace . . . much of life for many people, even in the heart of the first world, still consists of waiting in a bus-shelter with your shopping for a bus that never comes" (1992, 7–8). This certainly holds true in Daly City.

that have guided countless researchers after him, "the routine of a man's working day," or "the tone of conversational and social life around the village fires," or "the existence of strong friendships or hostilities" (1961, 18)—indeed, many of the affective elements that scholars of "the transnational" have neglected. I have focused more on discourse than on practice, to look at nationality and belonging as embodied in people's perspectives and in media images rather than in economic structures. These images are constructed and circulated, and in turn they shape the expectations of immigrants concerning their future lives in America. I have argued as well that public discourse directly contributes to the fashioning of a specifically immigrant identity for Pinoy immigrants in the United States.

And in contrast to the "imponderability" of the everyday, I focus on notions of ethnicity, assimilation, citizenship, colonialism, belonging, nationalism, and so on, that are indeed much pondered and debated in the pages of *Philippine News*, and also in everyday conversation. But they are nonetheless "imponderable" as well, in the sense that there are no fixed definitions or answers to the categories, issues, and questions I have raised.

For instance, the hypothetical transition from Filipino immigrants to Filipino Americans, or from nationality to ethnicity, is discussed both by the newspaper and by my interviewees. This transition is also structurally similar to the historical process by which immigrants move from being sojourners to being settlers. Such a "model" is of course riddled with exceptions, and "ethnicity" (or, more specifically, a form of Americanization) is in many ways dependent on individual self-definition.

When compared to assimilation, a "move" from nationality to ethnicity seems to involve a false evolutionary progression. The difficulty with assimilation and its corresponding melting pot theory is that the reality of race confounds the neatness of the metaphor. Native Americans, African Americans, and Asian Americans were historically excluded from citizenship (and, particularly the latter, from naturalization rights) and participation in the greater political and cultural process. Ethnicity theory did not take root in racial minority communities because the supposed end result, assimilation, would not and could not take place. Moreover, Filipinos (or at least, my interviewees) never really identified with Asian to begin with. They have also stubbornly resisted pressures to identify with the category of "Filipino American," much less to accept an Asian American identity, "radical" or otherwise. "Turning" Filipino American was not necessarily an ideal, just as U.S. citizenship did not seem to be an ultimate goal, either.

Nevertheless, it is a "process" that my interviewees were familiar with; many of them clearly distinguished between different categories (Filipino, American, and Filipino American) when referring to themselves, and spoke of markers (the conferral of citizenship, one's place of birth, biological parentage, length of stay in the United States, etc.) that signaled when one belonged to or entered such categories. The latter factor—length of stay—perhaps most directly relates to wanting to settle permanently and its analogous pairing with being Filipino American. Time, more than anything, seemed to influence when a Filipino immigrant "became" Filipino American. That is to say, some of the interviewees recognized themselves as belonging to relatively static categories, but also saw the possibility of "acceding" to another (i.e., Filipino American) in the future.

Such a transition, however, is neither inevitable nor completely idealized for Filipino immigrants. Whereas some see "becoming American" as a clear step up, other Daly City Filipinos regard citizenship with much ambivalence. Some immigrants, as do some Filipinos in the Philippines, see the act of immigration (and naturalization) as intrinsically linked to the abandonment of Filipino identity in place of another. Filipino popular culture almost consistently represents the U.S. balikbayan as a person who has forsaken her or his Filipino identity. Becoming American is an unquestioned change in social status, and, by the same token, a repudiation of being Pinoy.

Despite talk about Filipinos migrating to the United States only for the ultimate goal of U.S. citizenship, I found little evidence for such an accusation. Though many were inspired by dreams of material success (in turn fueled by the media), my interviewees were also quite realistic about the constraints and pressures of immigrant life in the United States. The world of "fast cars and blonde women," as Kiko Novero put it, or a country "where everyone was friendly to you," as Wally Curameng said approvingly, were genuine, if misguided, fantasies, as were streets paved with gold for earlier immigrants. At the same time, potential immigrants—through relatives' letters and the ubiquitous media—were well aware of the hardships that lay before them.

But there is no denying the fact that Filipinos do opt for American citizenship in mass numbers. The Philippines is the country of birth of one of the largest groups of people naturalizing per year. In 1999, for instance, 35,206 Filipinos were naturalized, third only to Mexicans (193,709) and Vietnamese (51,055); this number included more than 5,000 spouses of U.S. citizens and more than 500 World War II veterans who were naturalized under special provisions. A year later, in 2000, the Philippines dropped to fourth place, after the People's Republic of China, but with even more new citizens—a total of 46,563 (Immigration and Naturalization Service 2000).

The desire to migrate to the United States necessarily has its roots in the Philippines. The "doubleness" I have described among Daly City immigrants has its parallel back in the Philippines; Filipinos there too can see themselves in another country. Such a desire, mediated through letters, newspapers, movies, and balikbayan boxes, is simply part of a complex tangle of possibilities and motivations, whether it is a search for material success or the supposedly irresistible call of family obligation.

The constant invocation of family obligation—of immigration as response to kinship responsibility—is evident. As my Daly City interviewees related, family-reunification preferences were the main conduit by which immigration could be achieved; similarly, it was obligation towards the family (and economic circumstances) that prompted the move in the first place. Pinoys have also long cited the family—or rather, *their* family—as the primary site of their loyalties, and in this sense, kinship can be seen as obliquely opposed to the differently inflected paternal demands of the state. But to say that one had no choice but to pack up and follow her siblings or parents strikes the listener as somewhat disingenuous; some were, after all, fully employed adults in their thirties or forties who could make decisions on their own. (This was not the case, of course, with the so-called 1.5 generation (those who were born in the Philippines but arrived in the United States at a young age).

Blaming the call of family obligation seems a kind of defense mechanism to soften the blow of having to justify their decision to migrate. (In the case of the Bautistas, it may be seen as justification for their current lowered social standing.) It is not, however, just a reaction to accusations of being *walang pakisama*, as discussed in Chapter Five—"but I had no choice but to come," the answer comes; it is also a way of making themselves involuntary, as opposed to voluntary, migrants. What is involved in decision-making, as my interviewees indicate, is a mixture of the rational and irrational—the gamble, as it were, of making a life elsewhere. But the seeming passivity of the immigrants lets them distance themselves from the very heart of the gamble: in short, the financial and material (and therefore materialist) reasons for coming to the United States. One removes oneself from the cultural taint of money by attributing reasons to a higher cause—the family.

Why do Pinoys choose to take this gamble? The relative hardships of life in the United States are well known in advance, from films and from reports of previous immigrants. Government agencies inform overseas contract workers of the difficulties in advance. Countless films and television shows, not to mention friends and relatives' experiences and the numerous cases of employment abuse, all illustrate the privations of life overseas. Why, then, do immigrants persist in the face of an apparent illusion?

Part of the answer lies in the relative prosperity of Filipinos in the United States—relative to their previous lives in the Philippines. But economic success was largely achieved only by the first wave of doctors and engineers; the demographic differences between the later technical worker immigrants and family-reunification immigrants are stark. The phenomenon of Manila office workers leaving their jobs to be parking lot attendants in Daly City— or veterans leaving their families for slow, lonely deaths in Tenderloin apartments—is very real, and very tragic, and yet still does not stop the persistent migration.

The answer may lie more in my interviewees' images of America: as a benevolent nation, replete with material luxuries, and welcoming deserving immigrants with open arms. Wally Curameng's conception of an America where one did not have to work, Kiko Novero's vision of an America with its "fast cars and blonde women"—these images are part of the discourse about America that persists as much as immigrants, then and now, do. America opens up the option of a different belonging. People do not necessarily dream of settling in Saudi Arabia, or working as domestic helpers in Hong Kong; such fantasies are all envisioned and take place in the Philippines, where the fruits of material prosperity are more properly consumed. The United States, however, is quite different from other places because of the greater rewards of citizenship.

Such rewards come with certain obligations, of course. But Filipino immigrants seem to bear the burden of citizenship (or even the possibility of citizenship) lightly; it is, after all, just one of many formal options. If a transition to assimilation were ever "supposed" to take place, the Filipino example would have to be seen as a failure. Like other immigrants, Filipino immigrants are seen, even by themselves, as "flawed," unassimilable, and irresponsible citizens, clinging too tightly to homeland politics and culture, and refusing to take seriously the concerns of their adopted country. And indeed, their lack of political participation bears this out.

It is, on the surface, a condemnatory and even politically dangerous observation to make. I do not wish to suggest that the Filipino American community is characterized by opportunism or civic irresponsibility, or that love for America is somehow not genuine, or less heartfelt. People certainly come to the United States for a better life, in order to make money. There is also no doubt that people decide to become naturalized for very practical, self-serving reasons—merely to avoid the hassle of reapplying for an entrance visa, for instance. Such cynical sentiment, when taken to its extreme, is almost unthinkable to the ardent American patriot; surely becoming American requires more than memorizing answers to a few history questions! But the solemnity of nationhood and its rites of conferral have necessarily obscured the numbing bureaucracy involved in achieving citizenship.

Naturally the question of loyalty comes to mind. As noted above, it has often been immigrants whose loyalty is placed under suspicion, depending on the United States' relations with the immigrant's country of origin. But loyalty—that non-quantifiable measurement and product of nationalism—is inherently unstable, and can be seen as a mystified distillation of the complex emotions and obligations exacted by the state. Despite their emotionally elevated status, the external sacraments of nationhood have always concealed the inner workings of a coldly pragmatic, bureaucratic system. To use loyalty as a political and cultural gauge is to overlook different geopolitical conditions, different senses of belonging, and, perhaps, different conceptions of citizenship.

To be specific, it is a pragmatic citizenship, whose advantages and disadvantages are weighed, seen by Filipino immigrants as merely a mantle over an essentially Filipino core. U.S. citizenship, despite its marking an ideal change in behavior—as a passage into a different state of being, as it were—is not seen by Filipino immigrants to effect any changes in the person. It is a citizenship that provides a passport. It is a citizenship that, perhaps, provides a passage to the American Dream without the attendant responsibilities.

One may say that the rights and responsibilities of a citizen are being taken for granted by naturalized Filipino Americans, but the same may be said for practically anyone else. The burden of American citizenship has never been equally carried by all. Low voter turnout, for instance, is hardly the exclusive province of Filipino Americans, although failure to vote is seen as a glaring omission in a predominantly Filipino American community like Daly City. In a globalized age, when commodities, information, and sometimes people, circulate at faster speeds, the accessories of the homeland can be easily consumed from afar. Indeed, Filipinos in Daly City can still live very much as Filipinos in the Philippines do. Can one not allow for a sense of belonging that is not necessarily naturally linked to citizenship? My interviews bear this out: there is a clearly utilitarian aspect to gaining American citizenship. But instead of automatically condemning this apparent lack of civic responsibility, perhaps we should conceive of an alternate form of American belonging—a belonging that recognizes the complexities and contradictions of the immigrant experience.

We must separate the politico-legal definition of citizenship from its emotional and affective connotations. But it is also important to recognize the political consequences of an alternate American belonging. For the Filipinos of Daly City, becoming an American citizen is, ultimately, merely an alternative—an alternative that does not necessarily require the profession of a love for democratic ideals or everything for which America is supposed to stand. The option to be naturalized is perhaps the primary reason why some Filipinos in the United States hold citizenship in abeyance; it is an American belonging—and, perhaps most damagingly, a *commitment* perpetually deferred.

American citizenship is also an alternative that is embedded in everyday Filipino life, making it markedly different for Filipinos both in the United States and in the Philippines. This is different from the experience of many other nationals, whose countries' relationships to the United States are not nearly as violently intimate. The possibility of migrating to the United States is lodged deeply in the Filipino national imagination; as it did to Carlos Bulosan and some of my interviewees, America already looks like home from afar. One could then easily argue that a kind of colonial mentality drives Filipino migration to the United States, and some of the discourse I have analyzed in the previous chapters supports this conclusion. As Yen Le Espiritu argues, any study of Filipino migration to the United States, "must begin with . . . [the] history [of conquest, occupation, and exploitation]." Indeed, "contemporary Asian immigration to the United States can be better understood," she writes, quoting Lisa Lowe, "as 'the "return" of Asian immigrants to the imperial center'" (2003; 1, 5). Immigrants certainly saw America as the source of all things superior, a notion that, Filipino nationalist scholars argue, American colonial education propagated.

But my interviews complicate this facile notion. Much has been said about the aftereffects of the colonial relationship, and there is undeniably a connection between it and the elevation of America as another place to live. But with the exception of many Filipino World War II veterans (who feel that they *deserve* to live in the United States in return for military services rendered to the conflated colony-nation), it is unclear that colonialism still directly propels migration to take place decades after decolonization. Although some of my interviewees grew up, for instance, with the notion that anything "stateside" was superior to local Filipino products, it is not easy to differentiate what is specifically colonial from other factors affecting migration—most especially, America's economic dominance as a First World power. America, as a land of opportunity, also looms large in the dreams of many people around the world; this is an image that the United States itself cultivates. The United States has represented the same image to millions of immigrants and would-be immigrants around the world—and not just to Filipinos—since the 1880s. Filipino immigration to the United States also has to do with particular conjunctures of colonial history, economic conditions, stronger international networks, Philippine politics, and, perhaps most important, familial obligations.

Although the legacies of colonialism surely fuel the engines of immigration to the United States, the counterexample—seen everywhere else, in the evidence of the Filipino diaspora—is in my opinion more persuasive. The United States need not be central in conceptions of Filipino immigration studies. It is true that the movement of "population, armies, goods, capital, and culture", as Espiritu enumerates them (2003, 6), from the colonial center to the islands caused a powerful cultural and physical dislocation, but the same cannot be said for Rome or Singapore or freighters in the middle of the Atlantic.

Filipinos are bound to America not necessarily by a set of political tenets, but by a series of consumerist ideals fostered by postcolonialism and globalization and embodied in the material conditions and economic opportunities that America makes possible. Although these ideals may be attainable to a certain extent, the cost is having to bow down to the demands of work in the United States and as a consequence losing the "ease" possible in the Philippines. Most important, these consumerist ideals and the relinquishing of Filipino citizenship are also linked to a corresponding loss of Filipinoness. Pinoys in the Philippines may accuse emigrants to the United States of "betrayal." Pinoys in the United States, of course, do not see themselves as betrayers. Indeed, their attitude is perhaps reinforced by immigrants' parallel gatekeeping of Filipino identity; they view second-generation Filipino Americans, like many of the second generation in general, as even less Filipino in "manners" and language.

This is where the difference between Filipino immigrants (as well as other Asian and Latino immigrants) and immigrants from Europe lies: suspicions of betrayal rarely, if ever, haunt so-called Euro-Americans. This ambiguity, most often providing the basis for anti-immigrant rhetoric, engenders an untenable either-or position: one is required to choose, to prevent "regression" to nationality. Once again, assimilation exerts its force.

The *Philippine News* posits such a transition as ideal, but it also embodies the same ambivalent position that first-generation Filipinos in the United States seem to have. The immigrant predicament—the conflict between obligations to the homeland and obligations to the new home—is perfectly captured in the newspaper. Indeed, the newspaper represents a formalized embodiment of ambiguity, reproduced and circulated throughout the Pinoy community and ultimately maintained as official discourse. The transition into a "genuine" Americanness is seen specifically in terms of political empowerment and action; that is, a greater political participation is the key to a fuller American life. In this respect the role of *Philippine News* is very similar to that of ethnic newspapers at the turn of the twentieth century. Robert Park (1922) observed that the ethnic newspaper not only provided news, but also initiated immigrants into American life—or, as Oscar Handlin put it, the newspaper, like the mutual aid associations, "were not vestiges of any European forms, but steps in [immigrants'] Americanization" (2002, 165). At the same time, one can also argue that *Philippine News*'s prescriptive function is not merely to make "good Americans" out of its readers, but "good Filipinos" as well, befitting its fantasies of transnational status. Readers are constantly reminded of their "fellow countrymen" and their obligation, as Pinoys, to help them in times of need.

Much of the newspaper's agenda has been to keep the Filipino community informed, and it is chiefly in this sense that it performs a public service. As an ethnic newspaper, *Philippine News* practices advocacy journalism—in its case, supporting Filipino causes and businesses, and (selectively) championing the rights of Filipinos in America. Its editorials have, in general, urged its readers to political action, both in the United States and in the Philippines. But as I have pointed out, this purpose contradicts the subject matter for which the newspaper is most known: photographs of balls, weddings, baptisms, and parties, and pages of announcements for these events. Its display of middle-class materialism seemingly caters to the desire to be able to say "I was in the newspaper." Though the attention to social events seems to undermine the seriousness of the newspaper's politics, it is in keeping with the essence of *Philippine News*. In many ways, it is still a small community newspaper, though one involved with international political events. (And as I mentioned previously, much of the newspaper's driving force has been spent with the passing of the Marcos regime.)

The haziness of the newspaper's position is seen in the issues it covers—indeed, its recent increased dependence on reprinting articles from the *Philippine Daily Inquirer* emphasizes this transnational ambivalence. Even though the newspaper has long urged involvement in local political affairs, and has at times overenthusiastically celebrated the successes of Filipino Americans, the *Philippine News* has also spent an inordinate amount of time and space dealing with events in the Philippines. In this respect it is becoming more and more like a Filipino newspaper, albeit one that publicizes local community events in the United States.

Its dual image—both as small-scale, localized Filipino American newspaper and as ambitious, international Philippine-based newspaper—makes *Philippine News* ambiguous in a binational way. Advertisements, and by extension, the businesses using them, are almost equally divided between those based or oriented toward the United States (restaurants, real estate agencies, shops) or toward the Philippines (remittance and real estate agencies, airlines). The newspaper already reflects a readership attuned to events in the homeland, a reading community used to "repeated turning."

Ironically, the mass media are also responsible for the current image of the Filipino American community as more interested in politics—or, to be more specific, political gossip—in the Philippines than in the United States. Newspapers and TV circulate this image by producing discourse about the Philippines for their audience. Like The Filipino Channel, the *Philippine News* keeps talk about the Philippines going. Like its readership, the newspaper tries to be both "Filipino" and "Filipino American" at the same time. In this way the media both produce and reflect the transnational fantasy: both public and private discourse feed off each other. Not only do the media create a community of readers, they engender and encourage multiple loyalties as well.

Modern advances in communication and travel have brought other people's lives around the world closer than ever, in ways faster than ever—altogether quite a contrast to the situation only a handful of decades before, when a letter took weeks to reach its intended reader. Similarly, the role of the mass media in fashioning and disseminating these alternate possibilities cannot be underestimated; the presence of the homeland constantly interrupts the everyday, existing not only as a mere reminder, but as a constant, almost palpable force. Mass media and the liberalization of import laws have long changed the dynamic in such a way that one does not have to be a member of the elite to consume American commodities, or to include living in the United States or the Philippines in one's imaginings and life options.

Nevertheless, there has been no fundamental break in continuity with previous migration patterns or the ways in which immigrants lived their lives. The rise of the capitalist world-system has dispersed many populations throughout the world—people whose memories of and connections with their homelands have been no less strong than those of their present-day counterparts. Immigrants to America have also relied on complex and state-spanning networks, both formal and informal, to keep in contact with friends and relatives in the homeland. The lives of immigrants, then and now, are similarly oriented to two nations in varying degrees. We are not witnessing new migration patterns, merely an increase—in speed, in population, in money, in travel. The "transnational" is not the product of a hyperaccelerated, pastiche-oriented postmodernity, but merely the intensified continuation of historical processes of migration.

Daly City Filipinos demonstrate that people have rigid, essentialized conceptions of culture, and of what is Filipino and what is American; identity is nowhere nearly as malleable as some may believe. Moments of contact between cultures—whether through colonialism, or through everyday "transnationality"—place the borders between cultures in question, but they also tend to solidify them. Filipino culture could, in effect, be reduced to a set of specific "cultural" traits, or performed on special occasions; the Filipino events in the San Francisco Bay Area highlighted and facilitated this reductiveness.

Homesickness in Daly City was not embedded in material objects, but in specific people (not necessarily relatives), places, and events. Otherwise homesickness was more a generalized feeling of longing, an emotional thirst that could be temporarily quenched with a click of the television's remote control or a visit to one of the many Filipino restaurants. The awareness of loss that accompanied nostalgia and homesickness could not have been as acute as it was for past immigrants. Nor do today's Pinoy immigrants feel the sense of cultural isolation that plagued their counterparts earlier in the twentieth century, because the loss can be recovered easily in a place like Daly City; an "improved" Philippines is already around them, fashioned and refashioned by the community they reconstituted for themselves.

My interviewees almost always located the object of their nostalgia back in the Philippines. It is less a temporal distancing and more a spatial differentiation (thus more similar to homesickness). They missed the camaraderie and friendship—embodied in persons who could not be relocated—that they had back home, in great contrast to the pressures of work and suburban life in the United States. True to form, nostalgia is displayed and commodified in public discourse through various expressions of Filipino culture such as festivals and dances. Nostalgia changes the way in which the homeland is perceived, as it is cast in a more positive, rose-colored light. As Oscar Handlin wrote about European immigrants, "the Old World became a great mirror into which they looked to see right all that was wrong with the New" (2002, 232). Handlin continued, regarding nostalgic memories of the homeland, "The landscape was prettier, the neighbors more friendly, and religion more efficacious; in the frequent crises when [immigrants] reached the limits of their capacities, the wistful reflection came: This would not have happened there [in the homeland]" (2002, 233).

This would not have happened there. As Daly City residents observed, and as *Philippine News* told its readers weekly, it was the other way around. There is also an odd reverse nostalgia exhibited in the pages of *Philippine News*, and in much talk about the Philippines: that is, the homeland is almost always remembered as worse than it may actually be, as if to constantly confirm that Filipino immigrants' decisions to migrate were indeed right. One could read the Filipino newspaper and reflect, "This would not have happened *here* [in America]." As I pointed out in Chapter Seven, this "reverse nostalgia" assuages a certain kind of guilt: not just the guilt of abandonment, but also the guilt of making the wrong life decision. The phrase *love-hate relationship*, long used by Filipinos to describe the Philippines' relationship with the United States, can be equally applied to the attitudes of Filipinos in the United States toward the Philippines.

I began my research with an eye toward presenting the multiplicity of perspectives from Pinoy immigrants in Daly City. I had not expected how varied those viewpoints would be. But at least it is clear that economic success—not necessarily just economic stability, but an increase in status unavailable in the Philippines—is the main reason for migration. Couched in terms of the general objective of "buhay na maginhawa" (a comfortable life), this quest for a secure middle-class status has driven Filipinos to abandon their jobs and take their chances at seeking their fortune all around the world. In contrast, the ostensible reason for migration, family reunification, was not as significant as I had thought; many of my interviewees were unenthusiastic about reuniting with their relatives, and considered it another "risk" to take, like the act of moving itself.

My earlier insistence on not viewing immigrants as merely "rational, economic actors" was somewhat deflated; the emotional elements of transnationality—loyalty, nostalgia, love, and hate—were of course crucial to decision-making, but so were rational calculations of risk and the possibility of making more money. I had also initially looked at Pinoy immigrants as exemplifying a new kind of migration; my subsequent interviews proved me wrong, as the Daly City residents grappled with the same conflicted emotions, the same marginal position, and the same desire to belong in an increasingly connected world, as did immigrants before them.

I lived in Daly City, in an ethnic enclave perhaps much like other ethnic enclaves, for almost two years. After a while, it became easy to forget what the Filipino community in Daly City, with all its suburban failings, petty heroisms (to those outside), and apolitical sensibilities, had to offer to Filipinos far away from home: the rare option to speak to other people in one's own native tongue, the precious possibility to eat the food of home, the invaluable chance to be with one's fellow countrymen and women. These opportunities factor into those same rational and irrational decisions made by Pinoy immigrants every day.

The feeling of belonging to two places, however illusory, has become more of a possibility in a more connected age. This form of belonging has, however, engendered shifts in sentiment, in political participation, in the conceptualizations of citizenship and the borders of the nation-state. I end on a note of ambiguity and ambivalence as well, reflecting the nature of my subject. Pinoy immigrants in the United States, in their repeated turnings toward the homeland, have created places like home. But even in all their stubborn, fickle loyalty, they have still chosen to consume home from a safe distance.

BIBLIOGRAPHY

Abelmann, Nancy, and Lie, John. 1995. *Blue Dreams: Korean Americans and the Los Angeles Riots.* Cambridge, MA: Harvard University Press.

Abinales, Patricio N., and Amoroso, Donna J. 2005. *State and Society in the Philippines.* Lanham, MD: Rowman & Littlefield.

Agoncillo, Teodoro A., and Milagros C. Guerrero. 1987. *History of the Filipino People*, 7th ed. Quezon City: Garcia Publishing Co.

Aguilar, Filomeno V., Jr. 2002. Ritual Passage and the Reconstruction of Selfhood in International Labor Migration, 413–451. In *Filipinos in Global Migrations: At Home in the World?*, edited by Filomeno V. Aguilar. Quezon City: Philippine Migration Research Network.

Aljovin, Andrea. 1979. Yvonne Picked as Magandang Filipina in Dazzling Grand Finals. *Philippine News*, December 1–7, 1, 12.

Alvarez-Bihis, Ressie. 1973. Operation Homecoming. *Philippine Panorama*, October 17, 15, 21.

Anderson, Benedict. 1992. The New World Disorder. *New Left Review* 193:3–13.

———. 1994. Exodus. *Critical Inquiry* 20:314–327.

Ang Katipunan. 1975. Stand Up for the Homeland. October 10, 2.

———. 1979a. Don't Let Red-Baiting Stop the People's Movement. June 1–15, 2–3.

———. 1979b. Philippine News Gets Yellow Journalism Award. June 1–15, 2.

———. 1979c. Red-Baiting Won't Stop the People's Movement. June 16–30, 2, 12–13.

———. 1979d. Beauty Contests: An Exercise in Irrelevance. December 1–15, 3.

Appadurai, Arjun. 1990. Disjuncture and Difference in the Global Cultural Economy. *Public Culture* 2 (2): 1–24.

———. 1991. Global Ethnoscapes: Notes and Queries for a Transnational Anthropology. In *Recapturing Anthropology: Working in the Present*, edited by Richard G. Fox, 191–210. Santa Fe, NM: School of American Research Press.

————. 1993. Patriotism and Its Futures. *Public Culture* 5 (3): 411–429.

Aranda, Chris. 1992. Daly City: The New Manila. *Filipinas*, May, 30–34.

Ballescas, Ma. Rosario P. 1992. *Filipino Entertainers in Japan: An Introduction.* Quezon City: Foundation for Nationalist Studies.

Basch, Linda, Nina Glick Schiller, and Cristina Szanton Blanc. 1994. *Nations Unbound: Transnational Projects, Postcolonial Predicaments, and Deterritorialized Nation-States.* Langhorne, PA: Gordon and Breach.

Batino, Clarissa S. 2002. OFW Dollar Flows Hit $1.96B in First Quarter. *Philippine Daily Inquirer*, June 24, 1.

Beltran, Ruby P., Elena L. Samonte, and Lita Walker. 1996. Filipino Women Migrant Workers: Effects on Family Life and Challenges for Intervention. In *Filipino Women Migrant Workers: At the Crossroads and Beyond Beijing*, edited by Ruby P. Beltran and Gloria F. Rodriguez, 15–45. Quezon City: Giraffe Books.

Billig, Michael. 1995. *Banal Nationalism.* London: Sage Publications.

Bonus, Rick. 2000. *Locating Filipino Americans: Ethnicity and the Cultural Politics of Space.* Philadelphia: Temple University Press.

Bourdieu, Pierre. 1979. *Distinction: A Social Critique of the Judgement of Taste.* Trans. Richard Nice. Cambridge, MA: Harvard University Press.

Briones, Willy. 1979. Magandang Filipina U.S.A.: Esclamado's Glamorous Subscription Drive Exposed. *Ang Katipunan*, December 1–15, 1.

Bulosan, Carlos. 1973. *America Is in The Heart: A Personal History.* Seattle: University of Washington Press.

Calendar of Events. 1998. *Philippine News*, July 8–14, B2.

Campomanes, Oscar V. 1995. The New Empire's Forgetful and Forgotten Citizens: Un-representability and Unassimilability in Filipino-American Postcolonialities. *Critical Mass* 2 (2): 145–200.

Canlas, MC. 2002. *SoMa Pilipinas.* San Francisco: Arkipelago Books.

Catapusan, Benicio T. 1936. Filipino Repatriates in the Philippines. *Sociology and Social Research* 21 (1): 72–76.

Chambers, Iain. 1994. *Migrancy, Culture, Identity.* London: Routledge.

Chan, Sucheng. 1991. *Asian Americans: An Interpretive History.* Boston: Twayne Publishers.

Chandler, Samuel. 1973. *Gateway to the Peninsula: A History of the City of Daly City.* Daly City, CA: City of Daly City.

Cinel, Dino. 1982. *From Italy to San Francisco: The Immigrant Experience.* Stanford, CA: Stanford University Press.

Climaco, Augusto F. 1978. Let Us Help Our People Recover Their Freedom. *Philippine News*, April 1–7, 5.

Commission on Filipinos Overseas. 2006. Stock Estimate of Overseas Filipinos. From the Commission on Filipinos Overseas Statistics website, http://www.cfo.gov.ph/statistics.htm, last accessed January 21, 2008.

Constable, Nicole. 1997. *Maid to Order in Hong Kong: Stories of Filipina Workers.* Ithaca, NY: Cornell University Press.

Constantino, Renato. 1987. *The Miseducation of the Filipino.* Quezon City: Foundation for Nationalist Studies.

Cordova, Fred. 1983. *Filipinos: Forgotten Asian Americans.* Dubuque, IA: Kendall/Hunt Pub. Co.

Critical Filipina and Filipino Studies Collective. 2004. *Resisting Homeland Security: Organizing against Unjust Removals of U.S. Filipinos.* From http://www.sjsu.edu/depts/sociology/living/removal.html, last accessed January 16, 2008.

Cruz, Isagani R., and Lydia B. Echauz. 1993. *1001 Reasons to Stay in the Philippines.* Manila: Aklat Peskador.

Daly City/Colma Chamber of Commerce. 1992. *1992–93 Business Directory.* Daly City, CA: Daly City/Colma Chamber of Commerce.

Denton, Frank H., and Victoria Villena-Denton. 1986. *Filipino Views of America: Warm Memories, Cold Realities.* Washington, DC: Asia Fellows.

Department of Labor and Employment. 2007. Global Deployment of Filipinos Breaches 1M Mark. From the Philippine Department of Labor and Employment website, http://www.dole.gov.ph/news/details.asp?id=N000002145, last accessed January 18, 2008.

Donaldson, Scott. 1969. *The Suburban Myth.* New York: Columbia University Press.

Esclamado, Alex A. 1975a. On Being Anti-Marcos. *Philippine News,* April 3–9, 1, 2.

———. 1975b. The Story of the Marcos Coercion. *Philippine News,* October 4–10, 14, 15.

———. 1979. KDPs Are Communists! *Philippine News,* June 16–22, 1, 4.

———. 2000. Tribute to Community Organizations. *Philippine News,* August 30–September 5, 1995, 1, 4.

España-Maram, Linda. 2006. *Creating Masculinity in Los Angeles's Little Manila: Working-Class Filipinos and Popular Culture, 1920s–1950s.* New York: Columbia University Press.

Espiritu, Yen Le. 1992. *Asian American Panethnicity: Bridging Institutions and Identities.* Philadelphia: Temple University Press.

———. 1995. *Filipino American Lives.* Philadelphia: Temple University Press.

———. 2003. *Home Bound: Filipino American Lives across Cultures, Communities, and Countries.* Berkeley and Los Angeles: University of California Press.

Esposo, William C. 2007. The $500 Million "Desperate Housewives" Damage Suit: Is It for Filipino Pride or Greed? *The Philippine Star,* October 16, 13.

Featherstone, Mike. 1990. Global Culture: An Introduction. In *Global Culture: Nationalism, Globalization and Modernity,* edited by Mike Featherstone, 1–14. London: Sage Publications.

Filipino Americans Demand for Apology from ABC and Desperate Housewives. 2007. Online petition, http://www.petitiononline.com/FilABC/, last accessed January 21, 2008.

Fischer, Michael M. J. 1986. Ethnicity and the Post-Modern Arts of Memory. In *Writing Culture: The Poetics and Politics of Ethnography,* edited by James Clifford and George E. Marcus, 194–233. Berkeley and Los Angeles: University of California Press.

Fong, Timothy B. 1994. *The First Suburban Chinatown: The Remaking of Monterey Park, California.* Philadelphia: Temple University Press.

Fortich, Chic. 1991. *Escape!: Charito Planas, Her Story.* Quezon City: New Day Publishers.

Garcia, Tony. 1975. Westlake, Daly City, One of Best 15 US Suburbs, Developing into Veritable Filipino Town. *Philippine News,* September 20–26, 6.

———. 1976. Good Enough to Be Elected, But for Freedom, NO! *Philippine News,* March 13–19, 4.

Georges, Eugenia. 1990. *The Making of a Transnational Community: Migration, Development, and Cultural Change in the Dominican Republic.* New York: Columbia University Press.

Glick Schiller, Nina, Linda Basch, and Cristina Blanc-Szanton. 1992a. Towards a Definition of Transnationalism: Introductory Remarks and Research Questions. In Glick Schiller, Basch, and Blanc-Szanton 1992b, ix–xiv.

———, eds. 1992b. *Towards a Transnational Perspective on Migration: Race, Class, Ethnicity, and Nationalism Reconsidered.* New York: New York Academy of Sciences.

———. 1992c. Transnationalism: A New Analytic Framework for Understanding Migration. In Glick Schiller, Basch, and Blanc-Szanton 1992b, 1–24.

Gonzalves, Theo. 1995. "The Show Must Go On": Production Notes on the Pilipino Cultural Night. *Critical Mass* 2 (2): 129–144.

Griffiths, Stephen J. 1988. *Emigrants, Entrepreneurs, and Evil Spirits: Life in a Philippine Village.* Honolulu: University of Hawaii Press.

Gupta, Akhil. 1992. The Song of the Nonaligned World: Transnational Identities and the Reinscription of Space in Late Capitalism. *Cultural Anthropology* 7 (1): 63–79.

Gutierrez, Lito C. 1995. Network Aims to Reach All Filipinos Anywhere. *Philippine News.* June 28–July 4, 1, 12.

Hall, Stuart. 1991. The Local and the Global: Globalization and Ethnicity. In *Culture, Globalization and the World-System: Contemporary Conditions for the Representation of Identity,* edited by Anthony D. King, 19–39. Binghamton: State University of New York at Binghamton.

Handlin, Oscar. 2002. *The Uprooted.* 2nd ed. Philadelphia: University of Pensylvania Press.

Hannerz, Ulf. 1992. *Cultural Complexity: Studies in the Social Organization of Meaning.* New York: Columbia University Press.

Hing, Bill Ong. 1993. *Making and Remaking Asian America through Immigration Policy 1850–1990.* Stanford, CA: Stanford University Press.

Hobsbawm, Eric J. 1990. *Nations and Nationalism since 1780: Programme, Myth, Reality.* Cambridge: Cambridge University Press.

Ignacio, Emily Noelle. 2005. *Building Diaspora: Filipino Community Formation on the Internet.* Piscataway, NJ: Rutgers University Press.

Immigration and Naturalization Service. 2000. Naturalizations Fiscal Year 2000. In *2000 Statistical Yearbook of the Immigration and Naturalization Service.* www.dhs.gov/xlibrary/assets/statistics/yearbook/2000/NATZ2000text.pdf, last accessed July 21, 2008.

Jamero, Peter M. 1997. The Filipino American Young Turks of Seattle: A Unique Experience in the American Sociopolitical Mainstream. In Root 1997, 299–315.

JanMohamed, Abdul R. 1992. Worldliness-without-World, Homelessness-as-Home: Toward a Definition of the Specular Border Intellectual. In *Edward Said: A Critical Reader,* edited by Michael Sprinker, 96–120. London: Basil Blackwell.

Jimenez-Magsanoc, Letty. 1974. The "Darling Balikbayan". *Philippine Panorama,* n.d., 9.

Kearney, Michael. 1986. From the Invisible Hand to Visible Feet: Anthropological Studies of Migration and Development. *Annual Review of Anthropology* 15:331–361.

Kymlicka, Will, and Wayne Norman. 1995. Return of the Citizen: A Survey of Recent Work on Citizenship Theory. In *Theorizing Citizenship,* edited by Ronald Beiner, 283–315. Albany: State University of New York Press.

Langdon, Philip. 1994. *A Better Place to Live: Reshaping the American Suburb*. Amherst: University of Massachussetts Press.

Last, John. 1975. Underground Press Fills the Gaps in the Philippines. *Philippine News*, January 30–February 5, 9.

Lessinger, Johanna. 1992. Investing or Going Home? A Transnational Strategy among Indian Immigrants in the United States. In Glick Schiller, Basch, and Blanc-Szanton 1992b, 53–80. New York: New York Academy of Sciences.

Lowe, Lisa. 1996. *Immigrant Acts: On Asian American Cultural Politics*. Durham, NC: Duke University Press.

Luna, Victoria. 1979. "When We Get To America, Life Will Be . . ." *Ang Katipunan*, June 16–30, S1–S2.

Mabalon, Dawn B., Rico Reyes, the Stockton Chapter of the Filipino American National Historical Society, and the Little Manila Foundation. 2008. *Filipinos in Stockton*. San Francisco: Arcadia Publishing.

Macabenta, Greg B. 2006. America Is Our Country Too. *Filipinas*, November, 7.

Mahler, Sarah J. 1995. *American Dreaming: Immigrant Life on the Margins*. Princeton, NJ: Princeton University Press.

Malinowski, Bronislaw. 1961. *Argonauts of the Western Pacific*. New York: E.P. Dutton and Co.

Malkki, Liisa. 1992. National Geographic: The Rooting of Peoples and the Territorialization of National Identity among Scholars and Refugees. *Cultural Anthropology* 7 (1): 24–44.

Manalansan, Martin F. 1996. Searching for Community: Filipino Gay Men in New York City. In *Asian American Sexualities: Dimensions of the Gay and Lesbian Experience*, edited by Russell Leong, 51–64. New York: Routledge.

Mapa, Vic A. 1973. The Most Beautiful Country in the World. *Philippine News*, April 5–11, 1, 16.

Marcus, George. 1986. Contemporary Problems of Ethnography in the Modern World System. In *Writing Culture: The Poetics and Politics of Ethnography*, edited by James Clifford and George E. Marcus, 165–193. Berkeley and Los Angeles: University of California Press.

———. 1992. Past, Present and Emergent Identities: Requirements for Ethnographies of Late Twentieth-Century Modernity Worldwide. In *Modernity and Identity*, edited by Scott Lash and Jonathan Friedman, 309–330. Oxford: Basil Blackwell.

Massey, Doreen. 1992. A Place Called Home? *New Formations* 17:3–15.

Montoya, Concepcion A. 1997. Living in the Shadows: The Undocumented Immigrant Experience of Filipinos. In Root 1997, 112–120.

Morantte, P. C. 1984. *Remembering Carlos Bulosan*. Quezon City: New Day Publishers.

Morawska, Ewa. 1990. The Sociology and Historiography of Immigration. In Yans-McLaughlin 1990, 187–238.

Munasinghe, Viranjini. 2001. *Callaloo Or Tossed Salad?: East Indians and the Cultural Politics of Identity in Trinidad*. Ithaca, NY: Cornell University Press.

Naficy, Hamid. 1991. The Poetics and Practice of Iranian Nostalgia in Exile. *Diaspora* 1 (3): 284–302.

Nye, Joseph S. Jr., and Robert O. Keohane. 1971. Transnational Relations and World Politics: An Introduction. *International Organization* 25 (3): 329–349.

Omi, Michael, and Howard Winant. 1994. *Racial Formation in the United States: From the 1960s to the 1990s*. 2nd ed. New York: Routledge.

Ong, Aihwa. 1992. Limits to Cultural Accumulation: Chinese Capitalists on the American Pacific Rim. In Glick Schiller, Basch, and Blanc-Szanton 1992b, 125–143.

———. 1999. *Flexible Citizenship: The Cultural Logics of Transnationality*. Durham, NC: Duke University Press.

Ong, Jennifer S. 2000. FilAm Groups More Than Meet the Eye. *Philippine News*, August 30–September 5, 1995, 1, 12–13.

Ortigas, Gaston Z., and Sylvia L. Mayuga. 1994. *A Revolutionary Odyssey: The Life and Times of Gaston Z. Ortigas*. Manila: Anvil Publishing.

Pamatong, Elly Velez. 1976. Weep, My Broken Land. *Philippine News*, April 10–16, 5.

Park, Robert Ezra. 1922. *The Immigrant Press and Its Control*. New York: Harper and Brothers.

———. 1950. Human Migration and the Marginal Man. In *Race and Culture*, 345–356. Glencoe, IL: Free Press.

Parreñas, Rhacel Salazar. 2001. *Servants of Globalization: Women, Migration, and Domestic Work*. Stanford, CA: Stanford University Press.

———. 2005. *Children of Global Migration: Transnational Families and Gendered Woes*. Stanford, CA: Stanford University Press.

Patterson, Orlando. 1987. The Emerging West Atlantic System: Migration, Culture, and Underdevelopment in the United States and the Circum-Caribbean Region. In *Population in an Interacting World*, edited by William Alonso, 227–260. Cambridge, MA: Harvard University Press.

Pazzibugan, Dona and Clarissa Batino. 2002. Macapagal on Survey: "See Other Side of the News, Too." *Philippine Daily Inquirer*, June 27, 3.

Pertierra, Raul, ed. 1992. *Remittances and Returnees: The Cultural Economy of Migration in Ilocos*. Quezon City: New Day Publishers.

Philippine Daily Inquirer. 1996. Workers' Remittances Shoot Up by 67 Percent. *Philippine Daily Inquirer*, January 14, 4.

Philippine News. 1973. 150 Names in Blacklist. May 24–30, 1, 8.

———. 1975a. Are We Prepared to Meet History's Judgement? April 10–16, 4.

———. 1975b. Dictator's Revenge. June 12–18, 2.

———. 1975c. The US Can Redeem Its Honor in RP. April 24–30, 2.

———. 1976. History Repeats Itself. March 13–19, 2.

———. 1985. Philippine News Fights Back, Hits Reagan Administration. March 20–26, 1.

———. 1995. Your Strongest Link to the $52 Billion Filipino Market. Brochure.

———. 1996a. A Decade to Remember . . .'80s. September 18–24, S1–S12.

———. 1996b. Remembering the '70s. September 11–17, S1–S12.

———. 2002. Motoring Supplement advertisement, October, C3.

Philippine Overseas Employment Administration. 1996. *Overseas Filipino Workers Handbook*, 4th ed. Mandaluyong City, Philippines: Philippine Overseas Employment Administration.

———. 2006. OFW Presence: A Compendium of Overseas Employment Statistics. From the Philippine Overseas Employment Administration website, http://www.poea.gov.ph/html/statistics.html, last accessed January 20, 2007.

Phillips, James. 1985. Distance, Absence, and Nostalgia. In *Descriptions*, edited by Don Ihde and Hugh. J. Silverman, 64–75. Albany: State University of New York Press.

Pido, Antonio J. A. 1985. *The Pilipinos in America: Macro/Micro Dimensions of Immigration and Integration*. New York: Center for Migration Studies.

Pineda, Rosario J. 1979. The Filipino Communist Organizations in America. *Philippine News*, May 19–25, 1, 4.

Portes, Alejandro. 1990. From South of the Border: Hispanic Minorities in the United States. In Yans-McLaughlin 1990, 160–184.

Portes, Alejandro, and Jozsef Borocz. 1990. Contemporary Immigration: Theoretical Perspectives on Its Determinants and Modes of Incorporation. *International Migration Review* 23 (3): 606–630.

Prystay, Cris. 2002. Nurse Shortage in U.S. Drains Philippine Pool. *The Wall Street Journal*, July 18. Reprinted in Migration News, http://migration.ucdavis.edu/MN/more .php?id=2692_0_3_0, last accessed August 3, 2008.

Psinakis, Steve. 1976. Marcos Attacks US!!! What Is Behind the Apparent Attack? *Philippine News*, May 22–28, 4.

Querol-Moreno, Cherie M. 1994. FilAms 2nd Highest Income Producers among Asian-Pacs. *Philippine News*. January 26–February 1, 1, 15.

Rafael, Vicente L. 1994. The Cultures of Area Studies in the United States. *Social Text* 41:91–111.

Riesman, David. 1958. The Suburban Sadness. In *The Suburban Community*, edited by William M. Dobriner, 375–408. New York: G. P. Putnam's Sons.

Rimonte, Nilda. 1997. Colonialism's Legacy: The Inferiorizing of the Filipino. In Root 1997, 39–61.

Rodis, Rodel. 1996. FilAm Media Should Focus on Us. *Philippine News*, July 24–30, A4.

———. 2007. The Disconnect. *Philippine News*, October 24–30, A7.

Rodriguez, Dylan. 2006. "A Million Deaths?" Genocide and the "Filipino American" Condition of Possibility. In *Positively No Filipinos Allowed: Building Communities and Discourse*, edited by Antonio T. Tiongson, Jr., Edgardo V. Gutierrez, and Ricardo V. Gutierrez, 145–161. Philadelphia: Temple University Press.

Root, Maria P. P., ed. 1997. *Filipino Americans: Transformation and Identity*. Thousand Oaks, CA: Sage Publications.

Rosaldo, Renato. 1989. *Culture and Truth: The Remaking of Social Analysis*. Boston: Beacon Press.

Rotea, Hermie. 1972. U.S. Statehood for R.P.? *Philippine News*. June 1–7, 4–5.

Rouse, Roger. 1992. Making Sense of Settlement: Class Transformation, Cultural Struggle, and Transnationalism among Mexican Migrants in the United States. In Glick Schiller, Basch, and Blanc-Szanton 1992b, 25–52.

Safran, William. 1991. Diasporas in Modern Societies: Myths of Homeland and Return. *Diaspora* 1 (1): 83–99.

Said, Edward W. 1978. *Orientalism*. New York: Vintage Books.

Salido, Sheila C. 1995. Beamers. *Filipinas*, September, 26–28.

San Juan, E., Jr. 1991. Beyond Identity Politics: The Predicament of the Asian American Writer in Late Capitalism. *American Literary History* 3 (3): 542–565. Quoted in Campomanes 1995, 147.

———. 1994. *Allegories of Resistance: The Philippines at the Threshold of the Twenty-First Century*. Diliman: University of the Philippines Press.

San Mateo County Historic Resources Advisory Board. 1984. *San Mateo County . . . Its History and Heritage*. San Mateo, CA: San Mateo County Historic Resources Advisory Board.

Santiago-Irizarry, Vilma. 1996. Culture as Cure. *Cultural Anthropology* 11 (1): 3–24.

Santos, Hector. 1997. Did Philippine Indios Really Land in Morro Bay? In Sulat sa Tansô, at http://www.bibingka.com/sst/esperanza/morrobay.htm, last accessed August 3, 2008

Seeley, John R., Alexander Sim, and Elizabeth W. Loosley. 1956. *Crestwood Heights: A Study of the Culture of Suburban Life.* New York: Basic Books.

Shain, Yossi, and Mark Thompson. 1990. The Role of Political Exiles in Democratic Transitions: The Case of the Philippines. *Journal of Developing Societies* 6:71–86.

Shapiro, Michael J. 1994. Moral Geographies and the Ethics of Post-Sovereignty. *Public Culture* 14:479–502.

Stewart, Susan. 1993. *On Longing: Narratives of the Miniature, the Gigantic, the Souvenir, the Collection.* Durham, NC: Duke University Press.

Strobel, Leny Mendoza. 1997. Coming Full Circle: Narratives of Decolonization among Post-1965 Filipino Americans. In Root 1997, 62–79.

Takaki, Ronald. 1989. *Strangers from a Different Shore: A History of Asian Americans.* New York: Penguin Books.

Taylor, Carson. 1928. *History of Philippine Press.* From The United States and its Territories, http://name.umdl.umich.edu/acr6448.0001.001, last accessed January 18, 2008.

Tebbel, Robert. 1963. *The Slum Makers.* New York: Dial Press. Quoted in Chandler 1973, p. 130.

Tilly, Charles. 1990. Transplanted Networks. In Yans-McLaughlin 1990, 79–95.

Tololyan, Khachig. 1996. Rethinking *Diaspora*(s): Stateless Power in the Transnational Moment. *Diaspora* 5 (1): 3–36.

Torres, Vic. 1993. Duel in Daly City. *Filipinas*, August, 12–16.

U.S. Bureau of the Census. 1992. Current Population Report, Asian and Pacific Islander Population in the United States. Washington, D.C.: U.S. Bureau of the Census.

———. 1996. Percent of Population Voting by Citizenship Status and Selected Demographic Characteristics: November 1994. Washington, DC: U.S. Bureau of the Census.

———. 1999. Current Population Survey: March 1999. Washington, DC: U.S. Bureau of the Census.

———. 2003. Bay Area Census—City of Daly City. From http://www.bayareacensus.ca.gov/cities/DalyCity70.htm, last accessed July 26, 2008.

———. 2006. 2006 American Community Survey. Washington, DC: U.S. Bureau of the Census.

Vallangca, Roberto V. 1977. *Pinoy: The First Wave.* San Francisco: Strawberry Hill Press.

Vallangca, Caridad Concepcion. 1987. *The Second Wave.* San Francisco: Strawberry Hill Press.

Ventura, Rey. 1992. *Underground in Japan.* London: Jonathan Cape.

Verdery, Katherine. 1994. Beyond the Nation in Eastern Europe. *Social Text* 38:1–19.

Vergara, Benito M., Jr. 1999. Review of *Filipino Americans: Transformation and Identity*, edited by Maria P. P. Root. *The Journal of Asian Studies* 58 (2): 577–578.

Wei, William. 1993. *The Asian American Movement.* Philadelphia: Temple University Press.

Yans-McLaughlin, Virginia, ed. 1990. *Immigration Reconsidered: History, Sociology, and Politics.* New York: Oxford University Press.

INDEX

(continuing from page ii)

Ko-lin Chin, *Smuggled Chinese: Clandestine Immigration to the United States*

Evelyn Hu-DeHart, ed., *Across the Pacific: Asian Americans and Globalization*

Soo-Young Chin, *Doing What Had to Be Done: The Life Narrative of Dora Yum Kim*

Robert G. Lee, *Orientals: Asian Americans in Popular Culture*

David L. Eng and Alice Y. Hom, eds., *Q & A: Queer in Asian America*

K. Scott Wong and Sucheng Chan, eds., *Claiming America: Constructing Chinese American Identities during the Exclusion Era*

Lavina Dhingra Shankar and Rajini Srikanth, eds., *A Part, Yet Apart: South Asians in Asian America*

Jere Takahashi, *Nisei/Sansei: Shifting Japanese American Identities and Politics*

Velina Hasu Houston, ed., *But Still, Like Air, I'll Rise: New Asian American Plays*

Josephine Lee, *Performing Asian America: Race and Ethnicity on the Contemporary Stage*

Deepika Bahri and Mary Vasudeva, eds., *Between the Lines: South Asians and Postcoloniality*

E. San Juan, Jr., *The Philippine Temptation: Dialectics of Philippines-U.S. Literary Relations*

Carlos Bulosan and E. San Juan, Jr., ed., *The Cry and the Dedication*

Carlos Bulosan and E. San Juan, Jr., ed., *On Becoming Filipino: Selected Writings of Carlos Bulosan*

Vicente L. Rafael, ed., *Discrepant Histories: Translocal Essays on Filipino Cultures*

Yen Le Espiritu, *Filipino American Lives*

Paul Ong, Edna Bonacich, and Lucie Cheng, eds., *The New Asian Immigration in Los Angeles and Global Restructuring*

Chris Friday, *Organizing Asian American Labor: The Pacific Coast Canned-Salmon Industry, 1870–1942*

Sucheng Chan, ed., *Hmong Means Free: Life in Laos and America*

Timothy P. Fong, *The First Suburban Chinatown: The Remarking of Monterey Park, California*

Benito M. Vergara, Jr., is the author of *Displaying Filipinos: Photography and Colonialism in Early 20th-Century Philippines.* He lives and works in the San Francisco Bay Area.